C000171296

UNDERCOVER

500 ROLLING STONES COVER VERSIONS THAT YOU MUST HEAR!

Peter Checksfield

FOR CHARLIE

ACKNOWLEDGEMENTS

A huge thank you to all the musicians who very generously shared their time answering my questions: Art Alexakis (Everclear), The Allah-Las, Frank Allen (The Searchers), Allman Brothers Band, Marc Almond, Ian A. Anderson, Robyn Adele Anderson, JJ Appleton, John Batdorf, Kasper Bjørke, Bloodshot Bill, Derrick Bostrom (Meat Puppets), Bob Bradbury (Hello), Paul Brady, Vashti Bunyan, John Butler (Diesel Park West), Susan Cadogan, Tony Campbell (The Mighty Avengers), Gerald Casale (Devo), Tommy Castro, Jake Cavaliere (Lords Of Altamont), Louis Cennamo (The Herd), Roger Chapman (Family), Gilby Clarke (Guns N' Roses), Steve Conte, Julie Corbalis, Allison Crowe, Rodney Crowell, James Curtiss (Vitamin String Quartet), Diana Darby, Eric Davidson (The New Bomb Turks), Tony Dekker (Great Lake Swimmers), Joel Van Dijk, Linda Draper, Jane Duboc, John Easedale (Dramarama), Ralph Ellis (The Swinging Blue Jeans), Steve Ellis (Love Affair), Mary Fahl, Lance Ferguson (The Bamboos), Lee Fields, Roxanne Fontana, Robert Forster, Mary Gauthier, Laurie Geltman, Bobby Goldsboro, Billy Goodman, Benny Gordini (The Slow Slushy Boys), Steve Harley (Cockney Rebel), Charlie Harper (The U.K. Subs), Lenny Helsing (The Wildebeests), Marcia Hines, Hooyoosay, Thelma Houston, Cary Hudson (Blue Mountain), Johnny Indovina (Human Drama), Crystal Jacqueline, Teresa James, Wendy James (Transvision Vamp), Anders Jarkell (Vinylbandet), Ignatius Jones (Jimmy and The Boys), Barbara Kessler, Jonathan King (Bubblerock), Kat Kramer, Steve 'Lips' Kudlow (Anvil), Robin Lane, Jeff Lang, Anita Livstrand (Anita Livs), Richard Lloyd, Ian McNabb (The Icicle Works), Manfred Mann, Marie Martens (Marie Martens and The Messarounds), Charlotte Martin, Kathy Mattea, Helge Mattenklodt (The Beatlesøns), Sarah Menescal, Andrew Molloy (Bum), Mike Montali (Hollis Brown), Wendy Ellison Mullen, Tomo Nakayama, Paul Nash (The Danse Society), Samantha Newark, Chris Norman (Smokie), Joe Nosek (The Cash Box Kings), Andrew O'Hazo (Eight n' Up), Christine Ohlman, Gale Paridjanian (Turin Brakes), Icarus Peel (Icarus Peel's Acid Reign), Tiffany Pollack, Jennifer Porter, Will Potter (Cud), Jan Preston, Greg Prevost (The Chesterfield Kings), John Primer, P.J. Proby, Frank Renshaw (The Toggery Five), Kimmie Rhodes, Chris Richards (Chris Richards and The Subtractions), Miranda Lee Richards, Mike Rimbaud, Alice Russell, Japhy Ryder (Celestial Bums), Fernando Saunders, Jill Saward (Shakatak), Rat Scabies (The Damned), Jeff Schroed (Altered Five), Nicolas Schuit (The Cosmic Carnival), Sandie Shaw, Bryan Shore (The Prisoner Of Mars), David Skinner (Twice As Much), Michael Snow (West Five), Gilles Snowcat, Brett Sparks (The Handsome Family), Chris Spedding, Lane Steinberg (Tan Sleeve), Andrew Strong, Justin Sullivan (New Model Army), Jesse Sykes, Larry Tamblyn (The Standells), Dick Taylor (The Rolling Stones / The Pretty Things), Jimmy Thackery, Joe Louis Walker, Dean Wareham (Luna), Mark Wenner (The Nighthawks), John Wheeler (Hayseed Dixie), Dani Wilde, Dave Wilson (Chatham County Line) and Sean Yseult (Rock City Morque).

I'd also like to thank the many agents, managers, historians and collectors who helped me: Rob Allum, Andre Calman, Rachel Cameron, Bruno Ceriotti, Pete Chambers, Robert Combs, Manja Dolan, Charles Driebe, Stephen Ford, Gordon Irwin, Lisa Jenkins, Paul Jonas, Ina Keilitz, Jennifer Kirtlan, Mark Langthorne, John Lappen, Bari Lieberman, Don London, Don McKay, Helen Milner, Lisa Primer, Frances Salmon, Natalia Sanhueza, Celeste Shepherd, Edwina Stuart and Morinaga Yuko.

Biggest thanks of all go to my long-suffering better half Heather. This book would never have been written without her love, support, patience and encouragement.

CONTENTS

DEAR DOCTOR
[84] The Beatlesøns
[85] Lee Harvey Osmond & Mary Gauthier
DONCHA BOTHER ME
[86] Hollis Brown
DOO DOO DOO DOO (HEARTBREAKER)
[87] The Quireboys
[88] Buddy Guy with Mick Jagger
DOOM AND GLOOM
[89] Miles Kane
DOWN IN THE HOLE
[90] Frank Black & The Catholics
DOWNTOWN SUZIE
[91] Four Year Beard
EACH AND EVERY DAY OF THE YEAR
[92] Bobby Jameson
[93] Thee
EMOTIONAL RESCUE
[94] St. Vincent
EMPTY HEART
[95] Thee Midniters
[96] MC5
EVENING GOWN
[97] Jerry Lee Lewis with Mick Jagger
EXILE ON MAIN ST. BLUES
[98] Chuck E. Weiss
FACTORY GIRL
[99] Tom Jones
FAR AWAY EYES
[100] The Handsome Family
FLIGHT 505
[101] Darrell Bath
FOOL TO CRY
[102] Taylor Dayne
[103] Tegan & Sara
GET OFF OF MY CLOUD
[104] Bubblerock
[105] Alexis Korner with Keith Richards
[106] Jimmy & The Boys
[107] Richard Lloyd

[108] The Meteors
[109] The Flying Pickets
GIMME SHELTER
[110] Merry Clayton
[111] Ruth Copeland
[112] Steve Ellis
[113] The Sisters Of Mercy
[114] Inspiral Carpets
[115] New Model Army Feat. Tom Jones
[116] Cud with Sandie Shaw
[117] Samantha Newark
[118] Kathy Mattea
[119] Paul Brady & The Forest Rangers
[120] Leanne Faine
GIVE ME YOUR HAND
[121] Teddy Green
GOIN' HOME
[122] Hollis Brown
GOMPER
[123] The Prisoner Of Mars
GOOD TIMES, BAD TIMES
[124] Roland Van Campenhout
GOODBYE GIRL
[125] The Preachers
GOTTA GET AWAY
[126] The Flys
GROWN UP WRONG
[127] The Johnnys
HAND OF FATE
[128] Uncle Ray feat. Imaani
HAPPY
[129] Nils Lofgren
[130] The Pointer Sisters
[131] Steve Conte
HAVE YOU SEEN YOUR MOTHER, BABY, STANDING IN THE SHADOW?
[132] Lord Sitar
[133] Tina Harvey
[134] John Batdorf & James Lee Stanley
HEART OF STONE
[135] The Andrew Oldham Orchestra

[136] Joe Louis Walker
[137] The Allman Brothers Band
HEAVEN
[138] Kasper Bjørke
HIGH AND DRY
[139] Bloodshot Bill
HONKY TONK WOMEN
[140] Ike & Tina Turner
[141] Waylon Jennings
[142] Joe Cocker
[143] Albert King
[144] Elton John
[145] Humble Pie
[146] Alexis Korner
[147] Taj Mahal & James Cotton
[148] Jerry Lee Lewis with Kid Rock
[149] Jan Preston
HOT STUFF
[150] The Mighty Mocambos with Afrika Bambaataa, Charlie Funk & Deejay Snoop
I AM WAITING
[151] The Quiet Five
[152] Jennifer Warnes
[153] Them
[154] Ollabelle
[155] Lindsey Buckingham
[156] Tomo Nakayama feat. Jesse Sykes
I GO WILD
[157] Omar Coleman
I GOT THE BLUES
[158] Solomon Burke
[159] Aloe Blacc & Joel Van Dijk
I JUST WANT TO SEE HIS FACE
[160] The Blind Boys of Alabama
I WANNA BE YOUR MAN
[161] The Beatles
I'D MUCH RATHER BE WITH THE BOYS
[162] The Toggery Five

[163] Donna Lynn
[164] Johnny Thunders
[165] Ronnie Spector
I'M FREE
[166] Chris Farlowe
[167] Wilmer & The Dukes
[168] The Soup Dragons
I'M NOT SIGNIFYING [I AIN'T SIGNIFYING]
[169] Greg 'Stackhouse' Prevost
IN ANOTHER LAND
[170] 57
IT SHOULD BE YOU
[171] George Bean
IT'S NOT EASY
[172] Blue Öyster Cult
IT'S ONLY ROCK 'N ROLL
[173] Rita Lee
[174] Rebecca Lynn Howard
JE SUIS UN ROCK STAR [JE SUIS UNE DOLLY]
[175] Dolly Rockers
JIGSAW PUZZLE
[176] Melanie
[177] Billy Goodman
JIVING SISTER FANNY
[178] Izzy Stradlin
JUMPIN' JACK FLASH
[179] Thelma Houston
[180] Alex Harvey
[181] Johnny Winter
[182] Leon Russell
[183] Peter Frampton
[184] Marcia Hines
[185] Aretha Franklin with Keith Richards & Ronnie Wood
[186] Guns 'n' Roses
[187] Motörhead
[188] Rodney Crowell
LADY JANE
[189] Glynt Johns
[190] David Garrick
[191] Trini Lopez
[192] Jane Duboc
THE LANTERN

[193] Mac Rybell
THE LAST TIME [BITTER SWEET SYMPHONY]
[194] The Andrew Oldham Orchestra
[195] The Who
[196] Dada
[197] Bobby Bare
[198] Transvision Vamp
[199] Dwight Yoakam
[200] The Tractors
[201] The Andrew Oldham Orchestra & Vashti Bunyan
[202] Chatham County Line
[203] The U.K. Subs
LET IT BLEED
[204] Johnny Winter
[205] Joan Jett & The Blackhearts
[206] John Primer
LET'S SPEND THE NIGHT TOGETHER
[207] Muddy Waters
[208] David Bowie
[209] Fanny
[210] Hello
[211] Melanie Harrold
[212] Roger Chapman
LITTLE BY LITTLE
[213] The Bintangs
[214] The Count Bishops
LIVE WITH ME
[215] Girlschool
[216] Sheryl Crow with Mick Jagger
LOCKED AWAY
[217] Robert Forster
LONG, LONG WHILE
[218] The Idols
LOVING CUP
[219] Nanette Workman with Peter Frampton
[220] The Bittersweets
LUXURY
[221] The Hammersmith Gorillas
MAKE NO MISTAKE

[222] Kat Kramer
MELODY
[223] Bill Wyman & The Rhythm Kings
MEMO FROM TURNER
[224] The Nighthawks
[225] Dramarama
MEMORY MOTEL
[226] Ian McNabb
MIDNIGHT RAMBLER
[227] Larry McCray
MISS AMANDA JONES
[228] The March Violets
MISS YOU
[229] Ann Peebles
[230] Sugar Blue
[231] Etta James
[232] Dani Wilde
MONKEY MAN
[233] Crazy Baldhead
[234] Gov't Mule
[235] The Lords Of Altamont
MOONLIGHT MILE
[236] The 5th Dimension
[237] Alvin Youngblood Hart
[238] Turin Brakes
[239] Lee Fields
[240] Cowboy Junkies
[241] Kimmie Rhodes
[242] Lucinda Williams
MOTHER'S LITTLE HELPER
[243] Gene Latter
[244] Liz Phair
[245] Linda Draper
MY OBSESSION
[246] Hooyoosay
19TH NERVOUS BREAKDOWN
[247] The Standells
[248] Jason & The Scorchers
[249] Teresa James
[250] Chris Norman
[251] Sarah Menescal
NO EXPECTATIONS
[252] Joan Baez
[253] Odetta
[254] Johnny Cash

[255] Anita Livs
[256] Nanci Griffith
[257] Chris Spedding
[258] George Thorogood
[259] Tiffany Pollack & Eric Johanson
[260] Icarus Peel's Acid Reign
NOW I'VE GOT A WITNESS
[261] The Lyres
OFF THE HOOK
[262] The Pete Best Combo
[263] Tommy Vance
[264] The Cash Box Kings
ON WITH THE SHOW
[265] The Prisoner Of Mars
ONE HIT (TO THE BODY)
[266] The Stone Coyotes
100 YEARS AGO
[267] Head Of Femur
ONE MORE TRY
[268] The Silks
OUT OF CONTROL
[269] Carlos Johnson
OUT OF TIME
[270] Chris Farlowe
[271] P.J. Proby
[272] Arthur Brown
[273] Dan McCafferty
[274] Del Shannon
[275] Andrew Strong
[276] Elvis Costello & The Imposters
[277] Steve Harley
PAINT IT BLACK
[278] The Standells
[279] Chris Farlowe
[280] Eric Burdon & The Animals
[281] Eric Burdon & War
[282] Ian A. Anderson
[283] The Mo-Dettes
[284] Anvil
[285] Echo & The Bunnymen
[286] The Meteors
[287] U2
[288] David Essex
[289] Marc Almond

[290] Thee Headcoatees
[291] Vanessa Carlton
[292] Chalice
[293] Hayseed Dixie
[294] Ali Campbell
[295] Robyn Adele Anderson
PARACHUTE WOMAN
[296] The Piggies
PARTY DOLL
[297] Mary Chapin Carpenter
[298] Kat Kramer with Billy Preston
PLAY WITH FIRE
[299] Clefs Of Lavender Hill
[300] Twice As Much
[301] The Beau Brummels
[302] John Fred & His Playboys
[303] Ruth Copeland
[304] Dana Valery
[305] Manfred Mann's Earth Band
[306] The Pretty Things
[307] Crystal Jacqueline
[308] La La Brooks
[309] Billy Boy Arnold
PLEASE GO HOME
[310] Izzy Stradlin
[311] The Wildebeests
RAIN FALL DOWN
[312] Ana Popovic
RESPECTABLE
[313] The Shop Assistants
RIDE ON BABY
[314] Chris Farlowe
[315] Joe Louis Walker
RIP THIS JOINT
[316] Tommy Castro
[317] Chuck Leavell
ROCKS OFF
[318] Jimmy Thackery
[319] Old 97's
[320] Bason feat. Badflower
RUBY TUESDAY
[321] Bobby Goldsboro
[322] The Rotary Connection
[323] Melanie

[324] Julian Lennon
[325] Rod Stewart
[326] The London Symphony Orchestra feat. Marianne Faithfull
[327] Deana Carter
[328] The Corrs & Ron Wood
[329] Twiggy
[330] Mary Fahl
SAD DAY
[331] Tan Sleeve
SAINT OF ME
[332] Debbie Clarke
[333] Nathalie Alvim
SALT OF THE EARTH
[334] The Rotary Connection
[335] Joan Baez
[336] Dandy Livingstone
[337] Johnny Adams
[338] Judy Collins
[339] Robin Lane
[340] Bettye Lavette
(I CAN'T GET NO) SATISFACTION
[341] Otis Redding
[342] Chris Farlowe
[343] The Beach Boys
[344] The Ventures
[345] Mary Wells
[346] The Supremes
[347] Manfred Mann
[348] Aretha Franklin
[349] José Feliciano
[350] Ken Boothe
[351] Jerry Lee Lewis
[352] Bubblerock
[353] The Troggs
[354] Devo
[355] Sam & Dave
[356] Junior Wells
[357] Britney Spears
[358] The Heptones
[359] Jill Saward
SHANG A DOO LANG
[360] Adrienne Poster
SHATTERED
[361] Rock City Morgue

SHE SMILED SWEETLY
[362] Love Affair
[363] Lindsey Buckingham
SHE WAS HOT
[364] The Karl Hendricks Trio
SHE'S A RAINBOW
[365] The Glass Menagerie
[366] Molly Tuttle
SHE'S SO COLD
[367] Vitamin String Quartet
SHINE A LIGHT
[368] Jennifer Warnes
[369] Allison Crowe
SILVER TRAIN
[370] Johnny Winter
[371] Carla Olson & Mick Taylor
SING THIS ALL TOGETHER
[372] The Orange Bicycle
THE SINGER NOT THE SONG
[373] Pan's People
[374] Alex Chilton
[375] Patti Palladin
SISTER MORPHINE
[376] Marianne Faithfull
[377] Ren Harvieu
SITTIN' ON A FENCE
[378] Twice As Much
(WALKIN' THRU THE) SLEEPY CITY
[379] The Mighty Avengers
[380] Luna
SO MUCH IN LOVE
[381] The Mighty Avengers
[382] The Swinging Blue Jeans
[383] The Herd
[384] The Inmates
[385] Roxanne Fontana
SOME GIRLS
[386] Kristi Argyle
SOME THINGS JUST STICK IN YOUR MIND
[387] Vashti
[388] Dick & Dee Dee
SOMETHING HAPPENED TO ME YESTERDAY
[389] The Lairds

THE SPIDER AND THE FLY
[390] James Cotton & Kenny Wayne Shepherd
STAR, STAR
[391] Joan Jett & The Blackhearts
[392] Rikki Rockett
START ME UP
[393] Toots & The Maytels
[394] Beverley Skeete
[395] Manic Street Preachers
STONED
[396] The Lyres
[397] Allah-Las
THE STORM
[398] The Screws
STRAY CAT BLUES
[399] Johnny Winter
[400] Soundgarden
[401] Chrissy Amphlett & Chris Cheney
STREET FIGHTING MAN
[402] Rod Stewart
[403] The Ramones
[404] The Chesterfield Kings
[405] Oasis
[406] Hayseed Dixie
STREETS OF LOVE
[407] Matthew Ryan
STUPID GIRL
[408] Ellen Foley
[409] Sue Foley
[410] The Slow Slushy Boys
SUMMER ROMANCE
[411] The New Bomb Turks
SURPRISE, SURPRISE
[412] Lulu & The Luvvers
[413] Rubber City Rebels
SWAY
[414] Laurie Geltman
[415] Alvin Youngblood Hart
[416] Jesse Malin
[417] Black Joe Lewis & The Honeybears
SWEET BLACK ANGEL
[418] The Wailing Souls
[419] Otis Taylor

SWEET VIRGINIA
[420] Ronnie Lane & Slim Chance
[421] Jeff Lang
[422] Jerry Lee Lewis with Keith Richards
[423] The Cosmic Carnival
SYMPATHY FOR THE DEVIL
[424] Sandie Shaw
[425] Bryan Ferry
[426] Linda Kendrick
[427] Guns 'n' Roses
[428] Ozzy Osbourne
[429] Motörhead
[430] Billy Branch
TAKE IT OR LEAVE IT
[431] The Searchers
[432] Vinylbandet
TELL ME (YOU'RE COMING BACK)
[433] The Grass Roots
[434] Cassell Webb
THAT GIRL BELONGS TO YESTERDAY
[435] Gene Pitney
THINK
[436] Chris Farlowe
THIS PLACE IS EMPTY
[437] Gilles Snowcat
TILL THE NEXT GOODBYE
[438] Human Drama
TOPS
[439] Eight n' Up
TORN AND FRAYED
[440] The Black Crowes
[441] Blue Mountain
TUMBLING DICE
[442] Owen Gray
[443] Linda Ronstadt
[444] Diesel Park West
[445] Johnny Copeland
[446] Julie Corbalis
2000 LIGHT YEARS FROM HOME
[447] The Danse Society
[448] Robin Danar feat. Rachael Yamagata

INTRODUCTION

Mick and Keith learned fast. Initially Rhythm 'n' Blues purists who believed that only ageing black Americans could write decent songs, they released their first original song 'Stoned' (a group-composed near-instrumental) as the UK B-side of their version of Lennon-McCartney's 'I Wanna Be Your Man' in November 1963; within 18 months they had written and recorded '(I Can't Get No) Satisfaction', and had become The Beatles' biggest musical rivals. Now *that* is fast!

In the 60 years since they started, there have been *thousands* of Rolling Stones cover versions. I listened to most of them (so you don't have to), and have come up with my favourite 500, in a staggering variety of genres: Rock, Blues, Soul, Garage, Psych, Prog, Beat, Reggae, Ska, Pop, Funk, Disco, Country, Folk, Bluegrass, Rockabilly, Glam, Metal, Punk, New Wave, Indie, Gothic, Grunge, Rock 'n' Roll, Bossa Nova, World, Gospel, Electronica, Boogie Woogie, Jazz, even Cabaret, Polka and Classical.

Inevitably, the vast majority of the songs covered are from the period up to and including 'Tattoo You', with *almost* every song from the Decca years represented here (can someone *please* cover 'If You Let Me'!). That said, none of the albums recorded since then have been totally ignored, and neither have their solo material.

I've also interviewed a mammoth 130 of the musicians involved. Which former Rolling Stone recorded 'Play With Fire' in the 90s? Who's favourite album is 'Jamming with Edward'? What legendary Punk group wanted to cover the entire 'Satanic Majesties Request' but ran out of time after 1 song? Read on!

Peter Checksfield (November 2022)

www.peterchecksfield.com

UNDERCOVER

[1] **ALL DOWN THE LINE - Christine Ohlman** (2003)

(Jagger-Richards)

Rolling Stones original: Exile On Main St. (1972) + US B-side (1972)

Blues-Rock singer, songwriter and guitarist from The Bronx, New York City, USA. Dubbed 'The Beehive Queen', she is the long-running vocalist for the 'Saturday Night Live Band'. Additionally, she was one of the backing vocalists for the 1975 'Metamorphosis' album, helping to overdub RS demos with producer Andrew Loog Oldham prior to release.

Christine Ohlman's powerful version of 'All Down The Line' sticks largely to the Rolling Stones' original template, with the most notable difference being a Bobby Keys-style saxophone solo instead of the expected guitar. It is a notable highlight of the 2003 'Exile On Blues St' various artists CD.

What made you choose this song?

"I've always loved it, and the record label also suggested it. We performed this song in The Scratch Band, which is a band I had with GE Smith before the two of us both ended up in the 'Saturday Night Live Band' on NBC."

Do you perform the song live?

"Yes, I have in the past. I also was part of the Carnegie Hall tribute to the Stones a few years back, where I sang '19th Nervous Breakdown' with Ian Hunter. Loved that!"

Were The Rolling Stones a big influence on your music?

"HUGE... I was much more a Stones fan right off the bat than a Beatles fan, truth be told. As time has gone on, I've come to love them more and more. My version of 'Out Of Time' WITH the Stones, from the 'Once Upon A Time In Hollywood' Quentin Tarantino soundtrack, was used in its entirety in the film. That version comes off the 'Metamorphosis' LP."

[2] **ALL I WANT IS MY BABY - Bobby Jameson** (1964)

(Oldham-Richards)

Rolling Stones original: unavailable (probable demo)

Robert Parker Jameson (b. 1945 - d. 2015). Pop and Rock singer and guitarist from Glendale, California, USA.

A friend of US expat P.J. Proby, his 1964 single 'All I Want Is My Baby' b/w 'Each and Every Day Of The Year' was recorded in London by producer Andrew Loog Oldham, with the A-side even promoted on 'Ready, Steady, Go!', but despite this, it failed to chart. The song is a mediocre Pop-Soul offering, though Bobby Jameson gives it his all.

[3] **ALL SOLD OUT - The Spinanes** (1999)

(Jagger-Richards)

Rolling Stones original: Between The Buttons (1967)

Rebecca Gates (vocals and guitar), Joanna Bolme (b. 1968 - bass) and Jerry Busher (drums). Indie Rock band from Portland, Oregon, USA. They disbanded in 2000.

'All Sold Out' has a very similar arrangement to The Stones' original, right down to the distorted guitar, with just the harmonised vocals being quite different. Released as a single, the B-side was another 'Between The Buttons' gem, namely 'She Smiled Sweetly'.

[4] **ALL THE WAY DOWN - Bernard Fowler** (2019)

(Jagger-Richards)

Rolling Stones original: Undercover (1983)

R. Bernard Fowler (b. 1960). Rock, R&B, Blues and Jazz singer from New York City, USA. Best known for being featured on the majority of both group and solo Rolling Stones albums and tours since the '80s, he has also worked with a diverse selection of other artists, including Herbie Hancock, Public Image Ltd, Duran Duran, Yoko Ono, Alice Cooper and even The Smurfs.

An integral and important part of The Stones' live concerts, the 2019 'Inside Out' album, consisting entirely of Rolling Stones covers, was much anticipated. Sadly, they are all spoken-word deconstructions, with most songs all but ruined ('Sister Morphine' has to be heard to be believed). 'All The Way Down' is one of the more palatable tracks, perhaps because the original was also partially semi-spoken.

[5] **ALMOST HEAR YOU SIGH - Mike Rimbaud** (2011)

(Jagger-Richards-Jordan)

Rolling Stones original: Steel Wheels (1989) + UK/US A-side (1990)

Rock and Anti-Folk singer, guitarist and painter from New York City, USA.

A song that started life as an unissued Keith Richards solo track from the 'Talk Is Cheap' sessions, Mike Rimbaud's version, from his 'Can't Judge A Song By It's Cover' album, is performed a little faster than the Stones' original, with his appealingly gravelly vocals enhanced by some fine harmonica.

What made you choose this song?

"I covered the Stones' 'Almost Hear You Sigh' from 1989's 'Steel Wheels' album, because I love that song and didn't believe it's been covered before."

Have you performed the song live?

"I have not performed it live yet, but would love to sometime."

Were The Rolling Stones a big influence on your music?

"Yes, The Rolling Stones have always been and continue to be a big influence to my music and songwriting. I've always admired the guitar playing, guitar sounds and styles from Keith, Ronnie and Mick Taylor. I love Mick Jagger's vocals too, nobody sings like Mick. Their records are timeless."

[6] ANGIE - Womack and Womack (1983)

(Jagger-Richards)

Rolling Stones original: Goats Head Soup (1973) + UK/US A-side (1973)

Cecil Dale Womack (b. 1947 - d. 2013 - guitar, piano and vocals) Linda Womack (née Cooke, b. 1953 - vocals). R&B and Soul duo from USA. Later known as The House of Zekkariyas.

This beautiful duet features Cecil and Linda trading verses, backed by acoustic guitars, bass and percussion. It was a highlight of their 1983 debut album 'Love Wars'.

[7] ANGIE - Tori Amos (1992)

(Jagger-Richards)

Rolling Stones original: Goats Head Soup (1973) + UK/US A-side (1973)

Myra Ellen Amos (b. 1963). Alternative Rock and Chamber Pop singer and pianist from Newton, North Carolina, USA.

Tori Amos included a simple vocals and piano version of 'Angie' on her 1992 'Crucify' vinyl EP, and whilst her Kate Bush-influenced voice can be a bit of an acquired taste, this is refreshingly different to all other versions.

[8] **ANGIE - Sammy Kershaw** (1997)

(Jagger-Richards)

Rolling Stones original: Goats Head Soup (1973) + UK/US A-side (1973)

Samuel Paul Kershaw (b. 1958). Country singer and guitarist from Kaplan, Louisiana, USA.

Performed in a lower key than the Stones' original, the arrangement is otherwise basically the same, albeit with added steel guitar and fiddle, and Sammy's distinctive Southern twang. It was released on the 'Stone Country' various artists compilation.

[9] **ANGIE - The Stereophonics** (1999)

(Jagger-Richards)
Rolling Stones original: Goats Head Soup (1973) + UK/US A-side (1973)

Kelly Jones (b. 1974 - vocals, guitar and piano), Richard Jones (b. 1974 - bass, harmonica and vocals) and Stuart Cable (Stuart James Cable, b. 1970 - d. 2010 - drums and vocals). Alternative Rock and Brit-Rock band from Cwmaman, Wales.

A bonus track on the CD single 'Hurry Up and Wait' (a No. 11 UK hit), this is basically a Kelly Jones solo performance, featuring just his vocal and guitar. The end result is not unlike a more restrained Rod Stewart.

[10] **ANGIE - Beta Hector** (2011)

(Jagger-Richards)

Rolling Stones original: Goats Head Soup (1973) + UK/US A-side (1973)

Simon Hill. Funk and Soul multi-instrumentalist, producer and DJ from the UK.

Featuring an uncredited Dionne Charles (a Soul singer from Brighton who deserves to be far wider known), this is a slow, soulful Blues arrangement, complete with a blistering guitar solo. It is one of several highlights on 'Sticky Soul Fingers: A Rolling Stones Tribute', a CD given away free with 'Mojo' magazine.

[11] **ANYBODY SEEN MY BABY? - The Sound Of Camden Feat. Mutya Buena** (2010)

(Jagger-Richards-Lang-Mink)

Rolling Stones original: Bridges To Babylon (1997) + UK/US A-side (1997)

R&B, Rock and Soul studio project from London, featuring ex-Sugarbabes singer Rosa Isabel Mutya Buena (b. 1985).

There is an annoying keyboard riff, but Mutya Buena's soulful voice doesn't overdo the melisma, and the guitars still manage to sound remarkably Stones-like. It was released on the 2010 album 'The Sound of Camden'.

[12] **AS TEARS GO BY - Marianne Faithfull (1964)**
(Jagger-Richards-Oldham)

Rolling Stones original: 1964 Demo ('As Time Goes By'): Bootleg only; 1965 re-cut: December's Children (and Everybody's) (1965) + US A-side (1965) + UK B-side (1966)

Marianne Evelyn Gabriel Faithfull (b. 1946). Pop, Rock, Folk and Jazz singer from London, UK.

Contrary to myth, this wasn't Jagger-Richards (and Oldham)'s 1st self-composed song, and it may or may not have been specially written for Marianne Faithfull. What *is* undoubtedly true though, is that this is the first *great* song written by Mick and Keith, and the one song that Marianne Faithfull will always be remembered for, above all others. Her version is also the one that all others are compared to, though few have equaled her combination of innocence and regret or Mike Leander's stunning arrangement. Marianne's debut single, it peaked at No. 9 in the UK and No. 22 in the USA.

Marianne Faithfull performing 'As Tears Go By' on 'Hullabaloo', 1965 [US TV]

[13] **AS TEARS GO BY - Nancy Sinatra** (1966)

(Jagger-Richards-Oldham)

Rolling Stones original: December's Children (& Everybody's) (1965) + US A-side (1965) + UK B-side (1966)

Nancy Sandra Sinatra (b. 1940). Pop and Rock singer from Jersey City, New Jersey, USA.

Very much a stylist rather just a copyist, Nancy Sinatra rarely did straight covers of other peoples' songs, and 'As Tears Go By' is no exception. With a Bossa Nova rhythm, and backed by little more than guitar, vibes and percussion, Nancy's rather cool version was included on 'Boots', her first and highest-selling album from 1966.

Nancy Sinatra performing 'As Tears Go By' on 'Shivaree!', 1966 [US TV]

[14] **AS TEARS GO BY - Esther Phillips** (1966)

(Jagger-Richards-Oldham)

Rolling Stones original: December's Children (& Everybody's) (1965) + US A-side (1965) + UK B-side (1966)

Esther Mae Jones (b. 1935 - d. 1984). Rhythm 'n' Blues, Pop, Jazz and Soul singer from Galveston, Texas, USA.

With her distinctive high vibrato, Esther Phillips beautiful Jazz and Soul arrangement was featured on her 1966 album 'Esther Phillips Sings'.

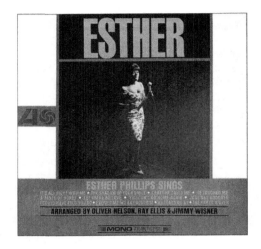

[15] **AS TEARS GO BY - Pat Boone** (1966)

(Jagger-Richards-Oldham)

Rolling Stones original: December's Children (& Everybody's) (1965) + US A-side (1965) + UK B-side (1966)

Patrick Charles Eugene Boone (b. 1934). Pop, Rock 'n' Roll, Country and Gospel singer from Jacksonville, Florida, USA.

It is hard to think of artists as different to each other as The Rolling Stones and Pat Boone - or indeed, Marianne Faithfull and Pat Boone, but his pleasant crooned cover appeared on the 1966 album 'Great Hits of 1965'.

[16] **AS TEARS GO BY - Bobby Goldsboro** (1966)
(Jagger-Richards-Oldham)

Rolling Stones original: December's Children (& Everybody's) (1965) + US A-side (1965) + UK B-side (1966)

Robert Charles Goldsboro (b. 1941). Country and Pop singer and guitarist from Marianna, Florida, USA.

In an arrangement that features prominent percussion, strings and female backing vocals, it is easy to image Roy Orbison utilising the same backing. Which is not surprising, as Bobby Goldsboro was Roy Orbison's ex-guitarist. It can be found on his 1966 album 'It's Too Late'.

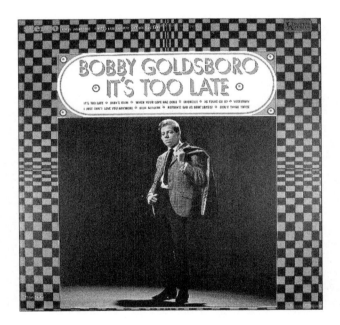

What made you record these songs?

"I thought the songs fit my voice so I recorded them."

Have you ever performed these or any other Stones songs live?

"I don't recall ever singing either of the songs live."

Have you ever met any members of The Rolling Stones?

"I was the opening act for the Stones on their first American tour. We spent about ten days together on a tour bus. I got to know them pretty well. Keith Richards wrote in his book about a blues guitar progression I showed him during our time on the tour bus together."

[17] **AS TEARS GO BY - The Pupils [The Eyes]** (1966)

(Jagger-Richards-Oldham)

Rolling Stones original: December's Children (& Everybody's) (1965) + US A-side (1965) + UK B-side (1966)

Terry Nolder (Terrance Robert Nolder, b. 1946 vocals), Chris Lovegrove (guitar), Phil Heatley (guitar), Barry Allchin (bass) and Brian Cocoran (drums). Better known as The Eyes, The Eyes/The Pupils were a Mod and Psych band from Ealing, London, UK. They disbanded in 1967.

Under the name The Pupils, London group The Eyes cut a whole album of Rolling Stones covers for the US market. Some of these are embarrassingly inept, but amongst the dross is this gem, which features a mid-tempo beat and a full band sound, complete with, unbelievably, prominent fuzz guitar.

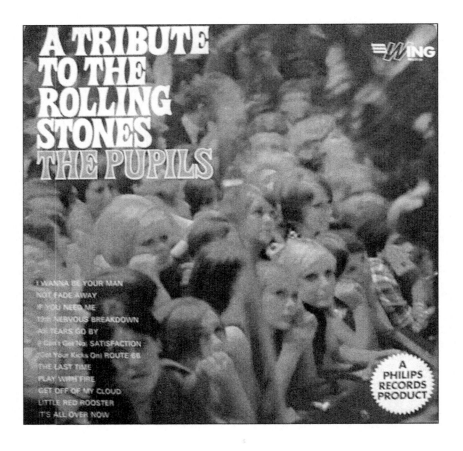

[18] **AS TEARS GO BY - P.P. Arnold** (1968)
(Jagger-Richards-Oldham)

Rolling Stones original: December's Children (& Everybody's) (1965) + US A-side (1965) + UK B-side (1966)

Patricia Ann Cole (b. 1946). Soul, Rock and Pop singer from Los Angeles, California, USA.

Canny businessman that he is, Andrew Oldham was keen for the artists on his Immediate label to record songs that he would profit by. A good example of this is 'As Tears Go By', recorded by both Twice As Much and ex-Ikette P.P. Arnold. Soulfully sung and beautifully orchestrated, it was released on her 2nd album 'Kafunta'.

[19] **AS TEARS GO BY - The Primitives** (1988)
(Jagger-Richards-Oldham)

Rolling Stones original: December's Children (& Everybody's) (1965) + US A-side (1965) + UK B-side (1966)

Tracy Tracy [aka Tracy Cattell] (Tracy Louise Spencer, b. 1967 - vocals and tambourine), Paul Court (Paul Jonathan Court - guitar and vocals), Steve Dullaghan (Steven Anthony Dullaghan, b. 1966 - d. 2009 bass) and Tig Williams (Richard Williams - drums). Indie Pop band from Coventry, UK.

For their 1988 'Sick Of It' CD single, The Primitives included an up-tempo jangly New Wave arrangement of 'As Tears Go By', introducing the song to a whole new generation.

[20] AS TEARS GO BY - Susan Cadogan (2002)
(Jagger-Richards-Oldham)

Rolling Stones original: December's Children (& Everybody's) (1965) + US A-side (1965) + UK B-side (1966)

Alison Anne Cadogan (b. 1951). Reggae singer from Kingston, Jamaica.

A legend in Reggae thanks to her '70s UK and '80s Jamaican hits, Susan Cadogan's version of 'As Tears Go By' is only slightly spoilt by the gimmicky squelchy bass. It was released on the 2002 'Paint It Black: A Reggae Tribute To The Rolling Stones' various artists compilation.

What made you record this song?

"I was asked to sing this song many years ago in Jamaica by Wayne Armond of Chalice Band who were covering 'Paint it Black'. I think Wayne was working with the producer in Jamaica getting covers done... his name was Henry something, not quite sure. It was some years after I saw the song released on a CD put out by Madacy Records in Canada. I managed to chase up Henry in Florida, where I was, and got a contract and US$500.00 advance and have never heard about it since."

Have you performed this (or any other Stones songs) live?

"I have never performed this track live... never thought they really liked it anyway."

Have you ever met any members of The Rolling Stones?

"I have never met any of the Rolling Stones but wish I'd have got 'Wild Horses' to sing... I love that. I do remember dancing away wildly to 'Satisfaction' when I was young... The Boogaloo!"

[21] **AS TEARS GO BY - Melanie** (2002)

(Jagger-Richards-Oldham)

Rolling Stones original: December's Children (& Everybody's) (1965) + US A-side (1965) + UK B-side (1966)

Melanie Anne Safka (b. 1947). Folk and Pop singer and guitarist from Queens, New York, USA.

Melanie's interpretations of Rolling Stones songs are always memorable, and her version of 'As Tears Go By' is no exception. Accompanied just by her acoustic guitar until the halfway mark, it then unexpectedly goes into a New Age Dance version, complete with trip-hop beat and full band backing. It was released on her 2002 'Moments From My Life' album, as well as on a Netherlands-only single.

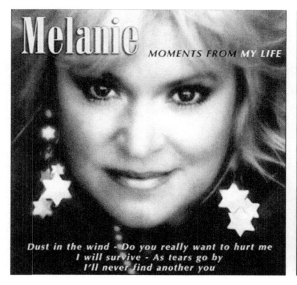
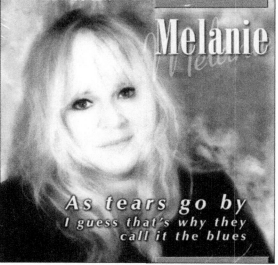

[22] **BACK STREET GIRL** - Nicky Scott (1967)

(Jagger-Richards)

Rolling Stones original: Between The Buttons [UK version] (1967) + Flowers (1967)

Pop singer from Birmingham, UK.

Mick Jagger doesn't have much affection for 'Between The Buttons', but one track that *does* receive his praise is 'Back Street Girl'. He believed in the song at the time too, as he produced a version by Nicky Scott, which was released as a single on the same day as the Stones' album. Sung in a lower key and orchestrated, it failure to chart.

[23] **BACK STREET GIRL** - Bobby Darin (1967)

(Jagger-Richards)

Rolling Stones original: Between The Buttons [UK version] (1967) + Flowers (1967)

Walden Robert Cassotto, b. 1936, d. 1973. Pop, Rock 'n' Roll, Swing and Folk singer, guitarist and pianist from Harlem, New York City, USA.

Bobby Darin was equally at home with a wide variety of musical genres, and this included Pop Folk. Sung in the same lower key as Nicky Scott's version, it is otherwise slower and more gentle. It was issued on his 1967 album 'Inside Out'.

[24] **BACK STREET GIRL - Jennifer [Warnes]** (1969)
(Jagger-Richards)

Rolling Stones original: Between The Buttons [UK version] (1967) + Flowers (1967)

Jennifer Jean Warnes (b. 1947), Country Rock and Pop singer from Seattle, Washington, USA.

Long before charting with movie duets in the '80s, Jennifer Warnes (credited as just 'Jennifer' here) put out a string of country-tinged records. Backed by some fine electric and acoustic guitar picking and strings, Jennifer's classy version of 'Back Street Girl' can be found on her 2nd album 'See Me, Feel Me, Touch Me, Heal Me'.

[25] **BACK STREET GIRL - Social Distortion** (1988)
(Jagger-Richards)

Rolling Stones original: Between The Buttons [UK version] (1967) + Flowers (1967)

Mike Ness (Michael James Ness, b. 1962 vocals and guitar), Dennis Danell (Dennis Eric Danell, b. 1961 - d. 2000 - guitar), John Maurer (b. 1961 - bass and vocals) and Christopher Reece (b. 1959 - drums). Punk Rock band from Fullerton, California, USA.

Not every cover of 'Back Street Girl' feature gently-picked acoustic guitars, as Social Distortion prove with their frantic and noisy Punk rendition. It works surprisingly well, and was released as a bonus track on their 1990 'Story Of My Life' CD single.

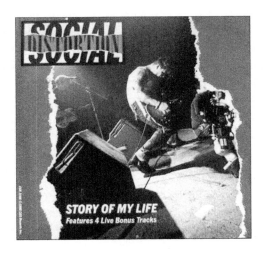

[26] BACK STREET GIRL - Fernando Saunders and Marianne Faithfull (2006)
(Jagger-Richards)

Rolling Stones original: Between The Buttons [UK version] (1967) + Flowers (1967)

(b. 1957). Bassist, guitarist and singer from Detroit, Michigan, USA, and, Marianne Evelyn Gabriel Faithfull (b. 1946). Pop, Rock, Folk and Jazz singer from London, UK.

Marianne Faithfull's versions of 'As Tears Go By' and 'Sister Morphine' are well known, but these aren't the only Rolling Stones-related songs that she's recorded. In more recent decades, there have also been fascinating versions of 'Ruby Tuesday' and the song here, 'Back Street Girl'. A duet with former Lou Reed sideman Fernando Saunders, the two of them trade lines over a gentle backing of percussion, pulsing bass, acoustic guitar and keyboards, while Marianne Faithfull's mature voice adds to the poignancy of the lyrics. It is on Fernando's 2006 album 'I Will Break Your Fall'. [Interview is with Fernando Saunders]

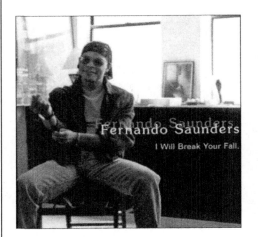

How did your collaboration with Marianne Faithfull come about?

"I was working with Marianne Faithfull and many other people, as they all wanted to record at my flat. Then she brought Evan over, Evan Dando from The Lemonheads, and that was the original idea of the song. Evan was playing the guitar, I'm playing drums and bass, and Kevin Hurn from the Bare Naked Ladies is playing keyboards. Anyway, for some reason it didn't work with Evan. So I called Marianne Faithfull and her manager and I said, well, I think you know what I would like to do. Instead of Evan's voice being there, I would like your voice there and use it for my album. So that's what happened."

Who suggested 'Back Street Girl'?

"Marianne Faithfull wanted to do the song. I guess her and Evan wanted to do the song together. And it ended up on my album."

Have The Rolling Stones been an influence on your music?

"That's a strange and interesting question because I'm from Detroit originally, so we already had this feeling for the music. The Stones weren't from America, right? They were inspired by blues, American blues, and Motown and stuff like that. But I liked what the Rolling Stones were doing. As time went on, the Rolling Stones developed their own sound, and it really inspired me."

[27] **BEAST OF BURDEN - Bette Midler** (1983)

(Jagger-Richards)

Rolling Stones original: Some Girls (1978) + US A-side (1978)

(b. 1945). Pop and Musical Comedy singer from Honolulu, Hawaii, USA.

One of the more timeless songs from the largely New Wave-inspired 'Some Girls' album, Bette Midler's suitably gender-reversed version has a typically 80s "Big Drum" sound that dates it far more than many 60s and 70s recordings. Get past that though, and it's a great version, with Bette Midler proving herself a fine Rock singer. Released as a single and promoted by a memorable video featuring Mick Jagger, it peaked at No. 71 on the US Billboard charts.

Bette Midler with Mick Jagger performing 'Beast Of Burden' (Promo Video, 1983)

[28] **BEAST OF BURDEN - Little Texas** (1997)
(Jagger-Richards)

Rolling Stones original: Some Girls (1978) + US A-side (1978)

Tim Rushlow (Timothy Ray Rushlow, b. 1966 - vocals and guitar), Porter Howell (guitar and vocals), Dwayne O'Brien (guitar and vocals), Duane Propes (bass and vocals), Jeff Huskins (fiddle, keyboards and vocals) and Del Gray (drums). Country Rock band from Nashville, Tennessee, USA.

Apart from singer Tim Rushlow's gritty twang, Little Texas' version sticks surprisingly close to the Stones' original arrangement, and it can be found on the various artists 'Stone Country' album.

[29] BEAST OF BURDEN - Altered Five (2008)
(Jagger-Richards)

Rolling Stones original: Some Girls (1978) + US A-side (1978)

Jeff Taylor (vocals), Jeff Schroedl (guitar), Mark Solveson (bass), Raymond Trevich (keyboards) and Scott Schroedl (drums). Blues band from Milwaukee, Wisconsin, USA. Now known as Altered Five Blues Band.

Starting off with a bass guitar riff, it is obvious straight away that this version is going to be something special, and they do not disappoint. With Jeff Taylor's powerful very "black" sounding vocal and Jeff Schroedl's jazzy blues guitar, it could easily be mistaken for the late B.B. King - which is a heck of a compliment indeed! Altered Five's cover is on their debut album 'Bluesified'. [Interview is with Jeff Schroedl]

Whose idea was it to record this song?

"We arranged our version of 'Beast of Burden' when our band first started rehearsing way back in 2002. We all suggested ideas for creative covers, and wanted to try something by the Rolling Stones. I don't recall exactly which member floated the idea of trying 'Beast of Burden' but it worked, and eventually we recorded it."

Do you perform this (or any other Stones songs) live?

"We performed it live often from about 2002-2012. We don't perform it much these days but I recall we dusted it off at a show a year or two ago. People really like it. It sometimes takes them a few seconds to realize what song we're playing but it always goes over well live."

Were the Rolling Stones an influence on you?

"All the guys in the band are fans of the Stones. A long time ago, we also performed a unique arrangement of 'You Can't Always Get What You Want' but 'Beast of Burden' is the main song we've covered."

[30] **BEAST OF BURDEN - Pure X** (2015)
(Jagger-Richards)

Rolling Stones original: Some Girls (1978) + US A-side (1978)

Nate Grace (vocals and guitar), Matty Tommy Davidson (guitar), Jesse Jenkins V (bass and vocals) and Austin Youngblood (drums). Indie Rock band from Austin, Texas, USA.

Sung in a dreamy echo-drenched falsetto and swamped by guitar and keyboards special effects, Pure X's cover was suitably released on 'Stoned: A Psych Tribute to The Rolling Stones'.

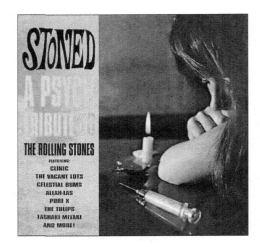

[31] **BEAST OF BURDEN - Jimmy Burns featuring Keith Richards** (2018)
(Jagger-Richards)

Rolling Stones original: Some Girls (1978) + US A-side (1978)

(b. 1943). Soul Blues singer and guitarist from Dublin, Mississippi, USA.

Played as a barely recognizable mid-paced shuffle complete with slide electric guitar and harmonica, Jimmy Burns' authentic-sounding Chicago Blues is one of many highlights on the various artists 'Chicago Plays The Stones' album.

[32] **BEAST OF BURDEN - Jennifer Porter** (2018)
(Jagger-Richards)

Rolling Stones original: Some Girls (1978) + US A-side (1978)

Jennifer Nichole Porter (b. 1968). Jazz, Blues and Classical singer, pianist and actress from Springfield, Maine, USA.

A unique combination of relaxed Jazz-tinged vocals and what can only be described as a Reggae Blues, Jennifer Porter's version of 'Beast Of Burden' is on her 2018 album 'These Years'.

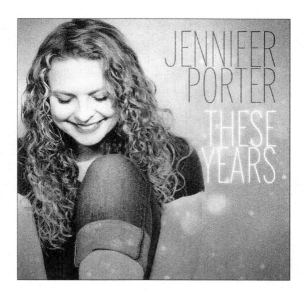

Whose idea was it to record this song?

"It was my idea to record the song. Before I recorded it, I would perform the song, as part of live concerts, in various ways- slow mournful blues with just me playing piano and singing, or the slightly more rocking blues as we performed the song on my album 'These Years'."

Were the Rolling Stones an influence on you?

"I wasn't so much influenced by The Rolling Stones, as I was by some of the jazz greats like Billie Holiday and Ella Fitzgerald. But, like the Rolling Stones, I was also influenced by blues greats such as Pinetop Perkins, Dr. John, and Professor Longhair (being a singer who plays piano as I do!). When I heard 'Beast Of Burden', I could hear the same blues influences in their music that had moved me to create songs as well, and that's what drew me to performing and recording 'Beast Of Burden'. I appreciate the blues roots in their music very much."

[33] **BEFORE THEY MAKE ME RUN and THE SUPERSUCKERS- Steve Earle** (1997)
(Jagger-Richards)

Rolling Stones original: Some Girls (1978)

Stephen Fain Earle (b. 1955). Country, Rock and Folk singer, guitarist and actor from Ft. Monroe, Virginia, USA.

Apart from 'Happy' and maybe 'You Got The Silver', the autobiographical 'Before They Make Me Run' is probably the famous Rolling Stones song where Keith takes lead vocals, and was very much inspired by his 1977 bust for Heroin in Toronto (he was still awaiting a trial date at the time). The song could've been tailor made for Steve Earle, someone who has had his own drug-related legal issues in the past. Recorded with Southern Rock band The Supersuckers for an EP, their version could best be described as Country Grunge.

[34] BEFORE THEY MAKE ME RUN - Great Lake Swimmers (2011)

(Jagger-Richards)

Rolling Stones original: Some Girls (1978)

Folk Rock band from Wainfleet, Ontario, Canada, led by Tony Dekker (vocals and guitar).

A nice laid-back Country-Folk performance complete with fiddle, this is available on 'Paint It Black: An Alt Country Tribute To The Rolling Stones'. [Interview is with Tony Dekker]

Whose idea was it to record this song?

"We were invited to contribute a song to a compilation called 'Paint It Black: An Alt Country Tribute To The Rolling Stones.' My personal favourite Rolling Stones album is 'Some Girls' so it was an easy choice to pick something from that. I'm a big Keith Richards fan in particular, so that track, which features his lead vocals, was on our shortlist from the beginning. There is also the Toronto, Canada connection (where our band is based). My understanding is that the song is a response to Keith's arrest for heroin possession in Toronto in February, 1977, on route to a concert at Toronto's famed El Mocambo venue. He was later let off on probation by the Canadian judge after entering rehab. The Rolling Stones have a special connection to Toronto and that story definitely informed our choosing that particular song to cover."

Do you perform this (or any other Stones songs) live?

"We performed the song live a handful of times around the time that the compilation was released. We also cover 'Dead Flowers' on occasion."

Were the Rolling Stones an influence on you?

"Asking if the Rolling Stones are an influence on any musician is sort of like asking if the sun has an influence on the earth. We're all in orbit in one way or another because of the Stones! Their music is in my DNA."

[35] **BITCH - Herbie Mann [with Mick Taylor]** (1974)
(Jagger-Richards)

Rolling Stones original: Sticky Fingers (1971) + UK/US B-side (1971)

Herbert Jay Solomon (b. 1930 - d. 2003). Jazz, Bossa Nova and World Music flutist, saxophonist and clarinetist from New York City, USA.

First heard as the B-side to 'Brown Sugar', 'Bitch' remains one of the Stones' most enduring songs. With a little help from Mick Taylor, Herbie Mann's instrumental starts off sounding very much like the Stones' version, but once Herbie's flute kicks in it gets progressively weirder as he improvises further away from the melody. A highly prolific artist who had been releasing albums since 1954, 1974's 'London Underground' (featuring 'Bitch') was at least his 50th.

[36] **BITCH - Exodus** (1992)

(Jagger-Richards)

Rolling Stones original: Sticky Fingers (1971) + UK/US B-side (1971)

Steve Souza (b. 1964 - vocals), Gary Holt (Gary Wayne Holt, b. 1964 - guitars and vocals), Rick Hunolt (b. 1963 - guitar), Mike Butler (Michael Butler, b. 1961 - bass) and John Tempesta (b. 1964 - drums). Thrash Metal band from Richmond, California, USA.

Following the original template but doubling the speed and adding an aggressive-sounding vocal, Exodus' version of 'Bitch' was released on 1992's 'Force Of Habit'.

[37] **BITCH - Electric Family** (1998)

(Jagger-Richards)

Rolling Stones original: Sticky Fingers (1971) + UK/US B-side (1971)

German Krautrock band from Germany, led by Tom Redecker (b. 1958 - multi-instrumentalist and producer).

Mixing the retro with the new by playing the main riff on a sitar and utilising a modern dance beat, Electric Family's highly individual performance is on their 2nd album 'Tender'.

[38] **BITCH - Girls With Guitars** (2011)

(Jagger-Richards)

Rolling Stones original: Sticky Fingers (1971) + UK/US B-side (1971)

Electric Blues Supergroup, featuring: Samantha Fish (b. 1989 - vocals and guitar - from Kansas City, Missouri, USA), Cassie Taylor (b. 1986 - vocals and bass - from Boulder, Colorado, USA) and Dani Wilde (b. 1985 - vocals and guitar - from Hullavington, Wiltshire, UK).

Three successful Blues-Rock artists in their own right, Girls With Guitars were put together for a one-off album and tour, thrilling audiences wherever they played. Starting off with pounding drums, their hard-rocking version of 'Bitch' shows off their individual talents. It can be found on the album 'Girls With Guitars', while a live version (with Cassie Taylor replaced by Brighton bassist Victoria Smith) is on 'Girls With Guitars Live'. [Interview is with Dani Wilde]

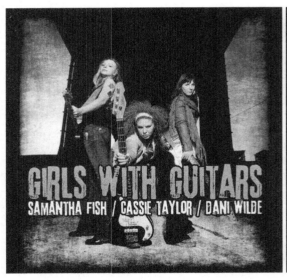

How did the collaboration with Samantha Fish and Cassie Taylor come about?

"I was signed to Ruf Records, who are one of the more successful independent blues labels internationally, and Thomas Ruf who runs the label signed these two amazingly talented American girls Samantha Fish and Cassie Taylor with the aim of putting us on a world tour in 2011 and 2012 (Europe, Canada, America). The tour was called 'Girls with Guitars' and it was a lot of fun. We played around 100 shows and got to see the world together. We were all endorsed by Fender and given some lovely new guitars to play. I played Luther Allison's beautiful Gold Top Les Paul for the studio guitar solo on 'Bitch' though. We shot the promo pics for the tour in Sam's hometown of Kansas City, Missouri which is where us girls first jammed together and where I was first introduced to blues musician Mike Zito who ended up flying over to Hamburg, Germany with us to produce our record in a vibey little studio on Frank Zappa Strasse."

Whose idea was it to record this song?

"I think it was producer Mike Zito's, although possibly it was Samantha's idea. I remember Thomas Ruf was keen to have us record the song when he heard it was on our list. Most of the tracks on our album were originals but we also wanted a few carefully selected covers. We were all Rolling Stones fans and so when this song idea came up I remember we were all excited to make it happen. For me, as a woman recording this song, the title took on a bigger meaning of really showcasing female musicianship. We are three strong women who can rock out with fierce rock n roll attitude and so the word 'Bitch' I think is one we proudly owned when we performed this song.

We shot the music video in the basement of the recording studio in Hamburg the day after we recorded the track. I remember finding it amusing as the vegetarian of the band that I got the verse with the lyric 'just ate a horse meat pie!' It became our most successful track from the album, reaching Number 1 in the ITunes blues chart in Italy and charting top twenty in many other European countries."

Do you perform this (or any other Stones songs) live?

"'Bitch' became the jokey nickname of our lovely drummer Denis Palatin on this tour - He was the only male musician in our group, bless him. We opened the show each night with this song.

Strangely enough, when Denis had to leave our tour due to a family emergency when we were performing in Vienna, Austria - I called upon my friend Martin Wright to fly out and finish off the tour with us. Martin is a British drummer who spent a huge chunk of his professional career touring with Ronnie Wood - He co produced one of Ronnie's solo albums in 2001. So in answer to your question, yes we played this song every night on tour and we played it with Ronnie Wood's drummer (but not Charlie Watts)."

Were the Rolling Stones an influence on you?

"Yes, I covered 'Miss You' on my 2010 album 'Shine' which was produced by Mike Vernon (Blue Horizon). How can anyone not love The Stones - they have so many amazing songs. 'Gimme Shelter' is a fave of mine - I love how session singer Merry Clayton's vocal worked so well next to Jagger's to take that song to a whole new level. I love how they took their huge passion for American Blues Music and combined it with their own British roots to create a new exciting sound. As a British Blues musician myself I find that collision of musical culture and sound really inspiring."

[39] **BLACK LIMOUSINE - JJ Appleton and Jason Ricci** (2015)

(Jagger-Richards-Wood)

Rolling Stones original: Tattoo You (1981)

Jon Jason Appleton (b. 1967), Blues and Rock singer and guitarist from Norwich, Vermont, USA, and, Jason Ricci (b. 1974), Blues and Rock singer and harmonica player from Portland, Maine, USA.

'Black Limousine' was Tattoo You's only real nod to the Rhythm 'n' Blues of old, albeit performed in a somewhat modern Blues-Rock style. JJ Appleton and Jason Ricci's acoustic slide guitar and harmonica performance make it instead sound like a lost Howlin' Wolf or Muddy Waters classic. It can be found on their 2015 album 'Dirty Memory'. [Interview is with JJ Appleton]

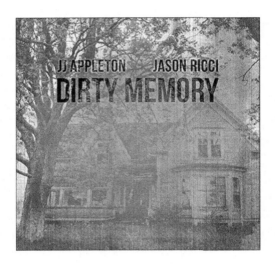

Whose idea was it to record this song?

"It was my idea - I've loved the 'Tattoo You' album since I was a kid. The song feels slightly biographical to me - I married and divorced a woman who was known to ride around in limousines!"

Do you perform this (or any other Stones songs) live?

"Indeed we do! From large outdoor blues festivals, to funky little blues dives - we perform 'Black Limousine' at almost every show."

Were the Rolling Stones an influence on you?

"Absolutely - honestly not so much when they play the blues (although it is good), but their songwriting which is obviously legendary. This particular song reminds me of New York City for some reason, maybe when some of them were living here in the 70's and 80's."

[40] **BLINDED BY LOVE - Kat Kramer** (2001)

(Jagger-Richards)

Rolling Stones original: Steel Wheels (1989)

Katherine Kramer. Actress, producer, activist, and Pop and Country singer from USA.

Perhaps better known for her acting work, Kat Kramer is also a fine Country-tinged Pop singer. Her evolving 'Gemstone' project (some of which was first released on a cassette called 'Hang On To Me Tonight') features mostly Mick Jagger solo songs, as well as a few Rolling Stones plus one Keith Richards solo song. Produced by Jagger collaborator Jimmy Rip, other guest musicians will be familiar to many Stones fans, including Billy Preston, Bernard Fowler, Ivan Neville, Waddy Watchtel, Ernie Watts and Ollie Brown. The song is an unusual combination of Tex-Mex and Country, and Kat's cover emphasises the Mexican feel further by featuring some nice Mariachi horns.

What made you choose this song in particular?

"I chose 'Blinded By Love' as part of my 'GEMSTONE' CD (it's still an evolving title) because I wanted to focus on deep cuts of the Rolling Stones and songs with a love theme. I mainly focus on Mick Jagger solo compositions on my album, because I feel his solo work has been largely under appreciated. I also covered Keith's solo song 'Make No Mistake' from 'Talk Is Cheap.'"

You cut an album of mostly Mick Jagger solo songs, was this your idea or producer Jimmy Rip's?

"The idea to record an album of mostly Mick Jagger solo songs was my idea, and I chose Jimmy Rip to produce and play on the tracks. I selected all the songs. Jimmy did weigh in, and of course arranged/created the styles of the cover versions."

Have members of the Stones (in particular Mick) ever commented on your versions?

"None so far. Mick supposedly has a copy and is more than likely waiting to hear more. I still have a couple more tracks to include."

Have you ever performed the songs live?

"I have performed Rolling Stones songs 'As Tears Go By' 'No Expectations' 'Tumbling Dice' (track from the album) and would love to eventually perform 'Blinded By Love' and other Rolling Stones/Mick Jagger solo songs 'live' in the future."

[41] **BLINDED BY RAINBOWS - Wendy Ellison Mullen** (2000)
(Jagger-Richards)

Rolling Stones original: Voodoo Lounge (1994)

Rock and Blues singer, guitarist and author from Seattle, Washington, USA.

A song that started life as an outtake from Mick Jagger's 1993 solo album 'Wandering Spirit', with a little reworking it became a highlight of 'Voodoo Lounge'. Wendy's strong vocal suits the song well, and can be found on her 2000 album 'Looking For My Kind'. *See [76] for interview!*

[42] **BLUE TURNS TO GREY - Tracey Dey** (1964)
(Jagger-Richards)

Rolling Stones original: 1964 Demo: Bootleg only; 1965 re-cut: December's Children (and Everybody's) (1965)

Nora Ferrari (b. 1943). Pop singer from Yonkers, New York City, USA, who retired from music in the late 60s.

Although The Rolling Stones first demoed the 'Blue Turns To Grey' in 1964, it wasn't until they re-cut it the following year that they considered the song worthy of release. Prior to that, three other artists cut versions of the song, and all are featured here. The first to be released was by Tracey Dey, whose innocent sounding version was on the B-side of her single in 'Didn't Ya' in December 1964.

[43] **BLUE TURNS TO GREY - The Mighty Avengers** (1965)

(Jagger-Richards)

Rolling Stones original: 1964 Demo: Bootleg only; 1965 re-cut: December's Children (and Everybody's) (1965)

Tony Campbell (guitar and vocals), Kevin 'Bep' Mahon (guitar and harmonica), Mike Linnell (vocals and bass) and 'Biffo' Beech (drums and vocals). Beat group from Coventry, UK.

A band that issued three singles in a row with (at the time) unreleased Jagger-Richards songs, their excellent version of 'Blue Turns To Grey' was their 2nd. Unfortunately, it didn't chart. [Interview is with Tony Campbell]

How on earth did you end up with several exclusive Jagger-Richards songs?

"The Mighty Avengers were a very popular Coventry based group and Pete Chambers [The Coventry Music Museum] has accurately written up our history in his books. We were signed to Kennedy Street Artistes in Manchester where we worked a lot, and managed by Danny Betesh who got us initially a record deal with Decca, and then with Andrew Loog Oldham who was managing the Stones. We met Mick and Keith at Andrew's flat, and Marianne Faithful who was with Mick at the time was also there. We recorded 'So Much In Love' and 'Blue Turns to Grey at Regent Sound in Denmark St., with John Paul Jones on piano and Jimmy Page on guitar. I played guitar, Dave Beech played drums, Kevin played tambourine. Mick Linnell played bass and sang lead vocal, with Dave and I on backing vocals. '(Walkin' Thru The) Sleepy City' was done with a live orchestra and we just had to put vocals on during Andrew's Phil Spector "Wall of Sound" phase."

Did any of the Stones attend your recording sessions?

"Mick and Keith did not attend any of the recording sessions, but might have been on the mix downs that we did not attend."

Did you perform these or any other Stones songs live?

"We played all three on stage to promote the records. Only 'So Much In Love' charted here, and also did well in Australia. Andrew has said that he was better known as The Avengers' recording manager in Australia than the Stones who were not so well known there at this time. 'Blue Turns To Grey' was a hit for Cliff, but Hank couldn't copy Jimmy's guitar solo (neither could I).

Dave (Biffo), Kevin and I became the core of Jigsaw in 1966, with the addition of Barrie from Pinkerton's Colours, Tony Britnel from the Fortunes and Clive Scott from the Antarctics."

[44] **BLUE TURNS TO GREY - Dick and Dee Dee** (1965)
(Jagger-Richards)

Rolling Stones original: 1964 Demo: Bootleg only; 1965 re-cut: December's Children (and Everybody's) (1965)

Dick St. John (Richard St. John Gosting, b. 1940 - d. 2003) and Dee Dee Sperling (Mary Spelling). Pop duo from Santa Monica, California, USA.

Using the same backing track as The Mighty Avengers' single, Dick and Dee's version was released on the flip side of another Jagger-Richards song, 'Some Things Just Stick In Your Mind'. It isn't entirely clear what the A-side was though, as they promoted both sides on TV.

Dick and Dee Dee performing 'When Blue Turns To Grey' on 'Hollywood A Go Go', 1965 [US TV]

[45] **BLUE TURNS TO GREY - Cliff Richard and The Shadows** (1966)

(Jagger-Richards)

Rolling Stones original: 1964 Demo: Bootleg only; 1965 re-cut: December's Children (and Everybody's) (1965)

Harry Rodger Webb (b. 1940, in Lucknow, India), with Hank Marvin (Brian Robson Rankin, b. 1941 - guitar and vocals), Bruce Welch (Bruce Cripps, b. 1941 - guitar and vocals), John Rostill (John Henry Rostill, b. 1942 - d. 1973 - bass) and Brian Bennett (Brian Laurence Bennett, b. 1940 - drums). Rock 'n' Roll and Pop singer with backing group from London.

Cliff Richard and The Shadows' version, with its fabulous harmonies, stomping beat and inspired Hank Marvin guitar solo, was only a moderate UK hit at No. 15. Despite this, it remains amongst Cliff's finest ever singles.

Cliff Richard and The Shadows performing 'Blue Turns To Grey' on 'The ABC of ABC', 1966 [UK TV]

[46] **BLUE TURNS TO GREY - Diana Darby** (2003)

(Jagger-Richards)

Rolling Stones original: 1964 Demo: Bootleg only; 1965 re-cut: December's Children (and Everybody's) (1965)

Folk, World and Country singer and guitarist from Houston, Texas, USA.

Diana Darby's gentle Folk arrangement, featuring just her soft, breathy vocals with a couple of guitars, captures the beauty of the melody and lyrics in a way that all the 60s versions didn't. It's a highlight of her 2nd album 'Fantasia Ball'.

Whose idea was it to record this song?

"The idea to record 'Blue Turns To Grey' came from my producer, Mark Linn. I'm a big Stones fan, especially the 60's hits and all of 'Exile On Main St.', but somehow I never had heard 'Blue Turns To Grey'. Mark had this great, vintage Stone's songbook and showed me the lyric and chords. I started playing it, but since I didn't have the Stones version in my head, what I came up with was really different. Mark immediately loved my version and encouraged me to include it on my second album, 'Fantasia Ball'."

Have you performed this (or any other Stones songs) live?

"I performed 'Blue Turns To Grey' a lot in 2003-5, at most every show, and I still play it regularly. 'Fantasia Ball' got picked up by an Italian label, that brought me to Italy for two extensive European tours, so it got played a lot! Ironically, that Italian label discovered me through a Kris Kristofferson cover I recorded for a tribute album ('Jesus Was A Capricorn'). I play lots of other Stone's songs at home, but I haven't performed them live."

Were the Rolling Stones an influence on your own music?

"Yes! I grew up listening to their music on the radio. I've always wished I could rock out more like the Stones or Velvets, but when I pick up my guitar and start writing and playing, that's never what comes out. I think I write more of an internal rock, where the beat pulses in my veins, and my whispers are silent screams. I was drawn to 'Blue Turns To Grey', because when I sang it I felt the deep remorse and sadness in the song. I literally could feel the blue shifting to grey, and that desperate feeling of looking for someone and realizing they are nowhere to be found and that what you had is gone forever."

[47] **BROWN SUGAR - Little Richard** (1971)

(Jagger-Richards)

Rolling Stones original: Sticky Fingers (1971) + UK/US A-side (1971)

Richard Wayne Penniman (b. 1932 - d. 2020). Rock 'n' Roll, Rhythm 'n' Blues, Gospel and Soul singer from Macon, Georgia, USA.

If Chuck Berry was Rock 'n' Roll's most influential guitarist, then the accolade of most influential vocalist belongs to Little Richard. A song now deemed controversial in these more sensitive times, Mick Jagger must've been thrilled to know that the first major cover was by one of his heroes. There is no piano, and the pace is moderate rather than frantic, but Little Richard's incredible voice is unmistakable. It was released on his modestly-titled 1971 album 'King of Rock and Roll'.

[48] **BROWN SUGAR - Thunder** (1990)

(Jagger-Richards)

Rolling Stones original: Sticky Fingers (1971) + UK/US A-side (1971)

Danny Bowes (Daniel John Bowes, b. 1960 - vocals), Luke Morley (b. 1960 - guitar, keyboards, harmonica and vocals), Ben Matthews (b. 1963 - guitar, keyboards and vocals), Mark 'Snake' Luckhurst (bass and vocals) and Gary Harry James (b. 1960 - drums, guitar and vocals). Hard Rock and Heavy Metal band from London.

A hard-rockin' live performance, there is no doubting the band's obvious love of the song. It was a bonus track on their 1990 'Dirty Love' single.

[49] **BROWN SUGAR - Collin Raye** (1997)

(Jagger-Richards)

Rolling Stones original: Sticky Fingers (1971) + UK/US A-side (1971)

Floyd Elliot Wray (b. 1960). Country singer and guitarist from De Queen, Arkansas, USA.

Basically Rock music sung with a slight twang, Collin Raye's cover is worth a listen for the excellent slide guitar. It is on the 1997 'Stone Country' CD.

[50] **BROWN SUGAR - Ken Boothe** (2002)

(Jagger-Richards)

Rolling Stones original: Sticky Fingers (1971) + UK/US A-side (1971)

Kenneth George Boothe (b. 1948). Reggae singer from Kingston, Jamaica.

Ken Boothe is mostly known for 'Lover's Rock' Reggae-style ballads. So it is a very pleasant surprise to hear his involved and inspired vocal on this excellent Reggae-fied performance. It is on the 'Paint It Black: A Reggae Tribute To The Rolling Stones' CD.

[51] **BROWN SUGAR - Honeywagon** (2005)

(Jagger-Richards)

Rolling Stones original: Sticky Fingers (1971) + UK/US A-side (1971)

Bryan Clark (vocals, guitar and dobro), Loren Ellis (mandolin and banjo), Ben Levine (acoustic bass) and Mike Drake (fiddle). Bluegrass and Country band from Hollywood, California, USA.

Unbelievably, this is performed as a very fast acoustic Bluegrass song, complete with a mandolin solo. It is available on the various artists 'Paint It Blue: A Bluegrass Tribute to The Rolling Stones' CD.

[52] **BROWN SUGAR - Alice Russell** (2011)

(Jagger-Richards)

Rolling Stones original: Sticky Fingers (1971) + UK/US A-side (1971)

(b. 1975). Soul, Funk and Nu Jazz singer from Suffolk, UK.

Country, Reggae, Bluegrass... and modern R&B? Why not, though Alice Russell's well-sung version can probably best be described as Soul-Rock. It can be heard on the fascinating 'Sticky Soul Fingers: A Rolling Stones Tribute' CD.

Whose idea was it to record this song?

"It was Mojo magazine, they wanted to make a tribute compilation of the Rolling Stones songs... Sticky Fingers! And we each got a song to tackle in our own way."

Do you perform this (or any other Stones songs) live?

"Do you know what I never have, if I were to it would probably be 'Beast Of Burden'... that was on heavy rotation as a teen."

Were the Rolling Stones an influence on you?

"So being totally honest they aren't ones that pop right up, and I feel a direct link that heavily made an impressive on the music I have gone on to make, but like all music through my ears... it all plays its part in our new tapestry so, yes, the main album I had was Exile On Main St.. I was a hip-hop head teen and from that found a lot of artists that had then been sampled, so then found all this other amazing shiz that blew my mind open!"

[53] **BROWN SUGAR - Steven Tyler and Nuno Bettencourt** (2018)
(Jagger-Richards)

Rolling Stones original: Sticky Fingers (1971) + UK/US A-side (1971)

Steven Victor Tallarico (b. 1948). Hard Rock and Blues Rock singer, harmonicist and pianist from New York City, USA, and Nuno Duarte Gil Mendes Bettencourt (b. 1966), Glam Metal and Hard Rock guitarist from Azores, Portugal. The singer from Aerosmith and the guitarist from Extreme.

Steven Tyler is sometimes compared to Mick Jagger, but apart the lips, he is far closer musically to Led Zeppelin. With a gloriously over-the-top vocal, creative guitar and punchy horns, what this cover of 'Brown Sugar' lacks in subtlety it more than makes up for in both enthusiasm and musicality. It is on the various artists 'Muscle Shoals: Small Town Big Sound' album.

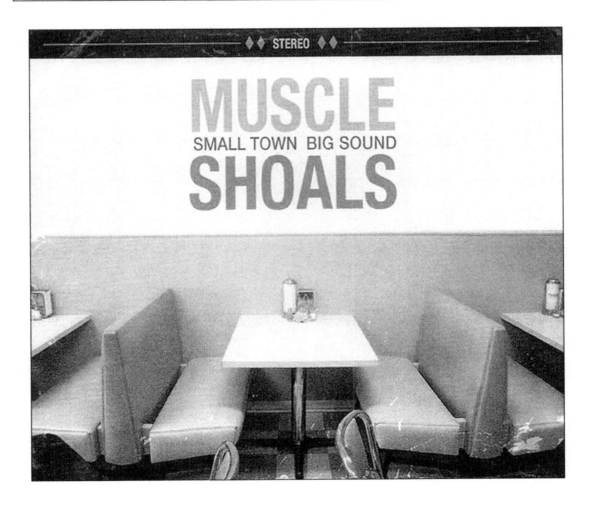

[54] **CAN'T BELIEVE IT - The Chesterfield Kings** (1994)

(Jagger-Richards)

Rolling Stones original (recorded 1966): Bootleg only

Greg Prevost (b. 1959 - vocals, guitarist, harmonica, tabla, sitar, maracas, theremin and percussion), Andy Babiuk (Andrew Michael Babiuk, b. 1963 - bass, guitar, sitar, dulcimer, mellotron, recorder and percussion), Paul Rocco (b. 1962 - guitar, piano, zither and autoharp) and Brett Reynolds (drums, congas, bongos, tambourine, maracas and percussion). Garage Rock and Psychedelic Rock band from Rochester, New York, USA. Disbanded in 2009.

Perhaps *the* greatest Rolling Stones outtake is a 'Between The Buttons' era song that has appeared on bootlegs under such titles as 'Get Yourself Together', 'I Can See It' and 'Can´t Believe'. Amazingly, two great cover versions of the song appeared in 1994, with The Chesterfield Kings' version, titled 'Can't Believe It', being the better known. Under the leadership of Stones fanatic Greg Prevost, the band always captured the sound and spirit of the Stones without resorting to impersonation or parody, and such is the case here. His powerful, assured vocal and the impeccable musicianship shows exactly what the Stones could've done with the song if they'd worked on it just a little longer. It is on their album 'Let's Go Get Stoned'. [Interview is with Greg Prevost]

Where did you first come across the unreleased Stones original?

"I was / still am a heavy collector of anything concerning the Stones - I had 100s of bootleg albums and that song always knocked me out. It was on at least 4 boots I had during the time I recorded that song with the Chesterfield Kings."

Did you need special permission to record it?

"No, as with most cover songs you just do them and credit the writers and place the publishing company name on the song. Since this was on a bootleg, no publishers were credited so I just credited the Stones' then current publishing company on the album."

Have any Stones members ever commented on your version?

"Only Mick Taylor, since we recorded 'I'm Not Talking' with him for the same album ('Let's Go Get Stoned') that 'Can't Believe It' is on. I initially asked him if he'd play on 'Can't Believe It' but he said he couldn't do this (a Stones song) out of respect for Keith Richards. He said he liked it a lot and would have liked playing on it. He instead opted to play on the Mose Allison number 'I'm Not Talking'. He also told me that what we were doing reminded him of the 'Exile' sessions."

Did you perform this or any other Stones songs live?

"Yes, too many Stones songs to remember over the 33 years the band existed. I can recall we also did 'All Sold Out', 'Midnight Rambler', 'Little T&A' and 'She Said Yeah' among several others."

[55] **CAN'T BELIEVE IT (GOT YOURSELF TOGETHER)** - Bum (1994)

(Jagger-Richards)

Rolling Stones original (recorded 1966): Bootleg only

Rob Nesbitt (guitar and vocals), Andrew Molloy (guitar and vocals), Kevin Lee (bass) and Graham Watson (drums), with Mike Ledwidge (piano). Pop-Punk band from Victoria, British Columbia, Canada.

Though perhaps lacking the power and crisp production of The Chesterfield Kings' version, Bum's cover, titled 'Got Yourself Together' is still more than worthwhile, particularly for the lead guitar and piano. Released on Bum's album 'I Am Superwoman', it would be more widely known if another band hadn't unintentionally stolen their thunder. [Interview is with Andrew Molloy]

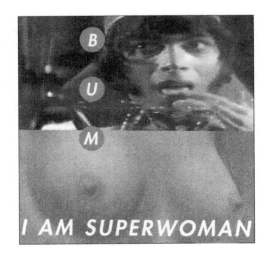

Did you learn the song via The Chesterfield Kings' version or from a Stones bootleg?

"I'm the Stones obsessive in the group and it was my idea to cover 'Got Yourself Together'. No, I hadn't already heard the Chesterfield Kings version, though I am a big fan of theirs. We recorded our version in December, '93 and it came out Spring '94 (May, I think?). I heard their version shortly after and my first thought was 'damn, someone else had the same great idea as me!'. I really like their take, especially Greg Prevost's vocal. We had played the song live a few times in the summer of '93 but our other guitar player, Rob, had been singing it (I think I had given him a tape of the version I had from a vinyl bootleg called Diverse Harmonics). When it came time to record in December of that year (we were recording a few covers for a compilation) Rob suggested I sing it since I was the Stones freak who had suggested it in the first place. So I did but I definitely feel like I would have done a better job on the vocal had I already been singing it live. My favourite thing about our version of 'Got Yourself Together' is the brilliant, Hopkins-inspired piano by our (dearly departed) friend, Mike Ledwidge. He had never heard the song before the day he came into the studio to lay his part down. He nailed it."

Have you performed this (or any other Stones songs) live?

"So yes, we had played it live a few times. We also played 'Bitch' and 'Miss Amanda Jones' a few times. In addition, we actually did three shows as Steel Wheels, our tribute to 80's Stones (only songs from their 80's oeuvre allowed). One of those sets was recorded from the audience by a friend and we included one song, 'Worried About You', as a hidden bonus track on the CD release 'I Am Superwoman' (the release which also contained 'Got Yourself Together'). One final bit of Stones-related ephemera: we did a split single that same year with our friends The Smugglers and the single was dubbed Tattoo Dave as the cover featured their guitarist, Dave Carswell, on the front in Tattoo You-inspired face makeup. Dave was our Jagger in the aforementioned Steel Wheels project. The b-side of that single contained a live version (recorded in Eugene, Oregon on tour) of 'Hang Fire' in which all members of both bands took the stage together. That was sort of the germ of the idea for the Steel Wheels project. It was borne of a mutual love of the Stones."

Were the Rolling Stones an influence on your own music?

"There were quite a few Stones touchstones for us back then. Which is kinda funny because we didn't really sound that way at all with our originals (more of a Ramones/Buzzcocks thing). So while I'm not sure how much the rest of the band would consider them to have been an influence (though they all certainly liked them - Charlie was our drummer's fave drummer) I would say they definitely were for me; it would be more evident stylistically in subsequent bands I put together. In short, the Rolling Stones are, and always will be, my favourite band."

[56] **CAN'T YOU HEAR ME KNOCKING - Santana and Scott Weiland** (2010)

(Jagger-Richards)

Rolling Stones original: Sticky Fingers (1971)

Latin Rock Band from San Francisco, California, USA, led by guitarist Carlos Santana (Carlos Augusto Santana Alves, b. 1947), and Hard Rock singer Scott Richard Weiland (b. 1967 - d. 2015). Guitarist for Santana and vocalist for Stone Temple Pilots.

A highlight of the consistently great 'Sticky Fingers' (and the only album they've performed in its entirety at a single gig), Santana and Scott Weiland's version unsurprisingly focuses more on Carlos' imaginative lead guitar than the hard riffing of the original, while Scott proves himself a sympathetic interpreter of the song. It is on Santana's 'Guitar Heaven - The Greatest Guitar Classics of All Time'.

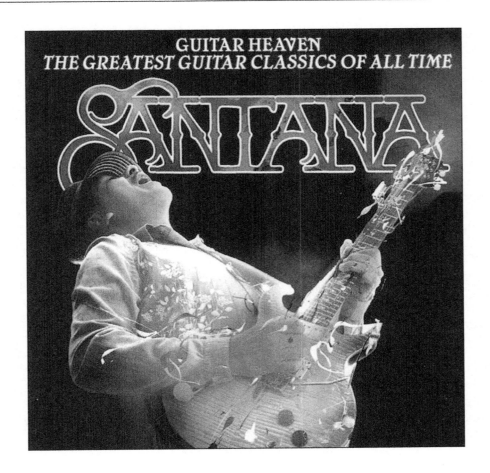

[57] CAN'T YOU HEAR ME KNOCKING - The Bamboos (2011)

(Jagger-Richards)

Rolling Stones original: Sticky Fingers (1971)

Funk and Soul band from Melbourne, Australia, led by guitarist, producer and songwriter Lance Ferguson and featuring Kylie Auldist (b. 1986) on vocals.

One of Australia's top bands, this fine Soul interpretation has horns instead of guitar playing the song's main riff, as well as a superb vocal by Kylie Auldist. It is on 'Sticky Soul Fingers: A Rolling Stones Tribute'. [Interview is with Lance Ferguson]

Whose idea was it to record this song?

"We were approached by Mojo Magazine to record this version, who were doing a 'Sticky Fingers' tribute for the free CD that accompanied the magazine at the time. Keith's guitar intro on this song is one of his classic moments on record - pure, unbridled blues-drenched raw greatness. It utilises his famous 5-string open G tuning technique (which he borrowed from Ike Turner). I was very weary of attempting to try to re-create this on guitar myself, so we put the line on the horns for our version and I think it gives it a point of difference."

Do you perform this (or any other Stones songs) live?

"After we recorded this version it got some good feedback, so we will still even now occasionally drop it into our live set."

Were the Rolling Stones an influence on you?

"The music of The Bamboos is rooted in Soul and Funk, but at times we have also skewed towards the rockier side of the spectrum. Working with Tim Rogers (You Am I) on the 'Rules Of Attraction' album brought us even closer to that sweet musical place where those soulful genres collide. The very first music book I had as a high school guitarist was the 'Big Hits (High Tide And Green Grass)' music transcription book so The 'Stones have always been with me."

[58] **CASINO BOOGIE - Casino Steel** (1990)

(Jagger-Richards)

Rolling Stones original: Exile On Main St. (1972)

Stein Groven (b. 1952). Rock singer and keyboardist from Trondheim, Norway.

Performed at a more lively pace than the original, Casino Steel's version of this 'Exile On Main St.' song features some inspired piano playing throughout, and would be even better if the guitar was mixed a tad higher. It is from his 2nd album, 1990's 'Casino Steel'.

[59] **'CAUSE I'M IN LOVE WITH YOU - Joey Paige** (1965)

(Wyman)

Rolling Stones original: unavailable, possibly never made

Joseph E. Sauseris (b. 1939). Pop-Rock and Garage Rock singer from Philadelphia, Pennsylvania, USA.

Bill Wyman's ''Cause I'm In Love With You' was recorded in 1964 by the totally obscure band Hi-Jinx, but that never got as far as a release. So instead, it was handed to Joey Paige, someone that Bill and Brian befriended on a US tour. The song isn't bad at all, with Joey's harmonized and harmonica-accompanied single sounding like a lost The Everly Brothers classic - an act that Joey had previously played bass for. [Joey Paige was traced during the research of this book, but declined to be interviewed as he is currently working on his own book]

[60] **CHILD OF THE MOON - Radon Daughters** (2001)
(Jagger-Richards)

Rolling Stones original: UK/US B-side (1968)

Bronwyn Rucker (vocals) and Woody Regan (piano). Pop and Cabaret duo from New York City, USA.

The B-side of 'Jumpin' Jack Flash' and the Stones' final nod towards psychedelia, 'Child Of The Moon' has long been a much-loved "deep cut" amongst fans. Backed just by a piano riff and keyboards, Radon Daughters' harmonised revival is on their sole album 'Glow'.

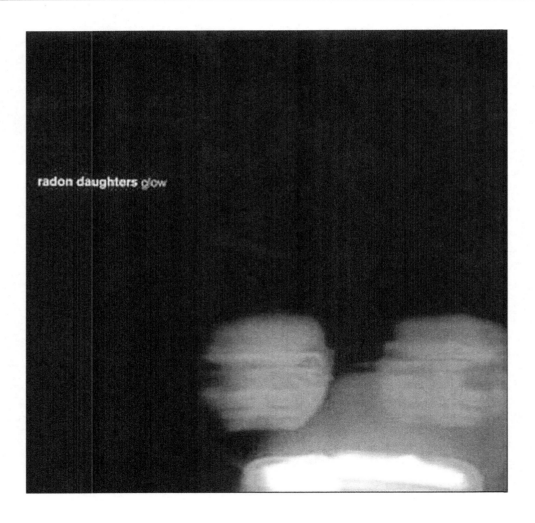

[61] **CHILD OF THE MOON - Celestial Bums** (2015)
(Jagger-Richards)

Rolling Stones original: UK/US B-side (1968)

Japhy Ryder (vocals, guitar, bass and keyboards), David InFurs (guitar), Albert Segura (guitar), Augusto J. Marchetti (drums) and Lotte Blum (vocals, keyboards and percussion). Psychedelic Rock from Barcelona, Spain.

With a distorted guitar riff, a dreamy echo-laden vocal and a whole host of effects, Celestial Bums' version is very different to the original. It is part of 'Stoned: A Psych Tribute to The Rolling Stones'. [Interview is with Japhy Ryder]

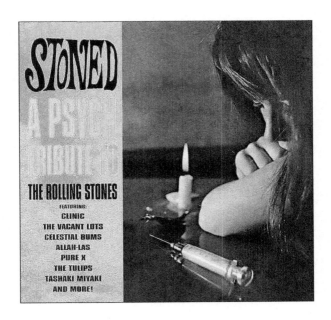

Whose idea was it to record this song?

"I brought up the idea as wanted to include a not very well-known song from their 'psychedelic' era."

Do you perform this (or any other Stones songs) live?

"Not much, however we are going to be playing this song in some concerts this fall."

Were the Rolling Stones an influence on you?

"Yes, big influence since the teenage years. Albums like 'Their Satanic Majesties Request' or 'Exile On Main St.' are key for us."

[62] **CITADEL - The Damned** (1981)

(Jagger-Richards)

Rolling Stones original: Their Satanic Majesties Request (1967)

Dave Vanian (David Lett, b. 1956 - vocals), Captain Sensible (Raymond Ian Burns, b. 1954 - guitar, keyboards and vocals), Algy Ward (Alasdair Mackie Ward, b. 1959 - bass) and Rat Scabies (Christopher John Millar, b. 1955 - drums and vocals). Punk and Gothic Rock band from London.

Probably the most musically accomplished band to come out of the original Punk era, The Damned weren't shy about revealing their love of '60s Psychedelia, including 'Satanic Majesties' era Rolling Stones. Their version of 'Citadel' is a little faster than the Stones' and Vanian's voice is quite different to Jagger's, but otherwise the arrangement is basically the same apart from some very '60s backwards guitar after the fade. It was released on their 1981 'Friday 13th' EP. [Interview is with Rat Scabies]

Whose idea was it to record/perform these songs?

"It was the Captain's idea to record 'Citadel', he actually wanted to re-record the whole of 'Satanic Majesties' but we didn't have time."

Did you perform these (or any other Stones songs) live?

"We played 'The Last Time' on a reunion show and 'We Love You' was always a popular encore."

Were the Rolling Stones an influence on you?

"Not on me so much as the rest of the band, but they've made so many records that you would be hard pressed not to find a couple of tracks that you thought were great."

[63] **COCKSUCKER BLUES - Daddy Long Legs** (2010)

(Jagger-Richards)

Rolling Stones original: Bootleg only (recorded 1970)

Brian Hurd (vocals, harmonica and guitar), Murat Aktürk (slide guitar) and Josh Styles (drums and percussion). Blues-Rock band from New York City, USA.

When the Stones terminated their contract with Decca, they were told that they were obliged to give them one final single. So Mick offered this *extremely* X-rated acoustic blues with explicit descriptions of homosexual practices, knowing full well that it would be totally un-releasable! Daddy Long Legs' cover was released as a single on Norton records, a company that (mostly) specialised in cover versions of Decca-era Rolling Stones songs.

[64] **COMING DOWN AGAIN - Anders Parker** (2011)

(Jagger-Richards)

Rolling Stones original: Goats Head Soup (1973)

(b. 1970). Indie Rock and Folk singer and guitarist from New York, USA.

The Stones' version is a piano-led ballad with one of Keith Richards' finest vocal performances. Anders Parker's version features just his gravelly vocals and a detuned acoustic guitar, making him sound like he really is coming down again. It is one of the more adventurous selections from 'Paint It Black: An Alt Country Tribute To The Rolling Stones'.

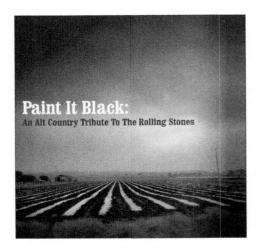

[65] **COMPLICATED - The Grays** (1994)

(Jagger-Richards)

Rolling Stones original: Between The Buttons (1967)

Jason Falkner (b. 1968 - vocals, guitar, bass and keyboards), Jon Brion (b. 1963 - vocals, guitar, keyboards and bass), Buddy Judge (vocals and guitar) and Dan McCarroll (drums). Rock and Pop band from Los Angeles, California, USA. Disbanded in 1994.

The Grays' cover of 'Complicated' starts with pounding drums, handclaps and a distorted guitar riff, sounding almost like a Gary Glitter record until the vocal kicks in. This excellent stomper was issued as part of the band's 1994 'Same Thing' single.

[66] **COMPLICATED - Bettye Lavette** (2015)

(Jagger-Richards)

Rolling Stones original: Between The Buttons (1967)

Betty Jo Haskins (b. 1946). Soul and Rhythm 'n' Blues singer from Muskegon, Michigan, USA.

Ably supported by simple yet effective guitar, bass, drums and keyboards, Bettye Lavette's expressive, mature and soulful voice help make this cover of 'Complicated' a highlight of her suitably-titled 2015 album 'Worthy'.

[67] COMPLICATED - Chris Richards and The Subtractions (2015)
(Jagger-Richards)

Rolling Stones original: Between The Buttons (1967)

Chris Richards (vocals and guitar), Todd Holmes (bass) and Larry Grodsky (drums). Power Pop band from Livonia, Michigan, USA.

With its sprightly tempo, jangly guitars, and an exciting breakdown (with a sneaky 'Hey Jude' inspired "Na na na na"), Chris Richards and The Subtractions' version of 'Complicated' is very fine indeed. It is on their '3peat! - That Covers That' EP. [Interview is with Chris Richards]

Whose idea was it to record this song?

"We have been making digital-only cover EPs 'That Covers That' (three volumes) in-between records for the last decade or so. Covering bands that have meant a great deal to us - including the Stones as well as Elvis Costello, the Kinks, The Who, Big Star and many more."

Do you perform this (or any other Stones songs) live?

"Years ago an early power pop band I had in the 80's (Hippodrome) did a pretty cool version of 'She's A Rainbow' as I was utterly obsessed with 'Their Satanic Majesties Request' and still am to this day! One of my first ever 4 track recordings was a (rough) version of 'Angie'... I was smart enough never to try and pull that off live."

Were the Rolling Stones an influence on you?

"Absolutely... as I mentioned, my love of TSMR, I also cannot get enough of 'Aftermath', 'Between The Buttons', 'Sticky' and 'Exile'... an amazing band with an amazing catalog of songs. Breathtaking when you take it all in."

[68] **CONGRATULATIONS - West Five** (1965)

(Jagger-Richards)

Rolling Stones original: 12 X 5 (1964) + US B-side (1964)

Barry Summerfield (vocals and guitar), Colin 'Bone' Charles (vocals and guitar), Michael Snow (vocals and keyboards), Don Broughton (vocals and bass) and Gerry Wood (vocals and drums). Pop and Rock group from London, known as West Four until Liverpool-born Michael Snow joined them. Disbanded in 1965.

Though not without its charm, The Rolling Stones' original of 'Congratulations' sounds like little more than a rough run-through, and wasn't even considered worthy of release in the UK. West Five polished the song up considerably for their single release, adding some stunning harmonies, as well as a gloriously over-the-top guitar solo that a young Jimmy Page would've been proud of. [Interview is with Michael Snow]

The Stones' version wasn't issued in the UK at the time... how did you come across it?

"West Five had just been signed to the Tommy Sanderson Agency when I joined them from Liverpool. Tommy had The Hollies and The Zombies under contract, so when Doris Troy's hit 'Just One Look' was covered by The Hollies, she was invited to be the guest star on that first Stones / Hollies tour, and Doris chose West Five as her backing band... a position I held as her bandleader/ Musical director for the next twenty five years. Lucky Me! When we returned from that tour, having met Loog and the boys a lot, Andrew sent an acetate of 'Congratulations' to Tommy for us as, we'd just signed with HMV. Well, their demo was rubbish, but there were very talented players and arrangers in West Five, and we had been killing audiences with our quintet harmonies on the American song 'Just Like Romeo and Juliet' (by The Reflections). So our drummer/leader, Gerry Wood, built this great vocal arrangement on his American perception of R&B, with Barry Summerfield playing an amazing, pre Hendrix guitar solo. It still sounds like The Four Seasons in heaven with Jimi to me!"

[69] **CONNECTION - Eric Burdon and The Animals** (1967)
(Jagger-Richards)

Rolling Stones original: Between The Buttons (1967)

Eric Burdon (Eric Victor Burdon, b. 1941 - vocals), Vic Briggs (Victor Harvey Briggs III, 1945 - d. 2021 - guitar), John Weider (b. 1947 - guitar and violin), Danny McCulloch (Daniel Joseph McCulloch, b. 1945 - d. 2015 - bass) and Barry Jenkins (Colin Ernest Jenkins, b. 1944 - drums). Rock, Rhythm 'n' Blues and Psychedelia band who originated in Newcastle-upon-Tyne, UK.

When The Rolling Stones first started out, Keith Richards was vocally silent, with all of their 1st EP and nearly all of their 1st LP featuring Brian and Bill on backing vocals. However, by the time of 'Between The Buttons' Keith's confidence had grown enough for him to do what are effectively two duets with Mick Jagger. One of these is 'Something Happened To Me Yesterday', and the other song is this one, 'Connection'. It was rumoured at the time to have also been offered to Eric Burdon and his newly-revamped Animals, but sadly only a slightly iffy-sounding BBC radio recording has surfaced to date. Despite this, the performance is excellent, with vocal stylist Eric making the song very much his own. It can be found on several CD collections of dubious legality.

[70] **CONNECTION - Ramblin' Jack Elliott (1968)**

(Jagger-Richards)

Rolling Stones original: Between The Buttons (1967)

Elliot Charles Adnopoz (b. 1931). Folk, Country and Bluegrass singer and guitarist from Brooklyn, New York, USA.

Making the song sound like it was written by Bill Monroe 30 years earlier, Ramblin' Jack Elliott's cover is an up-tempo Bluegrass treatment. It is featured on his 1968 album 'Young Brigham'.

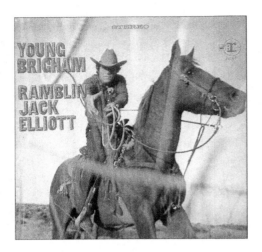

[71] **CONNECTION - Arlo Guthrie (1976)**

(Jagger-Richards)

Rolling Stones original: Between The Buttons (1967)

Arlo Davy Guthrie (b. 1947). Folk and Folk Rock singer, guitarist, pianist and harmonicist from Brooklyn, New York City, USA.

Not an imitation of Ramblin' Jack Elliott's arrangement as perhaps expected, instead Arlo Guthrie transforms the song into a mid-tempo very 70s-sounding Pop-Rocker. This can be found on his 1976 album 'Amigo'.

[72] **CONNECTION - Richard Lloyd** (1981)

(Jagger-Richards)

Rolling Stones original: Between The Buttons (1967)

Richard Lloyd (b. 1951). Rock, Punk Rock and New Wave singer and guitarist from Pittsburgh, Pennsylvania, USA.

Best known as a former member of Art-Punk band Television, Richard Lloyd's cover has lots of discordant, creative and prominently mixed guitar. It was released as a single, b/w 'Get Off Of My Cloud'.

Whose idea was it to record these songs?

"My idea."

Do you perform these or any other Stones songs live?

"Sometimes."

Were the Rolling Stones an influence on your own music?

"Big influence. I was a Stones fan since 1964."

[73] **CONNECTION - Everclear** (1993)
(Jagger-Richards)

Rolling Stones original: Between The Buttons (1967)

Art Alexakis (Arthur Paul Alexakis, b. 1962 - vocals and guitar), Craig Montoya (Craig Aloysius Montoya, b. 1970 - bass and vocals) and Scott Cuthbert (drums and vocals). Alternative Rock, Punk and Grunge band from Portland, Oregon, USA.

The song's mixture of Garage Rock and melodic Pop made it an ideal song to revive for the Grunge era, as heard on Everclear's suitably unsubtle version. It is on their 1993 'Nervous & Weird' single. [Interview is with Art Alexakis]

Whose idea was it to record this song?

"It was my idea… growing up in the '60s as the youngest of 5 children I was immersed in pop radio as far as I can remember. The album 'Between The Buttons' in particular was a huge fave in my household, but this was always one of my favourites. Even as a child, I loved the swagger and melodies."

Do you perform this (or any other Stones songs) live?

"Everclear recorded this as a b-side back in 1993. We used to play it a lot but I don't think we have played it since the late '90s."

Were the Rolling Stones an influence on you?

"The Rolling Stones were and still are a huge influence on me! I never acquiesced to the stupid debate of Beatles vs The Stones… if you love rock and roll, how could you not love both? I have covered other Rolling Stones songs in various bands, 'Dead Flowers', 'Jigsaw Puzzle', 'Far Away Eyes'…"

[74] COOL, CALM AND COLLECTED - The Grassmasters (2005)

(Jagger-Richards)

Rolling Stones original: Between The Buttons (1967)

Bill Hullett (guitar), Vic Jordan (banjo), Andy Lewis (fiddle), Fred Newell (guitar and mandolin), David Spicher (bass and guitar), Charlie Chadwick (bass) and Tommy White (dobro). Nashville studio-based Country and Bluegrass band from Nashville.

The Grassmasters released a whole album of Bluegrass instrumentals with Rolling Stones songs, though 'Cool, Calm and Collected' is the most unexpected. It even speeds up to a discordant 'crash' at the end, followed by the band's laughter - just like the Stones' original.

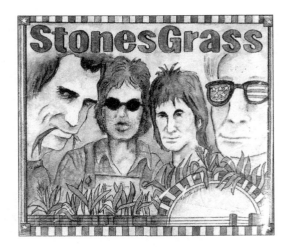

[75] COUNTRY HONK - Smoking Stones Trio (2016)

(Jagger-Richards)

Rolling Stones original: Let It Bleed (1969)

Vocals, Piano and Drums RS Tribute Band, from Barcelona, Spain.

The Rolling Stones' version of 'Country Honk' is an old-time country arrangement of 'Honky Tonk Women', just the way the song was originally conceived before being revamped into the Rock style of the famous single. Smoking Stones Trio's stripped down and guitar-less cover features a Jagger-esque vocal and some nice Johnnie Johnson/Ian Stewart style piano. It is on their album 'Naked Stones'.

[76] DANCE (PT. 1) - Wendy Ellison Mullen (2004)

(Jagger-Richards-Wood)

Rolling Stones original: Emotional Rescue (1980)

Rock and Blues singer, guitarist and writer from Seattle, Washington, USA.

The author of the *essential* Rolling Stones book 'Ronnie Wood's Smile (and where it led)' and webmaster of one of the very first fan sites in the mid-90s, Wendy also cut a whole album of Ronnie Wood-related songs. As well as his solo songs and some Faces classics, included are the Stones' 'It's Only Rock 'n' Roll', 'Black Limousine', and this one, 'Dance (Pt. 1)'. Wendy's version stays faithfull to the original, with her powerful and androgynous-sounding voice suiting the song well. It can be found on her 2004 album 'Ode to Ronnie Wood'.

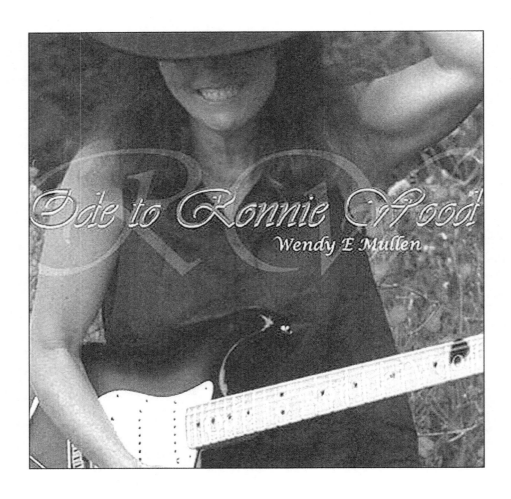

You recorded a whole album of Ronnie Wood-composed songs 'Ode to Ronnie Wood'... what prompted that?

"I wrote a book... It won a Real Contest! 'Ronnie Wood's Smile' was the Winner of the 2005 '13th Annual Writer's Digest International Self-Published Book Awards' in the category 'Life Stories' (serendipitously, you chose the song that is actually describing the last episode in the book!). Because I became fascinated with Ronnie's guitar work, I also learned to play the electric guitar!"

Has Ronnie ever commented on the album?

"Sadly, no. He's never commented on the songs. I've tried to give them to him... who knows?

He has never commented on my book either, but I know he has it (or had it). A friend placed it in his hand at an art show. Another friend placed it in Keith's hands too, and said he'd give it to Ronnie (the book, not the CD)."

Do you perform this or any other Stones songs live?

"I joined a band as lead singer and rhythm guitarist. We played at Bumbershoot (a big Seattle festival) among many other bars and parties in town. We did a lot of Stones songs... including 'Live With Me' and 'Satisfaction' and 'Sway' (think Karla Bonoff and Mick Taylor). That lasted many years, say 1999-2010. I then formed a duo with my lead guitarist and we did A LOT of Stones songs... a favourite is 'Spider and The Fly'. We played in bars and restaurants here in Seattle until Covid. Last May 30th (2022), I played with just a percussionist at the Folklife Festival. I had limited time and did 'Spider and The Fly' and 'Heart of Stone' ('Eleanor Rigby' brought the house down, though)."

Were the Rolling Stones an influence on your own music?

"Yes, of COURSE, the Stones were an influence. The big influence was, of course, me returning to the guitar and then "plugging in"... and eventually led to my best song, 'Stand Up! Fight Back!'."

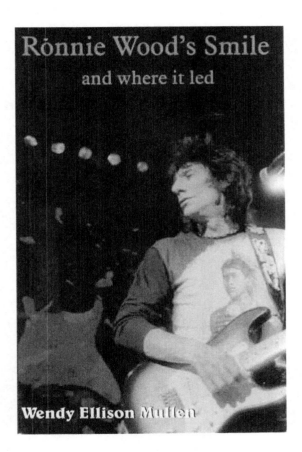

[77] **DANCING WITH MR. D. - Two Sheds** (1991)
(Jagger-Richards)

Rolling Stones original: Goats Head Soup (1973) + US B-side (1973)

Göran Magnusson (vocals and guitar), Ulf Larsen (guitar and trumpet), Rikard "Tåzt" Nilsson (bass guitar) and Anders "Lappen" Rosendahl (drums). Alternative Rock band from Malmo, Sweden. Disbanded in 1995.

The Rolling Stones' original of 'Dancing With Mr. D.' always seemed like a poor relation of 'Sympathy For The Devil', with little of the menace of its predecessor. Swedish metal merchants Two Shed's deconstruction completely alters the melody and riff, and in the process comes up with something that sounds genuinely frightening. It is on their 2nd album 'Out Of Our Sheds'.

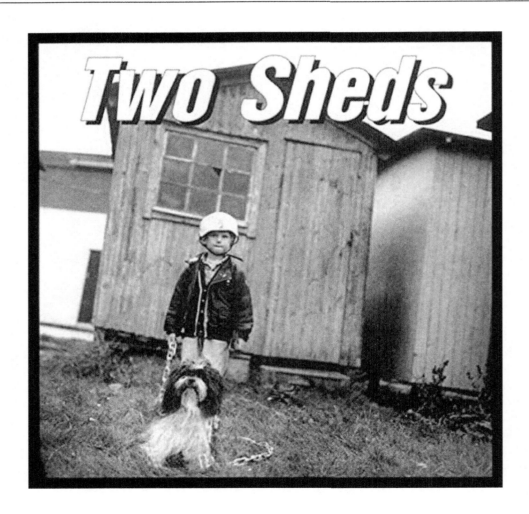

[78] **DANDELION - Miranda Lee Richards** (2001)
(Jagger-Richards)

Rolling Stones original: UK B-side and US A-side (1967)

(b. 1965). Folk Rock, Country Rock and World singer and guitarist from San Francisco, California, USA.

Perhaps the less remembered side of the Stones' '67 'Summer of Love' single (despite it being the A-side in the USA), Miranda Lee Richards' version starts with discordant faded-in strings, followed by a nice mixture of retro (harpsichord and sweet harmonies) and modern (a very 90s/00s sounding drums and guitar). It was included on her debut album 'The Herethereafter' in 2001.

What made you choose to record this song?

"My record company at the time, Virgin Records, actually suggested it! My first choice was 'She's a Rainbow' or 'No Expectations'."

Have any Stones members commented on your version?

"I met Mick Jagger once and told him I covered the song. His reply was, 'Really?'."

Do you ever perform the song live?

"Yes, during the tour to promote my first album, 'The Herethereafter', we performed it every night. I haven't since, but I have been known to throw 'No Expectations' (which I haven't recorded) into the set."

[79] DEAD FLOWERS - New Riders Of The Purple Sage (1974)

(Jagger-Richards)

Rolling Stones original: Sticky Fingers (1971)

John Dawson (John Collins Dawson IV, b. 1945 - d. 2009 - guitar and vocals), David Nelson (b. 1943 - guitar and vocals), Buddy Cage (b. 1946 - d. 2020 - pedal steel guitar), Dave Torbert (David Edwin Torbert, b. 1948 - d. 1982 - bass and vocals) and Spencer Dryden (Spencer Charles Dryden, b. 1938 - d. 2005 - drums). Country Rock band from San Francisco, California, USA.

Mick and Keith (and later Ronnie) have long had a genuine affection for Country music, and have written several songs with a strong Country influence that have since become standards in the genre. A good example of this is 'Dead Flowers'. A band that started off as a Grateful Dead spin-off, New Riders Of The Purple Sage's cover remains faithful to the original. It was first released in a live version on the 1974 album 'Home, Home On The Road', while a studio version surfaced 2 years later on 'New Riders'.

[80] DEAD FLOWERS - Cowboy Junkies (1990)

(Jagger-Richards)

Rolling Stones original: Sticky Fingers (1971)

Margo Timmins (b. 1961 - vocals), Michael Timmins (b. 1959 - guitar), Alan Anton (b. 1959 - bass) and Peter Timmins (b. 1965 - drums). Americana, Alt-Country, Country Rock and Folk Rock band from Toronto, Ontario, Canada.

Slowed down, accompanied by prominent mandolin and beautifully sung by vocalist Margo Timmins, Cowboy Junkies' cover was buried away as a bonus track on the limited edition cassette single of 'Sun Comes Up, It's Tuesday Morning'. It deserves to be far more widely heard.

[81] **DEAD FLOWERS - Gilby Clarke** (1994)

(Jagger-Richards)

Rolling Stones original: Sticky Fingers (1971)

Gilbert J. Clarke (b. 1962). Hard Rock singer and guitarist from Cleveland, Ohio, USA. Probably best-known as a former member of Guns N' Roses.

Marginally more Rock than the original, Gilby Clarke's version of 'Dead Flowers' features excellent guitar and some nice harmonies. It can be heard on his album 'Pawnshop Guitars'.

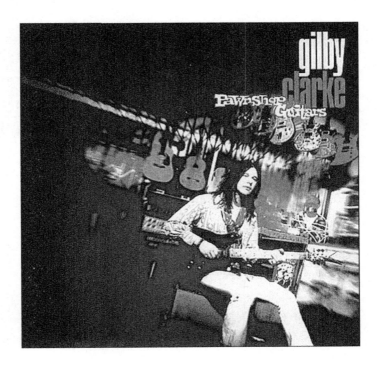

Whose idea was it to record this song?

"It was my idea. I used to play the song in jam settings, then we started playing it live in GNR during the acoustic portion of the set."

Do you perform this (or any other Stones songs) live?

"Yes, I do 'Dead Flowers' and 'It's Only Rock and Roll' live."

Were the Rolling Stones an influence on you?

"Yes, I would say the Stones were in my top 3 favourite bands/artists."

[82] **DEAD FLOWERS - Jerry Lee Lewis [with Mick Jagger]** (2010)

(Jagger-Richards)

Rolling Stones original: Sticky Fingers (1971)

(b. 1935 - d. 2022). Rock 'n' Roll and Country singer and pianist from Ferriday, Louisiana, USA.

The highlight of Jerry Lee Lewis' 2006 album 'Last Man Standing' was his duet with Mick Jagger on 'Evening Gown', and one of the better tracks on the follow-up 'Mean Old Man' was another Jerry and Mick duet, 'Dead Flowers', played in a suitably Honky Tonk arrangement complete with a steel guitar solo.

[83] **DEAD FLOWERS - Jimmy Burns** (2018)

(Jagger-Richards)

Rolling Stones original: Sticky Fingers (1971)

(b. 1943). Soul and Blues singer and guitarist from Dublin, Mississippi, USA.

Jimmy Burns' Blues version is given a Howlin' Wolf styled mid-tempo makeover with stinging guitar licks, and is on the consistently excellent 'Chicago Plays The Stones' CD.

[84] **DEAR DOCTOR - The Beatlesøns** (2004)
(Jagger-Richards)

Rolling Stones original: Beggars Banquet (1968)

Thorsten Sellheim (vocals), Monique Maasen (vocals), Michael Hack (guitar, banjo and mandolin), Thomas Schneider (guitar), Helge Mattenklodt (accordion), Jürgen Kramer (banjo), Sven Winterpagt (bass), Markus Schlapeit (drums) and Phillip Kerßenboom (saxophone). Alternative Folk-Punk and Trash Polka band from Düsseldorf, Germany.

With its comic-sad lyrics and waltz tempo, 'Dear Doctor' was one of the more light-hearted songs on 'Beggars Banquet'. The Beatlesøns' increase the fun quota on their mid-tempo cover, which features male-female duetting vocals with instrumentation that includes a twangy electric guitar, banjo, saxophone and lively drums. It can be found on their 2004 album 'Entertainment'. [Interview is with Helge Mattenklodt]

Whose idea was it to record this song?

"One concept of the Beatlesøns is to perform famous songs in another way. Every 'new' song is a band decision. The song 'Dear Doctor' was part of our own Rølling Stønes concert in 1998."

Do you perform this (or any other Stones songs) live?

"In 1998 the Stones did a concert in our town (Düsseldorf) and we did our own 'additional concert'. Ok, it was not quite as well attended as the original concert… But it was a great show with many weird Stones cover versions.

Some songs ('Dear Doctor', 'Anybody Seen My Baby', 'Paint It Black') we still had in the program for some time after the concert."

Were the Rolling Stones an influence on you?

"I think everyone who grew up in the seventies is also kind of Rolling Stones influenced, but our main influences are more punk rock based."

[85] DEAR DOCTOR - Lee Harvey Osmond and Mary Gauthier (2011)

(Jagger-Richards)

Rolling Stones original: Beggars Banquet (1968)

Psychedelic Folk band from Ontario, Canada, fronted by Tom Wilson (Thomas Cunningham Wilson, b. 1959 - vocals and guitar), with Mary Veronica Gauthier (b. 1962), Folk, Country and Americana singer and guitarist from New Orleans, Louisiana, USA.

An excellent vocal duet, Lee Harvey Osmond and Mary Gauthier's cover sticks close to the Stones' arrangement. The *big* difference though is that Mick Jagger's over-exaggerated vocal made theirs sound like a send-up, whereas this is the real deal. It is on 'Paint It Black: An Alt Country Tribute To The Rolling Stones'. [Interview is with Mary Gauthier]

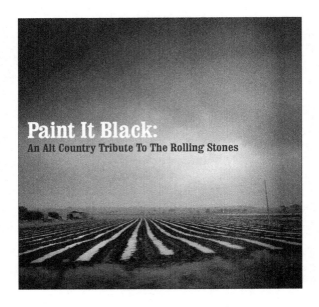

How did the collaboration with Lee Harvey Osmond come about?

"That was produced my Michael Timmons, of the Cowboy Junkies. It was his idea."

Do you perform this (or any other Stones songs) live?

"I do not perform this song live very often, but have sung it on stage with Lee Harvey Osmond."

Were the Rolling Stones an influence on you?

"I love the Stones, have loved them my whole life!"

[86] **DONCHA BOTHER ME - Hollis Brown** (2022)

(Jagger-Richards)

Rolling Stones original: Aftermath (1966)

Mike Montali (vocals and guitar), Jonathan Bonilla (guitar and vocals), Chris Urriola (bass and vocals), Adam Bock (keyboards) and Andrew Zehnal (drums). Rock band from Queens, New York, USA.

Recorded in one mammoth 24 hour session, Hollis Brown's 'In The Aftermath' covers the *entire* 'Aftermath' album (the US version rather than the UK one, so it includes 'Paint It Black' but there's no 'Mother's Little Helper', 'Take It Or Leave It' and 'What To Do'). It is an absolute delight, with the band adding just enough of their own touches to keep things interesting whilst retaining the spirit and feel of the originals. The biggest difference to the Stones' original of 'Doncha Bother Me' is that Hollis Brown's version has the added attraction of some excellent harmonica. *See [122] for interview!*

[87] DOO DOO DOO DOO (HEARTBREAKER) - The Quireboys (1990)

(Jagger-Richards)

Rolling Stones original: Goats Head Soup (1973) + US A-side (1973)

Spike (Jonathan Gray, b. 1966 - vocals), Guy Griffin (guitar and vocals), Guy Bailey (guitar), Nigel Mogg (bass) and Nick Connell (drums). Hard Rock and Blues Rock band from London.

One of the best songs from 'Goats Head Soup', The Quireboys' live cover of 'Doo Doo Doo Doo Doo (Heartbreaker)' is performed in a higher key than the Stones' original, making it sound almost like The Faces. It was a bonus track on their 1990 'There She Goes Again' single.

[88] DOO DOO DOO DOO (HEARTBREAKER) - Buddy Guy [with Mick Jagger] (2018)

(Jagger-Richards)

Rolling Stones original: Goats Head Soup (1973) + US A-side (1973)

George Guy (b. 1936). Blues singer and guitarist from Lettsworth, Louisiana, USA.

Blues legend Buddy Guy's excellent slow version features some truly blistering guitar, as well as an occasional duet vocal from Mick Jagger. It is yet another highlight of the various artists 'Chicago Plays The Stones' CD.

[89] **DOOM AND GLOOM - Miles Kane** (2013)

(Jagger-Richards)

Rolling Stones original: GRRR! (2012) + UK/US A-side (2012)

Miles Peter Kane (b. 1986). Indie Rock and Mod Revival singer and guitarist from Birkenhead, Merseyside, UK.

One of the few Stones originals to emerge since the (rather good) 2005 'A Bigger Bang' album, Miles Kane's cover is just fine, albeit without really adding anything to the original. It was a bonus track on his 2013 'Better Than That' single.

[90] **DOWN IN THE HOLE - Frank Black and The Catholics** (2003)

(Jagger-Richards)

Rolling Stones original: Emotional Rescue (1980) + UK/US B-side (1980)

Frank Black, aka Black Francis (Charles Michael Kittridge Thompson IV. b. 1965). Alternative Rock singer and guitarist from Boston, Massachusetts, USA, with backing band.

The closest The Rolling Stones got to the blues on 'Emotional Rescue' was 'Down In The Hole', a somewhat rambling and unfocused minor key song with weaving guitars and a persistent harmonica. Frank Black and the Catholics' very different version is up-tempo, with a discordant electric guitar, prominent acoustic rhythm, and a weird, eerie falsetto lead vocal. The end result is unsettling but curiously fascinating. It was released as part of the 2003 'Everything Is New' CD single.

[91] **DOWNTOWN SUZIE - Four Year Beard** (2007)

(Wyman)

Rolling Stones original: Metamorphosis (1975) (recorded 1969)

Alternative Rock and Experimental artist from New Jersey, USA.

Bill Wyman only had two of his songs recorded and released by the Rolling Stones; 'In Another Land', and, several years after it was recorded, 'Downtown Suzie'. Four Year Beard's noisy revival is a strong candidate for the most unlikely ever Stones cover! It can be found on 'Get Yer Wah-Wahs Out!: The Main Man Records Tribute to The Rolling Stones'.

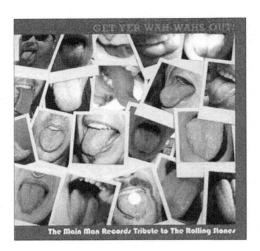

[92] **EACH AND EVERY DAY OF THE YEAR - Bobby Jameson** (1964)

(Jagger-Richards)

Rolling Stones original: 1964 Demo: Metamorphosis (1975)

Robert Parker Jameson (b. 1945 - d. 2015). Pop and Rock singer and guitarist from Glendale, California, USA.

The B-side of Oldham-Richards' 'All I Want Is My Baby', the arrangement is largely identical to the Rolling Stones' demo that was released on 'Metamorphosis', albeit with a slightly lighter production.

[93] **EACH AND EVERY DAY OF THE YEAR - Thee** (1965)

(Jagger-Richards)

Rolling Stones original: 1964 Demo: Metamorphosis (1975)

Andy Mitchell (vocals and guitar), Robert Betts (guitar), Tony Savva (bass) and Peter Balding (drums). Beat group from Hampstead, London. They later (minus Robert Betts) changed their name to The New Breed.

Lacking the orchestration of the Rolling Stones and Bobby Jameson versions, Thee's single has a far more palatable guitars, bass and drums arrangement, as well as a nice vocal that sounds similar to The Hollies' Allan Clarke.

[94] **EMOTIONAL RESCUE - St. Vincent** (2015)

(Jagger-Richards)

Rolling Stones original: Emotional Rescue (1980) + UK/US A-side (1980)

Anne Erin Clark (b. 1982). Pop and Indie Rock singer, guitarist and keyboardist from Tulsa, Oklahoma, USA.

With Mick's falsetto vocal and the Funk/Disco rhythm, the brilliant 'Emotional Rescue' was dismissed by some as a belated Bee Gees tribute. St. Vincent's version has a marginally slower tempo, a more modern dance beat and a non-falsetto female vocal, but otherwise the arrangement is pretty much the same as the Stones' original. It is on the 'A Bigger Splash' soundtrack album.

[95] EMPTY HEART - Thee Midniters (1965)

(Nanker-Phelge)

Rolling Stones original: Five By Five [EP] (1964) + 12 X 5 (1964)

Little Willie G. (Willie Garcia - vocals), George Dominguez (guitar), Roy Marguez (guitar), Jimmy Espinoza (bass), George Salaza (drums), Ronny Figuero (organ), Larry Rendon (saxophone) and Romeo Prado (trombone). Chicano Rock and Pop band from Los Angeles, California, USA.

'Empty Heart' was one of two Stones originals on their 2nd UK EP 'Five By Five' (which was expanded to a full album in the USA). Thee Midniters' fabulous cover is played at a faster tempo, and features cheesy organ, distorted guitar, a stomping beat and soulful vocals. One of the greatest ever Stones covers, it was released on their debut album in 1965.

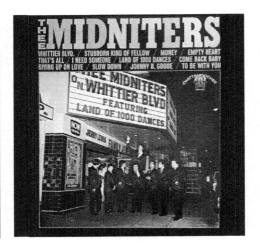

[96] EMPTY HEART - MC5 (1972) *(Not released until 1995)*

(Nanker-Phelge)

Rolling Stones original: Five By Five [EP] (1964) + 12 X 5 (1964)

Rob Tyner (Robert W. Derminer, b. 1944 - d. 1991 - vocals), Wayne Kramer (Wayne Kambes, b. 1948 - guitar and vocals), Fred 'Sonic' Smith (Frederick Dewey Smith, b. 1948 - d. 1994 - guitar and vocals), Michael Davis b. (1943 - d. 2012 - bass) and Dennis Thompson (b.. 1948 - drums). Hard Rock, Garage Rock and Proto-Punk band from Lincoln Park, Michigan, USA.

An absolute stormer of a cover and a band live favourite, the MC5's frantic and powerful version of 'Empty Heart' was belatedly released on 'Thunder Express' in 1995.

[97] EVENING GOWN - Jerry Lee Lewis [with Mick Jagger and Ronnie Wood] (2006)

(Jagger)

Rolling Stones original: Wandering Spirit [Mick Jagger solo album] (1993)

(b. 1935 - d. 2022). Rock 'n' Roll and Country singer and pianist from Ferriday, Louisiana, USA.

A wonderful country song that is every inch as great as the more acclaimed 'Sweet Virginia' and 'Far Away Eyes', Mick Jagger initially wrote it as a Jerry Lee Lewis-styled honky tonk ballad. So he must've been thrilled when The Killer himself recorded it for a project that would become his best-selling ever album 'Last Man Standing'. Jerry does a great job on it too, with Mick contributing just enough not to dominate proceedings, and it is arguably the album's highlight.

[98] **EXILE ON MAIN ST. BLUES - Chuck E. Weiss** (2014)

(Jagger-Richards)

Rolling Stones original: NME Flexi disc (1972)

Charles Edward Weiss (b. 1945 - d. 2021). Blues and Rock singer from Denver, Colorado, USA.

To promote 'Exile On Main St.', music paper the N.M.E. (New Musical Express) included a free flexi-disc featuring excerpts of album tracks, intercut with an ad-libbed blues by Mick Jagger on vocals and piano. Chuck E. Weiss made a whole song out of this, lasting almost 5 minutes. Starting off sounding similar to Mick's original, after a minute or so a full New Orleans Rhythm 'n' Blues band kicks in. It is on his 2014 album 'Red Beans and Weiss'.

[99] **FACTORY GIRL - Tom Jones** (2015)

(Jagger-Richards)

Rolling Stones original: Beggars Banquet (1968)

Thomas John Woodward OBE (b. 1940). Rhythm 'n' Blues, Country, Soul and Pop singer from Treforest, Glamorgan, Wales.

Back in the '60s and '70s, Tom Jones, with his macho image and Las Vegas residencies, was the very anti-thesis of The Rolling Stones. Yet, he has always been a very versatile artist, both willing and able to tackle a whole variety of genres. With the acoustic guitar and fiddle backing contrasting nicely against his powerhouse vocals, Tom Jones' unique version of 'Factory Girl' is well-worth checking out. It can be found on his 2015 album 'Long Lost Suitcase'.

[100] **FAR AWAY EYES - The Handsome Family** (2001)
(Jagger-Richards)

Rolling Stones original: Some Girls (1978) + UK/US B-side (1978)

Brett Sparks (vocals, guitar and keyboards) and Rennie Sparks (bass, banjo and vocals). Gothic Country and Alt-Country duo from Chicago, Illinois, USA.

One of The Rolling Stones best country songs, the big difference with The Handsome Family's cover is Brett Sparks Johnny-Cash-meets-Iggy-Pop deep voice. It is on their collection of outtakes, demos and rarities, 'Smothered and Covered'. [Interview is with Brett Sparks]

Whose idea was it to record this song?

"Uncut magazine request."

Do you perform this (or any other Stones songs) live?

"No, we don't generally do covers."

Were the Rolling Stones an influence on you?

"Yes, very much so."

[101] **FLIGHT 505 - Darrell Bath** (2002)

(Jagger-Richards)

Rolling Stones original: Aftermath (1966)

(b. 1967 - d. 2021). Punk Rock and Blues Rock singer and guitarist from London, UK.

One of many great songs on 'Aftermath' that rarely gets covered, Darrell Bath's version has a few more Chuck Berry/Keith Richards guitar licks, but otherwise it stays true to the original right down to the Boogie Woogie piano intro. It is on his album 'Love and Hurt'.

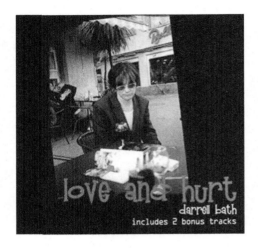

[102] **FOOL TO CRY - Taylor Dayne** (2008)

(Jagger-Richards)

Rolling Stones original: Black and Blue (1976) + UK/US A-side (1976)

Leslie Wunderman (b. 1962). Pop, Dance and Soul singer from New York City, New York, USA.

One of the Stones' most touching songs, Taylor Dayne turns it into a very modern-sounding R&B ballad, and it can be found on 2008's 'Satisfied'.

[103] **FOOL TO CRY - Tegan and Sara** (2013)

(Jagger-Richards)

Rolling Stones original: Black and Blue (1976) + UK/US A-side (1976)

Tegan Rain Quin (b. 1980) and Sara Keirsten Quin (b. 1980). Twin siblings Indie Pop and Folk Pop duo from Calgary, Alberta, Canada.

Sticking close to The Rolling Stones' original arrangement, Tegan and Sara's fine cover is on the various artists 'Girls - Volume 1: Music from the HBO Original Series'.

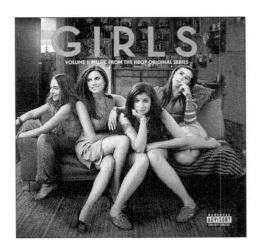

[104] **GET OFF OF MY CLOUD - Bubblerock** (1974)

(Jagger-Richards)

Rolling Stones original: December's Children (and Everybody's) (1965) + UK/US A-side (1965)

Jonathan King under a pseudonym (Kenneth George King, b. 1944). Pop singer, producer and music entrepreneur from Marylebone, London.

Jonathan King has issued records in a large variety of styles over the years, often under pseudonyms. These include two mid-'70s singles of Stones classics performed in a Country-Folk style. '(I Can't Get No) Satisfaction' was a hit, but the just-as-good 'Get Off Of My Cloud' failed to chart. *See [352] for interview!*

[105] **GET OFF OF MY CLOUD - Alexis Korner [with Keith Richards]** (1975)
(Jagger-Richards)

Rolling Stones original: December's Children (and Everybody's) (1965) + UK/US A-side (1965)

Alexis Andrew Nicholas Koerner (b. 1928 - d. 1984). Blues and Blues Rock singer and guitarist from Paris, France.

It is impossible to over-emphasise Alexis Korner's importance to The Rolling Stones. Without him, it is unlikely that Mick and Keith would ever have met Brian and Charlie, and he gave all four of them crucial early stage experience and encouragement. Indeed, the gravelly-voiced raconteuring Keith Richards of recent decades both looks and sounds like him! His slowed-down and bluesy revamp of 'Get Off Of My Cloud' (from the album of the same name), features Keith on both guitar and occasional duet vocals, and is well worth a listen. Far more impressive though is a live version from German TV's 'Musikladen', where Keith is substituted by former The Small Faces and Humble Pie front man Steve Marriott.

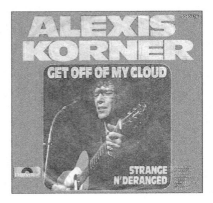

Alexis Korner with Steve Marriott performing 'Get Off Of My Cloud' on 'Musikladen', 1975 [German TV]

[106] **GET OFF OF MY CLOUD - Jimmy and The Boys** (1981)
(Jagger-Richards)

Rolling Stones original: December's Children (and Everybody's) (1965) + UK/US A-side (1965)

Ignatius Jones (Juan Ignacio Rafaelo Lorenzo Trápaga y Esteban, b. 1957 - vocals), Joe P. Rick (Joseph Joseph Attullah - guitar and vocals), Michael Vidale (bass), Joylene Thornbird Hairmouth (William O'Riordan - keyboards and vocals) and Scott Johnston (drums). Shock Rock and New Wave band from Sydney, Australia. Disbanded in 1982.

Camp, robotic and just plain bizarre, once heard, Jimmy and The Boys' unique cover can't be forgotten! [Interview is with Ignatius Jones]

Whose idea was it to record this song?

"I had always been very influenced by the Stones' 'attitude' songs. When Jimmy and the Boys came to do their second album the record company introduced us to this weird English producer called Danny Beckerman. The rest of the band didn't like him much but we got on immediately. We both ADORED the Flying Lizards and Devo, and I was starting my lifelong obsession with Giorgio Moroder and electronic music. Hence the weird gestation of that version of 'Get Off Of My Cloud'."

Did you perform any other Stones songs live?

"With Jimmy and the Boys that was the only one. We did a lot in my first rock band, Gomorrah."

Were the Rolling Stones an influence on your own music?

"Huge. I was a strange child. Until about 16 I only listened to Baroque composers like Lullly and Rameau, until around the same time I discovered Wagner. But as Captain of the Y10 Debating Team in Australia's most elite Catholic boys' school, I'd been hanging out with the stars of the Y11 and Y12 teams, guys who would later be Ministers of Education or Heads of Department in various govt ministries. They were actually really subversive. I remember when one of them played me 'Let It Bleed' on his parents' stereo while they were out. Blew my head off. Then I had a cousin who had every record the Stone ever made, in inch-thick import versions. (He was actually truly evil...) But he put 'Exile On Main St.' into my hands and said "Listen to this..." I ended up memorising that record, all four sides. I fell in love with 'It's Only Rock 'n' Roll', and my love affair continued till 'Black and Blue'. After that, it was Punk, and the Bones seemed to lose relevance."

[107] **GET OFF OF MY CLOUD - Richard Lloyd** (1981)

(Jagger-Richards)

Rolling Stones original: December's Children (and Everybody's) (1965) + UK/US A-side (1965)

Richard Lloyd (b. 1951). Rock, Punk Rock and New Wave singer and guitarist from Pittsburgh, Pennsylvania, USA.

Not as discordant as the flipside 'Connection' (also in this book), Richard Lloyd's revival of 'Get Off Of My Cloud' has exciting lead guitar work running throughout the entire song. *See [72] for interview!*

[108] **GET OFF OF MY CLOUD - The Meteors** (1981)

(Jagger-Richards)

Rolling Stones original: December's Children (and Everybody's) (1965) + UK/US A-side (1965)

P. Paul Fenech (guitar and vocals), Nigel Lewis (bass and vocals), and Mark Robertson (drums). Psychobilly band from London, UK.

With its '50s styled reverberating guitar and Punk-like vocals, Psychobilly pioneers The Meteors' version of 'Get Off Of My Cloud' is predictably crazed-sounding. It is on their 1981 album 'In Heaven'.

[109] **GET OFF OF MY CLOUD - The Flying Pickets** (1982)

(Jagger-Richards)

Rolling Stones original: December's Children (and Everybody's) (1965) + UK/US A-side (1965)

Brian Hibbard (b. 1946 - d. 2012), Ken Gregson, David Brett, Red Stripe, Rick Lloyd (b. 1947) and Gareth Williams. A cappella Pop group from London, UK.

Sounding like a cross between a '50s Doo Wop group and Chas 'n' Dave, this clever vocal-only arrangement was on The Flying Pickets' 1982 album 'Live At The Albany Empire!'. The following year, the band would hit the big time with their UK chart-topping cover of Yazoo's 'Only You'.

[110] **GIMME SHELTER - Merry Clayton** (1970)

(Jagger-Richards)

Rolling Stones original: Let It Bleed (1969)

(b. 1948). Soul and Gospel singer from New Orleans, Louisiana, USA.

Ask people to name their favourite Rolling Stones song, and there's a high chance that 'Gimme Shelter' will be near the top of the list - indeed, both 'Rolling Stone' magazine and the 'Ultimate Classic Rock' website have ranked it as the number one Rolling Stones song. Yet, it wasn't even released as a single! That is how good 'Gimme Shelter' is. A key element to the song's success was the soulful Gospel duet vocal - and that vocalist was Merry Clayton. She issued her own horn-drenched Soul-Rock version on a single the following year, when it got to No. 73 in the US Billboard Pop charts, but with or without The Rolling Stones, this will *always* be the song she'll be remembered for.

[111] **GIMME SHELTER - Ruth Copeland** (1971)

(Jagger-Richards)

Rolling Stones original: Let It Bleed (1969)

Kelly Michaels (b. 1946). Pop, Folk, Soul and Funk singer from Consett, Durham, UK.

Ruth Copeland's version starts off as a typical female-led early 70s Rock performance, complete with wah-wah guitar; then, around the half-way mark, she brings it down to almost a whisper for over a minute, before the expected big finale. This powerful and inspired performance is on her 1971 album 'I Am What I Am'.

[112] **GIMME SHELTER - Steve Ellis** (1971) *(Not released until 2013)*

(Jagger-Richards)

Rolling Stones original: Let It Bleed (1969)

Stephen John Ellis (b. 1950). Pop, Rock and Soul singer from Edgware, Middlesex, UK.

Ex-Love Affair front man Steve Ellis comes across sounding like a slightly more restrained Steve Marriott on this fine soulful Rock performance. Recorded in 1971 for a proposed solo project, it didn't see the light of day until the 2013 'Time Hasn't Changed Us' collection. *See [362] for interview!*

[113] **GIMME SHELTER - The Sisters Of Mercy** (1983)
(Jagger-Richards)

Rolling Stones original: Let It Bleed (1969)

Andrew Eldritch (Andrew William Harvey Taylor, b. 1959 - vocals, guitar and drum programming), Gary Marx (Mark Frederick Pearman, b. 1958 - guitar) and Craig Adams (Craig David Adams, b. 1962 - bass). Gothic Rock and Post-Punk band from Leeds, Yorkshire, UK.

Deep voiced, with distant reverb guitar and loud brittle-sounding electronic drums, The Sisters Of Mercy's doom-laden version makes the original sound positively upbeat! It was a bonus track on their 1983 single 'Temple Of Love'.

[114] **GIMME SHELTER - Inspiral Carpets** (1990)
(Jagger-Richards)

Rolling Stones original: Let It Bleed (1969)

Tom Hingley (Thomas William Hingley, b. 1965 - vocals), Graham Lambert (Graham Paul Lambert, b. 1964 - guitar), Martyn Walsh (Martyn John Walsh, b. 1968 - bass), Craig Gill (Craig Douglas Gill, b. 1971, d. 2016 - drums) and Clint Boon (Clinton David Boon, b. 1959 - keyboards and vocals). Indie Rock and Madchester band from Oldham, UK. Disbanded in 2016.

With slow verses and up-tempo, anthemic choruses, Inspiral Carpets' keyboard-dominated version is very much of its time. First released on the 1989 'Peel Sessions' EP, it turned up again the following year on 'Stoned Again - A Tribute to The Stones'.

[115] **GIMME SHELTER - New Model Army Feat. Tom Jones** (1993)
(Jagger-Richards)

Rolling Stones original: Let It Bleed (1969)

Justin Sullivan (Justin Edward Sullivan, b. 1956 - vocals and guitar), Dave Blomberg (guitar), Peter 'Nelson' Nice (bass), Robert Heaton (Robert Charles Heaton, b. 1961 - d. 2004 - drums) and Ed Alleyne-Johnson (b. 1959 - violin). Punk Rock, Post-Punk and Folk Rock band from Bradford, Yorkshire, UK. Thomas John Woodward OBE (b. 1940). Rhythm 'n' Blues, Country, Soul and Pop singer from Treforest, Glamorgan, Wales.

In 1993, Food Records released a series of 4 different CD singles by various bands and collaborations, all covering 'Gimme Shelter', for the 'Shelter' charity's 'Putting Our House in Order' homeless initiative. These were: 'Pop' (Voice of the Beehive and Jimmy Somerville, Heaven 17 with Hannah Jones), 'Alternative' (New Model Army and Tom Jones, Cud and Sandie Shaw, Kingmaker), 'Rock' (Thunder, Little Angels, Hawkwind and Samantha Fox)' and 'Dance' (808 State and Robert Owens, Pop Will Eat Itself vs Gary Clail vs Ranking Roger vs the Mighty Diamonds vs the On U Sound System, Blue Pearl mixed by Utah Saints). Not all of these were great (some were diabolical!), but two of the better ones have been selected for this book. Kicking off with some powerful harmonica, New Model Army featuring Tom Jones's solid and unpretentious cover works well, with Tom Jones' powerful voice perfectly complimenting the song's arrangement. [Interview on next page is with New Model Army's Justin Sullivan]

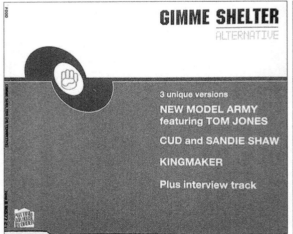
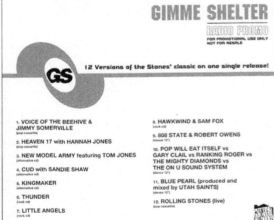

How did the collaboration with Tom Jones come about, and whose idea was it to record this song?

"In 1992 an organisation called 'Putting Our House In Order' (which was a kind of offshoot of Shelter) was set up to draw attention to the issue of homelessness. Somehow they obtained permission from Jagger/Richards to commission a number of cover versions of 'Gimme Shelter' and we were asked (among others). We immediately thought of having a guest vocalist and I think it was our secretary at the time, Sacha Walker, who thought of Tom Jones. Whatever else people might think, no one can deny the sheer power and quality of his voice. We thought that yes that could really work well musically. So we asked, he said yes and we set about making an arrangement in the key of his choice. I don't know if it was by chance or design that we ended up recording the backing track in London with sometime Rolling Stones producer Chris Kimsey (with whom we later recorded two albums) but that was perfect. We also decided to bring in our old friend, Mark Feltham, to play the extraordinary harmonica breaks.

Then, somehow it was me that flew over to Los Angeles to record Tom, finding myself in a studio suddenly acting producer. We had never met and I imagine that he was only half-aware of New Model Army but he was friendly, polite and of course brilliant. One of my all-time favourite musical memories came after three or four takes and he'd absolutely nailed it; he then said 'you're the singer in NMA... do you want to try it as a duet?' So we set up two microphones opposite each other and did it like that. I had always thought that I had a loud voice but I was totally out-gunned; still I loved every second. When Chris mixed the track later, he didn't use the duet take, going for pure Tom, but I do treasure that generously-given moment. The record did well (all the versions were grouped into two or three singles) and had attention for a short while. Sadly for us, it was a Jimmy Somerville version that got the most airplay at the time, but I still think that ours was the coolest."

Do/did you perform this (or any other Stones songs) live?

"We have done this once or twice but we discovered that you have to be quite careful about doing Stones songs, contractually... But I do have one vivid memory of finishing a particularly gruelling, difficult American tour by playing 'The Last Time' - although we did go back again eventually."

Were the Rolling Stones an influence on you?

"When I was about seven years old I was sent to stay with my Grandmother. On my arrival she exclaimed "Justin, your hair is so long, you look like a Beatle", to which I apparently answered, "I'm not a Beatle, Gran, I'm a Rolling Stone!". I don't actually remember this but it's a family story. So yes, they were a massive influence from the very beginning. I never saw them though, until about 5 years ago, when I was lucky enough to be at the very front and was totally blown away by the attack, the looseness and the attitude - the most punk-rock gig I'd seen for years. Strange and totally unique band. That they were also great song-writers, can be demonstrated by the many, many cover versions, but actually, no one has ever been able to copy their particular way of making music. Total respect."

[116] **GIMME SHELTER - Cud and Sandie Shaw** (1993)

(Jagger-Richards)

Rolling Stones original: Let It Bleed (1969)

Carl Puttnam (vocals), Mike Dunphy (guitar and keyboards), Will Potter (William Potter - bass) and Steve Goodwin (drums). Indie Rock band from Leeds, Yorkshire, UK, with Sandra Ann Goodrich (b. 1947). Pop singer from Dagenham, Essex, UK.

Sandie Shaw always had her finger on the pulse musically, as proven by her '80s collaborations with BEF and The Smiths. So putting her together with acclaimed Indie band Cud made perfect sense. Basically a duet between Cud singer Carl Puttman and Sandie Shaw (both a bit low in the mix), they are ably supported by funky-sounding guitar, bass and drums. [Interview is with Will Potter, and see also [424] for Sandie Shaw interview]

How did the collaboration with Sandie Shaw come about?

"The CUD recording with Sandie Shaw came about in 1993 as part of a UK fund-raising effort for the Shelter charity's 'Putting Our House in Order' homeless initiative. With the Stones' permission, several collaborations were arranged, some rather bizarre, all recording a version of 'Gimme Shelter' for separate single releases. The Stones provided a live version for the release.

We were originally offered a pairing with glamour model Sam Fox but turned that down (she then recorded a version of 'Gimme Shelter' with Hawkwind.) We asked about the possibility of Lulu or Marc Almond before Sandie Shaw's name came up. Sandie had given up recording since her '80s work with the Smiths and had moved into teaching. She asked her class about CUD and the positive response persuaded her to join the project.

We recorded and mixed our cover over two days in Ray Davies' Konk Studios in February 1993 based on a drum and guitar loop. Sandie was lovely to work with, though the session was interrupted by documentary recording. The finished single reached No.23 in the charts, with Voice of the Beehive and Jimmy Somerville performing their version on Top of the Pops."

Do/did you perform this (or any other Stones songs) live?

"Though we're happy with the recording, we never did play our version of 'Gimme Shelter' live, or any Stones songs. It was worked out in the studio and that's where it stayed. We did play a benefit concert for 'Putting Our House in Order', though."

Were the Rolling Stones an influence on you?

"Mike our guitarist and chief songwriter was/is a fan of the Stones, particularly of the 'Exile On Main St.' period, so if there is any influence on us, it will come through him."

CUD'S STACKED TO HELP THE HOMELESS

CUD, Orbital, Utah Saints and New Model Army are among the acts confirmed to play the "Putting Our House In Order" charity concerts in March. Although no band dates have been finalised the shows will take place between March 13-20 at London ULU. Organiser Jon Beast told the Maker, "other acts are getting involved on a daily basis. Both The Levellers and Carter have given their support and it's possible that they will play a date for us."

MELODY MAKER, January 16 1993

Cud said they thought she was going to be Dusty Springfield, Sandie Shaw said

she'd understood they were The Cult but, of course, pan-generational hugs ensued for the very good cause of contributing to the umpteen versions of Gimme Shelter which those nice people at Gallup agreed were all one record, so that Jon Beast's Putting Our House In Order campaign could take its message about the national disgrace of homelessness to the top of the charts for a week or two.

Q 81

NOT MORE BLOODY COVER VERSIONS present...

12 UNIQUE COLLABORATIONS
30 CREDIBLE ARTISTS
1 CATALOGUE NUMBER 1 AIM 1 MONSTER HIT SINGLE

INCLUDING

Hawkwind vs. Samantha Fox, New Model Army vs. Tom Jones, P.W.E.I. vs. On-U Sound System, Jimmy Sommerville vs. Voice of the Beehive, Utah Saints vs. Neneh Cherry, 808 State vs. Robert Owens...
- and much, much more -

POP CAS-SINGLE	ROCK C.D.	ALTER-NATIVE C.D.	DANCE 12"	All profits donated directly to homelessness charities

An unprecedented release! Twelve unique versions of **Gimme Shelter**. Featuring over 30 top artists including Tom Jones, New Model Army, Utah Saints, Neneh Cherry, Little Angels, Ricky Ross, Thunder, Pop Will Eat Itself, Gary Clail and the On-U Sound System, plus a whole bucketful more stars working together to help us help the homeless.

* Thanks to them all from Jon Beast *

HELP US TO HELP THE HOMELESS

Over 500 Live Events   Parties   Concerts   Huge Celebrity Memorabilia Auction

RELEASED
22nd March
Cat. No.
ORDER 1

VOLUNTEER!! Get involved in your area!!

PUTTING OUR HOUSE IN ORDER
Freepost Jon Beast, PO Box 21, London, W10 6XA

FOR AN EXCLUSIVE P.O.N.I.O. T-SHIRT, SEND A £10 CHEQUE/PO TO: C.H.I.L., PO BOX 1492, LONDON, W6 9PG.
Putting Our House In Order is a registered charity
(Number 1015664)

Sandie Shaw and Will Potter, 1993

(special thanks to Will for the photo and press cuttings)

[117] **GIMME SHELTER - Samantha Newark** (2003)

(Jagger-Richards)

Rolling Stones original: Let It Bleed (1969)

> (b. 1967). USA-based Pop and Rock singer and actress from London, UK.
>
> Probably best known for her voice-over work in the animated cartoon series 'Jem', Samantha Newark's version is done in a relaxed and mellow style, with acoustic guitar backing. It is on the various artists 'New Licks - A Tribute to The Rolling Stones'.

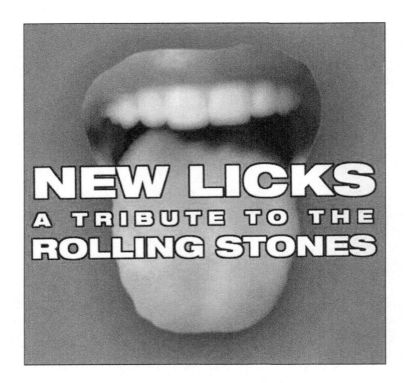

Whose idea was it to record this song?

"This project was such a while back when I was living in Los Angeles, and if memory serves, I was invited to perform the song by some female singers that knew me that were already involved."

Do you perform this or any other Stones song live?

"As far as performing any Stones covers, I haven't done that but I do love many Stones songs."

[118] **GIMME SHELTER - Kathy Mattea (2005)**

(Jagger-Richards)

Rolling Stones original: Let It Bleed (1969)

Kathleen Alice Mattea (b. 1959). Country and Country-Folk singer and guitarist from South Charleston, West Virginia, USA.

One of country music's finest and most successful artists, Kathy Mattea's heartfelt cover features a unique 'chiming' guitar riff. It was released on her 2005 'Right Out Of Nowhere' album, as well as on a various artists promotional CD.

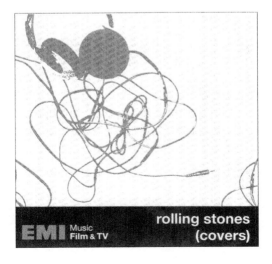

Whose idea was it to record this song?

"The invasion of Iraq had started, and we were talking about it on the bus. Bill Cooley, my guitarist/band leader for many years, said 'Gimme Shelter' keeps running through my head. It feels so relevant right now. And we talked about it a little bit. He started bugging me about it, about working it up with the band. And I was dragging my feet about it. Like I can do sometimes. That's part of why he was so good for me, he pushed me, musically. So I walk into a venue one afternoon while they're setting up, and he says 'Here are the lyrics to 'Gimme Shelter'. The CD is in the player on the bus. I'll see you at sound check.'

So, I went out and listened, made some notes, came in and, as usual, he had the whole arrangement worked up. That great acoustic guitar intro with the chimes, so good. And he taught me the chords to play, on the low strings of my guitar, when it was my turn to come in. Well, we got really excited about it at sound check, put it in the show that night and the crowd was just knocked out. We kept doing it, and when it came time to record the next album it was automatically on the list. By then we'd done it live so much that our arrangement was honed in and solid. I love it when a song comes back around. I think that's one of the most powerful things about living a life with music at its centre. A song can be written during one era, and the words can ring true in a different time. And it helps us have perspective on where we are, and have a sense of history, and the progress made... or not."

Have you ever performed this (or any other Stones songs) live?

"Well, this was a live thing that turned into a cut on my next album. I did do 'It's All Over Now' early in my stage shows, but I never recorded it. I loved how it could be bent in a direction that fit the Country Music genre, and people were familiar with it, but from an outside source. And, it was just fun to sing."

Were The Rolling Stones an influence on you?

"I was more of a Beatles girl. I was young when they all came out, and the Beatles were more structured and arranged, and less loose. It wasn't till later that I began to really appreciate the blues influence, the soulfulness, and the kind of freewheeling approach that they had to music. Especially when I dug into Keith Richards' guitar parts more, and the genius in his licks and how much they anchored the whole thing. I had a chance to go see them in Nashville, the head of my record label bought tickets (with backstage passes to go say hi) for all his artists. He wanted us to all be inspired. And of course, I was on the road that night, out of town with a gig of my own. I've never seen them live but would love to."

[119] GIMME SHELTER - Paul Brady and The Forest Rangers (2009)

(Jagger-Richards)

Rolling Stones original: Let It Bleed (1969)

Paul Joseph Brady (b. 1947). Folk, Irish Tradition, Pop and Rock singer, guitarist, pianist and mandolinist from Belfast, Northern Ireland, with band founded by Producer Bob Thiele Jr. (b. 1955), USA.

Paul Brady's powerful cover is given a modern Country Rock makeover complete with slide guitar, and can be found on the various artists 'Sons of Anarchy - Shelter' EP.

Whose idea was it to record this song?

"The idea came from Bob Theile Jr., who was the music supervisor on the series Sons Of Anarchy. We already knew each other as we'd written a song together 'Good Love' on my album 'Oh What A World' some years previously. He knew I was a Stones fan from the beginning and that I could handle this song vocally. He had a loose band The Forest Rangers that played a lot of the music on SOA soundtrack. They cut the track and sent it to me in Dublin. I recorded the vocal in my own studio. I also played the Irish tin whistle on the track."

Have you ever performed it live?

"I've played the song a few times here in Ireland on various fun jams but never officially cut it or included it in my own live set lists. My fave record of theirs is 'Black and Blue'."

[120] **GIMME SHELTER - Leanne Faine** (2018)

(Jagger-Richards)

Rolling Stones original: Let It Bleed (1969)

(b. 1939). Gospel singer from Inkster, Michigan, USA.

A hot up-tempo Rhythm 'n' Blues arrangement complete with robust Little Walter styled Chicago Blues harmonica, Leanne Faine's superb version is on the consistently brilliant 'Chicago Plays The Stones' various artists CD.

[121] **GIVE ME YOUR HAND - Teddy Green** (1964)

(Jagger-Richards)

Rolling Stones original: 1963 Demo: Bootleg only (excerpt)

(b. 1936). Actor, choreographer, dancer and singer from UK.

Reputedly written by Mick Jagger for The Beatles as a "Thank You" for 'I Wanna Be Your Man', the Fab Four must've had a good laugh if true! The song is quite dreadful, though to be charitable, Teddy Green's sub-Anthony Newley vocal doesn't help matters. It was issued as the B-side of his 1964 single 'Always'.

[122] GOIN' HOME - Hollis Brown (2022)

(Jagger-Richards)

Rolling Stones original: Aftermath (1966)

Mike Montali (vocals and guitar), Jonathan Bonilla (guitar and vocals), Chris Urriola (bass and vocals) and Andrew Zehnal (drums). Rock band from Queens, New York, USA.

The closing track of the US edition of 'Aftermath', Hollis Brown's version of the Stones' ground-breaking epic somehow manages to keep fairly faithfull to the original yet still sound like they're jamming. One of the many highlights of their 'In The Aftermath' tribute. [Interview is with Mike Montali]

Why did you cover 'Aftermath' (as opposed to, say, 'Beggars Banquet' or 'Sticky Fingers')?

"Covering an iconic band like the Rolling Stones can often come across like karaoke. We wanted to pick an album that had a lot of back wall, bluesy songs that the mass population weren't as familiar with. 'Aftermath' is an album where you can hear the band learning how to write together, it's a coming of age album and the songs felt very natural to us."

What song was the hardest to recreate?

"The hardest song to recreate was probably 'Lady Jane'. The Stones version has a very distinct arrangement, and we wanted to put our own flavour on the song."

Do you perform these or any other Stones songs live?

"We performed an entire tour, about 20 shows in total across the USA. It was a blast to see the reactions to the music."

[123] GOMPER - The Prisoner Of Mars (2011)
(Wyman)

Rolling Stones original: Their Satanic Majesties Request (1967) + US A-side (1967)

Bryan Shore. Psychedelic Rock, Acid Rock and Indie Rock singer and multi-instrumentalist from Cambridge, Cambridgeshire, UK.

The Rolling Stones' flawed but enduringly fascinating 'Their Satanic Majesties Request' has long been an album that has not just divided fans but the Stones themselves, with only Mick Jagger very occasionally praising it. Yet, there has been a growing appreciation of the album's contents over the years: '2000 Light Years From Home' and 'She's A Rainbow' are almost standards, while both 'Citadel' and '2000 Man' have been covered numerous times. However, there has just been only *one* artist who has been brave or foolhardy enough to record cover versions of the entire album, and that is The Prisoner Of Mars, AKA Bryan Shore, ex-guitarist of Alternative Rock band The Mutts. OK, his vocals are more Wyman than Jagger, and it all has a very home-made feel, but this just adds to its charm. The tracks that probably work best are the looser, more jam-like songs, particularly the Indian-influenced 'Gomper', but the entire 'The Prisoner of Mars Performs Their Satanic Majesties Request' can be heard via streaming sites.

What made you want to recreate the entire 'Satanic Majesties' album? Surely (say) 'Aftermath' or 'Beggar's Banquet' would've been far less daunting?

"I chose 'Majesties' as it was always an LP I loved despite it being one of the least popular. This opinion has changed in recent years thankfully! The other reason, was that, as it was not considered one of the high water marks of the Stones' cannon, I wouldn't get as much hate or dismissal from online Stones fans angry that I had desecrated a classic! Pussy Galore had already done Exile On Main St. which was another inspiration for covering a Stones album, but my Prisoner of Mars project was influenced broadly by Psychedelia in general so it made sense."

What was the hardest song to record?

"The hardest song to do was 'She's A Rainbow'. Mainly because of the piano part. I can't really play piano or drums, so I had to adapt the songs to fit my rudimentary playing on those instruments. This bothers me slightly on stuff like '2000 Man' or 'Citadel' which had I been a better drummer I could have made to rock harder. But that's OK."

And what's your favourite?

"My two favourite versions were 'Gomper' and 'Sing This Together (See What Happens)', both of which devolve into trancy drone freak-outs. On the latter track, I amassed as many sound effects as I could, lots of chanting and jungle sounds to give it that *Apocalypse Now* vibe. I got my wife to play as much percussion as possible, whatever was lying around, to build up the cacophony. She also sings on nearly every track.

For the strip club vibe of 'On With The Show', I used audio clips of Anthony Newley dialogue from the movie 'The Small World of Sammy Lee' about a Soho strip club compère who becomes disgusted and disillusioned with the whole scene. Seemed to fit nicely. I recorded everything by strumming the chords on an acoustic and building everything on top from there. 'In Another Land' was a song that worked best from this approach. I tried to lean further in to the Syd Barrett vibe that I'd always heard in this track.

My version of '2000 Light Years From Home' was used in a fashion catwalk show by designer Anna Sui. That was a big surprise! I initially got excited that it could lead to some sort of exposure, but then it struck me that they probably used my version as it wouldn't involve paying loads of money to Allen Klein! Still, it was pretty cool seeing the models strut about to something I'd recorded."

Have you attempted any of these songs live, or was this a studio-only project?

"This was a recording-only project, but after you asked me if it was ever a live thing, it would be nice to get a gang together and perform it on stage. One day maybe, I'll let you know if it ever happens!"

[124] **GOOD TIMES, BAD TIMES - Roland Van Campenhout** (2003)
(Jagger-Richards)

Rolling Stones original: UK and US B-side (1964)

(b. 1944). Blues, Folk and World singer and guitarist from Boom, Belgium.

The flipside to 'It's All Over Now', The Rolling Stones' original of 'Good Times, Bad Times' was the first time they recorded an acoustic blues, something they would do far more often of course in the late '60s. Former Rory Gallagher sideman Roland Van Campenhout instead plays the song on an electric guitar, adding some nice T-Bone Walker influenced licks. It is on his 2003 album 'Lime and Coconut'.

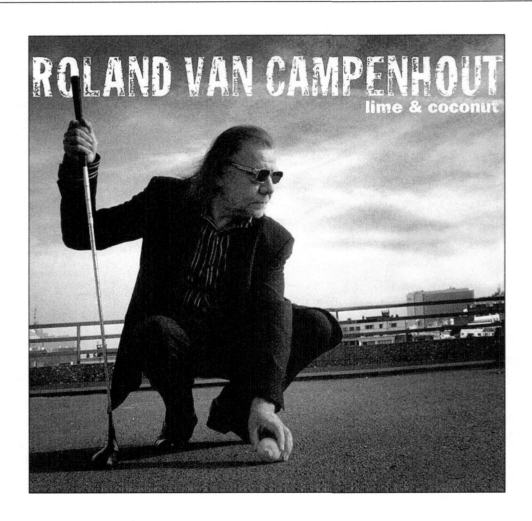

[125] **GOODBYE GIRL - The Preachers** (1965) *(Not released until 2010)*
(Wyman)

Rolling Stones original: Bootleg only (recorded 1964)

Peter 'Moon' Gosling (vocals and piano), Peter Frampton (Peter Kenneth Frampton, b. 1950 - guitar), Pete Attwood (bass), Tony Chapman (drums) and Ken Leamon (saxophone). Beat and Rhythm 'n' Blues group from Sydenham, London, UK.

The first Bill Wyman song that The Rolling Stones ever attempted, their tough Rhythm 'n' Blues performance, complete with a great Mick vocal, a lengthy Keith guitar solo, and piano from Ian Stewart, would've made a more than acceptable B-side or album track. Unfortunately, it was never released, so Bill donated the song to The Preachers, a band that featured drummer Tony Chapman - a former fellow band member in both The Cliftons and, briefly, The Rolling Stones. The Preachers' version is performed faster than the Stones', and features prominent piano and a saxophone, but it also lacks their power, and definitely comes off sounding 2nd best. Not that any of this mattered, as their version also stayed in the can, at least until it appeared on a various artists CD some 45 years later. [Note: The Preachers also recorded an earlier version of 'Goodbye Girl' with a different line-up in 1964. This remains unreleased and unheard]

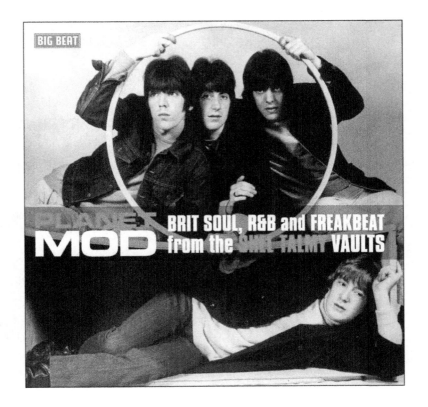

[126] **GOTTA GET AWAY - The Flys** (1966)

(Jagger-Richards)

Rolling Stones original: Out Of Our Heads [UK] (1965) + December's Children (and Everybody's) (1965)

Steve Widmeyer (vocals and guitar), Randy Dunham (guitar and vocals), Dave Reemsnyder (bass), Jim Arnholdt (drums) and Bill Lyons (keyboards and vocals). Garage band from McLean, Virginia, USA.

By 1965, Jagger-Richards were starting to write some great songs that were influenced by the Rhythm 'n' Blues they loved, yet that were also commercial and non-derivative sounding. 'Gotta Get Away' is a good example of their fast growing abilities. The Flys' version, released as a single, is essentially similar, but the faster tempo and lower key gives it a more Pop sound.

[127] **GROWN UP WRONG - The Johnnys** (1988)

(Jagger-Richards)

Rolling Stones original: 12 X 5 (1964) + Out Of Our Heads [UK] (1965)

Spencer P Jones (d. 2018 - vocals and guitar), Paul 'Slim' Doherty (guitar), Graham 'Hoody' Hood (bass and vocals) and Billy Pommer Jr. (drums). Cowpunk band from Sydney, Australia.

Though perhaps not the strongest of songs, the Stones' original of 'Grown Up Wrong' has a distinctive and powerful Blues riff. The Johnnys eschew that, and instead go for a faster, light-hearted, Country-Rock treatment. It is on their 1988 album of the same name.

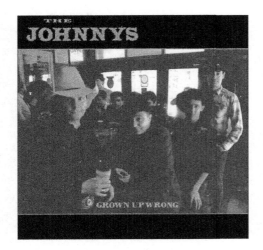

[128] **HAND OF FATE - Uncle Ray feat. Imaani** (2006)
(Jagger-Richards)

Rolling Stones original: Black and Blue (1976)

Studio-based Producer, with Melanie Crosdale (b. 1972). Pop and R&B singer from Nottingham, UK.

Following on from two patchy albums in 1973 and 1974, guitarist Mick Taylor announced his departure from the band just prior to the start of sessions for the next album. Instead, various guest players were brought in, to both play on the album and (potentially) audition for a place in The Rolling Stones. Ex-The Faces' Ronnie Wood of course eventually become the winning candidate. Despite all this, the resulting album 'Black and Blue' was generally regarding as their strongest and most cohesive work since 1972's 'Exile On Main St.'. Perhaps one of the album's lesser songs, Uncle Ray featuring Imaani's soulful update of 'Hand Of Fate' retains the original's guitar riff. It can be found on their 2006 album 'In Line with Mr. Jimmy'.

[129] **HAPPY - Nils Lofgren** (1977)
(Jagger-Richards)

Rolling Stones original: Exile On Main St. (1972) + US A-side (1972)

Nils Hilmer Lofgren (b. 1951). Roots Rock and Blues Rock singer, guitarist and keyboardist from Chicago, Illinois, USA.

The Rolling Stones' most famous song to feature Keith on lead vocals is almost certainly 'Happy', particularly in the USA where it was released as a No. 22 hit single. Nils Lofgren's cover is much slower, with a strange syncopated semi-dance beat, and is on his 1977 album 'I Came To Dance'.

[130] **HAPPY - The Pointer Sisters** (1979)
(Jagger-Richards)

Rolling Stones original: Exile On Main St. (1972) + US A-side (1972)

Ruth Pointer (Ruth Esther Pointer, b. 1946), Anita Pointer (Anita Marie Pointer, b. 1948) and June Pointer (June Antoinette Pointer, b. 1953 - d. 2006). Soul and Pop vocal group from Oakland, California, USA.

Surprisingly, The Pointer Sisters' version is a straight cover, without a hint of Disco. In fact, it Rocks! It is on their 1979 album 'Priority'.

[131] **HAPPY - Steve Conte** (2016)
(Jagger-Richards)

Rolling Stones original: Exile On Main St. (1972) + US A-side (1972)

(b. 1960). Rock singer and guitarist from New York City, USA. He was the lead guitarist for a latter-day version of the New York Dolls, amongst many other things.

With its raunchy rhythm guitar, excellent slide, and stomping Glam beat, Steve Conte's revival of 'Happy' is very fine indeed. It is on his 2016 album 'International Cover Up'.

Whose idea was it to record this song?

"Mine. I was doing an album of cover songs ('International Cover-Up') that my band was playing in live shows and this one was always a crowd pleaser. On that same album I also did an acoustic bluesy version of 'Play With Fire'."

Do you perform this (or any other Stones songs) live?

"Yes, many. In recent years on my original band shows I've done 'Happy' and 'Play With Fire', but on cover gigs (starting with my middle school bands up till present day) I have performed or *still* perform some of these: 'Heart Of Stone', 'Mother's Little Helper', 'Ruby Tuesday', 'Backstreet Girl', 'Street Fighting Man', 'Stray Cat Blues', 'Parachute Woman', 'Sympathy For The Devil', 'Midnight Rambler', 'Sway', 'Wild Horses', 'Bitch', 'Dead Flowers', 'Angie', 'Shattered', 'Miss You', 'Start Me Up', 'Let's Spend The Night Together', 'Paint It Black', 'Satisfaction', 'Get Off Of My Cloud', 'Honky Tonk Women', 'Country Honk',' Jumping Jack Flash', 'You Can't Always Get What You Want', 'Gimme Shelter', Live With Me', 'Brown Sugar', 'Had It With You'."

Were the Rolling Stones an influence on your own music?

"Totally. My rhythm playing is pure Keef - with a bit of Townsend and Page. You can hear the influence in songwriting and production going all the way back to my album 'Company Of Wolves' (Mercury Records, 1990) and more recently on my Steve Conte 'NYC Album' and 'Bronx Cheer'."

[132] HAVE YOU SEEN YOUR MOTHER, BABY, STANDING IN THE SHADOW? - Lord Sitar
(1967)

(Jagger-Richards)

Rolling Stones original: UK/US A-side (1966)

Session man Big Jim Sullivan under a pseudonym (James George Tomkins, b. 1941 - d. 2012). Guitarist and sitarist from Uxbridge, London, UK.

'Have You Seen Your Mother, Baby, Standing In The Shadow?', with its obscure lyrics, distorted guitars and vibrant horns, hasn't inspired anywhere near the same amount of covers as their other classic singles, and has been all but ignored by the band themselves (apart from around a dozen performances on their Autumn '66 UK tour, the only time it's been revived was by Mick Jagger for a one-off solo concert in 1993). That said, there are still a couple of interesting cover versions out there. Lord Sitar, AKA Big Jim Sullivan (who actually contributed guitar to some early Jagger-Richards demos), issued an intriguing instrumental version of the song on a 1967 single.

[133] HAVE YOU SEEN YOUR MOTHER, BABY, STANDING IN THE SHADOW? - Tina Harvey
(1973)

(Jagger-Richards)

Rolling Stones original: UK/US A-side (1966)

Folk Rock singer from Slough, Berkshire, UK.

An obscure artist, current whereabouts unknown, Tina Harvey reinvents the song as an acoustic ballad, with gentle finger-picked guitar and unobtrusive strings. It is on her only album, 1973's 'Tina Harvey'.

[134] **HAVE YOU SEEN YOUR MOTHER, BABY, STANDING IN THE SHADOW? - John Batdorf and James Lee Stanley** (2005)

(Jagger-Richards)

Rolling Stones original: UK/US A-side (1966)

John Batdorf (b. 1952). Singer, guitarist, bassist and keyboardist from Springfield, Ohio, USA, with James Lee Stanley (b. 1946). Singer and guitarist from Philadelphia, Pennsylvania, USA.

In 2005, John Batdorf and James Lee Stanley released a whole album of Stones covers - all of them played in a laid back, acoustic, harmonized, West Coast singer-songwriter style. 'Have You Seen Your Mother, Baby, Standing In The Shadow?' works surprising well in this form. [Interview is with John Batdorf]

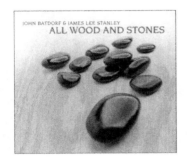

Whose idea was it to record two full albums of Stones covers?

"James Lee Stanley was at a wedding that had several singer/songwriters in attendance. After the wedding, because of the wealth of talent in the room, they wanted to sing something but nobody knew the other's song. Someone there broke out into 'Ruby Tuesday' and everyone joined in and James thought that maybe something like this would be a good idea for a CD project. The Stones had so many familiar hits and were much more melodic in the Brian Jones era. The Stones and Beatles seemed to be in a great healthy songwriting competition which made the groups strive to be better. James, who I knew but lost touch with in the 70s looked me up some 30 years later and we got together and gave it a whirl. It was instant magic! The record turned out way better than either of us originally imagined plus it was loaded with such great hits, unlike our previous projects. It was instantly put into the XM Radio rotation and we were off! Eventually we got around to recording a second CD 10 years later which rocked a little more than the first CD."

What Stones songs do you perform live?

"We played every song we recorded live except for 'Sympathy For The Devil'. We loved the version we cut but for some reason, never learned it to play live."

Were the Rolling Stones an influence on your own music?

"Ironically, I was a big Beatles guy. Although I liked the Stones very much, I loved the Beatles impeccable arrangements, production, singing, playing and their songwriting was through the roof. The Stones records were mostly pretty loose which left us room to maybe use the Beatles roadmap for the Stones arrangements but sung and played like CSN and their great California sound. What I did appreciate during the process was the songwriting skills of Mick and Keith in the new format. They were every bit as unique and special as the Beatles. It just took me a while to figure that out!"

[135] **HEART OF STONE - The Andrew Oldham Orchestra** (1966)
(Jagger-Richards)

Rolling Stones original: 1964 Demo: Metamorphosis (1975); 1964 re-cut: US A-side (1964) + The Rolling Stones, Now! (1965) + Out Of Our Heads [UK version] (1965)

Andrew Loog Oldham (b. 1944). Producer, Manager and Band Leader from London, UK.

A soulful ballad that was issued as a single in the USA but relegated to an album track in the UK, 'Heart Of Stone' is a much-loved fan favourite. Producer and early Manager Andrew Loog Oldham issued several semi-instrumental albums during the 60s, with the most notable being 'The Rolling Stones Songbook'. By far the most impressive tracks on the album were 'The Last Time' (featured elsewhere in this book), and this one, 'Heart Of Stone'. Heard in part on the 'Charlie Is My Darling' film soundtrack, the mixture of Rhythm 'n' Blues, brass orchestration and heavenly vocals was truly groundbreaking, far, far more so than George Martin's equivalent recordings of orchestrated Beatles covers issued around the same time. In 2013, Andrew recorded a follow-up album, 'The Andrew Oldham Orchestra and Friends Play The Rolling Stones Songbook Volume 2' - a mere 47 years after the first one.

[136] **HEART OF STONE - Joe Louis Walker** (1997)
(Jagger-Richards)

Rolling Stones original: 1964 Demo: Metamorphosis (1975); 1964 re-cut: US A-side (1964) + The Rolling Stones, Now! (1965) + Out Of Our Heads [UK version] (1965)

Louis Joseph Walker Jr. (b. 1949). Blues singer and guitarist from San Francisco, California, USA.

Joe Louis Walker's fabulous cover is a *very* Soulful Blues version. If Otis Redding had covered 'Heart Of Stone', it would've sounded just like this!

Did you choose these songs, or was it a producer/record company/etc?

"It was my idea... love those tunes and wanted to do my own versions."

Do you perform these songs (or any other Stones songs) live?

"No, never did them live on stage. Performed 'Around and Around' (Stones version) on quite a few occasions in the past."

Were the Rolling Stones a big influence on you?

"You could say every guitar player who heard 'Satisfaction' have been effected by them. That was a breakthrough for guitar sounds that *everyone* incorporated."

[137] **HEART OF STONE - The Allman Brothers Band** (2003)
(Jagger-Richards)

Rolling Stones original: 1964 Demo: Metamorphosis (1975); 1964 re-cut: US A-side (1964) + The Rolling Stones, Now! (1965) + Out Of Our Heads [UK version] (1965)

Gregg Allman (Gregory LeNoir Allman, b. 1947 - d. 2017 - keyboards, guitar and vocals), Warren Haynes (b. 1960 - guitars and vocals), Derek Trucks (b. 1979 - guitar), Oteil Burbridge (b. 1964 - bass), Butch Trucks (Claude Hudson Trucks, b. 1947 - d. 2017 - drums, percussion and vocals), Jaimoe (John Lee Johnson, b. 1944 - drums, percussion and vocals) and Marc Quiñones (b. 1963 - drums and vocals). Southern Rock, Blues Rock and Country Rock band from Jacksonville, Florida, USA.

The Allman Brothers Band included a superb Blues-Rock version of 'Heart Of Stone' on their 2003 'Hittin' The Note' album. [Interview is via the band's website]

Whose idea was it to record this song?

"The Allman Brothers Band had played 'Heart Of Stone' 5 times prior to recording it for the 'Hittin' The Note' release in 2003. The producers recalled the attempt, and proposed recording 'Heart Of Stone' with the idea of giving it a more Ray Charles feel which would bring out Gregg Allman's vocal style. The entire current band lineup thought it was an intriguing idea."

Did you perform this song (or any other Stones songs) live?

"'Heart Of Stone' is the only Rolling Stones authored song that comes to mind, the band played it 13 times over the years."

Were the Rolling Stones a big influence on you?

"The Allman Brothers Band original line-up were all motivated by the mid 60's British Invasion, inspiring each of them in some way to pursue their musical muse. They certainly were influenced in some ways by the Rolling Stones, as well as the Yardbirds, Spencer Davis Group among others. Since their founding they have played an instrumental version of Spencer Davis's 'Don't Want You No More', as well as being influenced by British bands guitarists and more importantly the blues artist they were uncovering early on. Big influence? Beyond Muddy Waters, Little Walter, Willie Dixon, Elmore James, Robert Johnson, John Coltrane, Miles Davis and their contemporaries, they never spoke of any other later band/musicians that a had a big influence in the development of the musical direction of the Allman Brothers Band. The later members of course all grew up listening to the Rolling Stones and to varying degrees were influenced by the Stones as well as all of the great musicians they have seen and heard during their lifetime."

[138] **HEAVEN - Kasper Bjørke** (2010)
(Jagger-Richards)

Rolling Stones original: Tattoo You (1981)

(b. 1975). Electronica musician, record producer and DJ from Copenhagen, Denmark.

A somewhat overlooked track from 'Tattoo You', the dreamy and ethereal 'Heaven' was covered in fine style by Danish musician and DJ Kasper Bjørke, with vocals by Louise Foo. As well as being a single (complete with an excellent Video), it was released on his album 'Standing On Top Of Utopia'.

Whose idea was it to record this song?

"I met my girlfriend in the Copenhagen nightlife in early 2009 and like me she was also DJ-ing. I got the idea to produce a cover version of 'Heaven' because she played the original version when we DJ´ed together and it became "our song" after that. At the time I was working on songs for my second album 'Standing On Top Of Utopia' and I asked some of my very talented musician friends of mine to be part of the recordings. The strings are performed by my friend and regular collaborator, the Italian composer Davide Rossi, who has collected multiple Grammys and has studied under Karlheinz Stockhausen and Robert Fripp. He is without parallel as a modern arranger, having worked with Alicia Keys, Frank Ocean, Jon Hopkins, The Verve, Goldfrapp, to name a select few - but may be best known for his long standing relationship with Coldplay (Davide did the strings on their hit 'Viva La Vida'). The vocals are performed by the artist Louise Foo, the little sister of Sharin Foo (The Raveonettes). I always loved her voice and knew it would fit perfectly on the cover of 'Heaven'. One of my best friends Anders 'Ormen' Christophersen performed the organ and guitar parts. It wasn't until years later that I realized that it was maybe a bit crazy to even attempt to cover such a classic, but to this day I am still very happy with the result and I have had great feedback over the years."

Do you perform this or any other Stones songs live?

"I played my cover version in many of my DJ sets over the years. I never managed to get all the musicians together for a live performance though, but maybe it's something I should look into again soon!"

Were the Rolling Stones an influence on your own music?

"I always loved The Stones as a fan since I was a teenager, and the more danceable side of Rolling Stones with 'Miss You' and 'Heaven' has certainly influenced me and always been a steady part of my DJ sets."

[139] **HIGH AND DRY - Bloodshot Bill** (2007)

(Jagger-Richards)

Rolling Stones original: Aftermath (1966)

Derek Rogers (b. 1976). Rockabilly and Country-Blues singer and guitarist from Montreal, Québec, Canada.

'High and Dry' is a song that owes more to Lonnie Donegan's Skiffle than Chicago Blues, and therefore it perfectly suits Bloodshot Bill's solo vocal/guitar style. With its echoing and hiccupping Rockabilly vocals, his cover was issued on a single for Norton.

What made you choose this song to record?

"Billy Miller chose it for me. He heard me play some song in my set and said 'You should try 'High 'n' Dry' like that.'"

Were the Stones an influence on your own music?

"Not really. I listen more to the blues records that influenced them."

Do you ever perform the song live?

"I may have done it a few times when the record came out, but haven't in years."

[140] **HONKY TONK WOMEN - Ike and Tina Turner** (1970)

(Jagger-Richards)

Rolling Stones original: UK/US A-side (1969)

Izear Luster Turner Jr. (b. 1931 - d. 2007 - guitar, keyboards and vocals) and Anna Mae Bullock (b. 1939 - vocals). Husband-and-wife Rhythm 'n' Blues, Soul and Rock duo from St. Louis, Missouri, USA. Separated in 1976.

The Rolling Stones' first single to feature Brian Jones' replacement was 'Honky Tonk Women' (it was actually released the day after Brian died, though he'd left the band 6 weeks earlier), and it has remained one of their most popular and most-performed songs. Ike and Tina Turner's fabulous Soul-Rock cover was issued as a single in 1970.

[141] **HONKY TONK WOMEN - Waylon Jennings** (1970)

(Jagger-Richards)

Rolling Stones original: UK/US A-side (1969)

Wayland Arnold Jennings (b. 1937 - d. 2002). Country, Country-Blues and Rockabilly singer and guitarist from Littlefield, Texas, USA.

'Honky Tonk Women' was originally conceived as a Country song, and indeed, a Country version later appeared on the 'Let It Bleed' album under the title 'Country Honk'. So it is not surprising that it is a song that has been very popular with Country artists over the years. Waylon Jennings' version, complete with a fiddle break, is both one of the earliest and one of the best. It is on his 1970 album 'Singer Of Sad Songs'.

[142] **HONKY TONK WOMEN - Joe Cocker** (1970)

(Jagger-Richards)

Rolling Stones original: UK/US A-side (1969)

John Robert Cocker (b. 1944 - d. 2014). Rock, Blues and Soul singer from Sheffield, Yorkshire, UK.

Backed by a cast of thousands (or so it seems), Joe Cocker's rather fast live version is featured in the 1970 film 'Mad Dogs & Englishmen', as well as on the soundtrack album.

[143] **HONKY TONK WOMEN - Albert King** (1971)

(Jagger-Richards)

Rolling Stones original: UK/US A-side (1969)

Albert Nelson (b. 1923 - d. 1992). Blues and Rhythm 'n' Blues singer and guitarist from Indianola, Mississippi, USA.

With relaxed vocals and stinging guitar licks, Albert King's mid-tempo Blues cover of 'Honky Tonk Women' is on his 1971 album 'Lovejoy'.

[144] **HONKY TONK WOMEN - Elton John (1971)**
(Jagger-Richards)

Rolling Stones original: UK/US A-side (1969)

Reginald Kenneth Dwight (b. 1947). Pop and Rock singer and pianist from Pinner, Middlesex, UK.

Although already a fine singer, songwriter and pianist, in his early days Elton John didn't have many exciting songs to liven up his stage shows. So, what better than a recent Stones classic? With an acapella intro, syncopated drumming and a fast ending, Elton's live cover of 'Honky Tonk Women' is on his 1971 album '17-11-70'.

[145] **HONKY TONK WOMEN - Humble Pie (1973)**
(Jagger-Richards)

Rolling Stones original: UK/US A-side (1969)

Steve Marriott (Stephen Peter Marriott, b. 1947, d. 1991 - vocals, guitar and harmonica), Clem Clempson (David Clempson, b. 1949 - guitar), Greg Ridley (Alfred Gregory Ridley, b. 1941, d. 2003 - bass and vocals) and Jerry Shirley (b. 1952 - drums). Rock band from Moreton, Essex, UK.

With *electrifying* high vocals from the late great Steve Marriott and inspired Rock backing, Humble Pie's live cover of 'Honky Tonk Women' can be found on side 4 of the sprawling 1973 double album 'Eat It'.

[146] **HONKY TONK WOMEN - Alexis Korner** (1979)
(Jagger-Richards)

Rolling Stones original: UK/US A-side (1969)

Alexis Andrew Nicholas Koerner (b. 1928 - d. 1984). Blues and Blues Rock singer and guitarist from Paris, France.

Featuring just his vocals and a rhythmic acoustic guitar, Alexis Korner's stripped down and raw version of 'Honky Tonk Women' is on his 1979 album 'Me'.

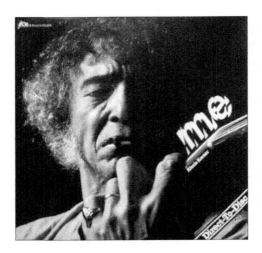

[147] **HONKY TONK WOMEN - Taj Mahal and James Cotton** (1997)
(Jagger-Richards)

Rolling Stones original: UK/US A-side (1969)

Henry St. Claire Fredericks Jr. (b. 1942). Blues, Blues-Rock and World Music singer and guitarist from Harlem, New York, USA, and James Henry Cotton (b. 1935 - d. 2017). Blues singer and harmonicist from Tunica, Mississippi, USA.

Sounding just like it was recorded on a Mississippi porch in the 1930s, Blues legends Taj Mahal and James Cotton's remarkable cover is on the 'Paint It, Blue: Songs of The Rolling Stones' album.

[148] **HONKY TONK WOMEN - Jerry Lee Lewis [with Kid Rock]** (2006)

(Jagger-Richards)

Rolling Stones original: UK/US A-side (1969)

(b. 1935 - d. 2022). Rock 'n' Roll and Country singer and pianist from Ferriday, Louisiana, USA, with Robert James Ritchie (b. 1971). Rock, Hip Hop and Country singer, rapper and guitarist from Romeo, Michigan, USA.

If one person can almost be guaranteed to come up with a very different version of a song, that person is Jerry Lee Lewis. Starting off slowly with just him and his piano, it quickly transforms into a fast modern Rock 'n' Roll song. It is debatable whether Kid Rock detracts from or enhances it, but 'Honky Tonk Women' can be found on The Killer's 2006 album 'Last Man Standing'.

Jerry Lee Lewis with Kid Rock performing 'Honky Tonk Women' (Promo Video, 2006)

[149] **HONKY TONK WOMEN** - Jan Preston (2013)

(Jagger-Richards)

Rolling Stones original: UK/US A-side (1969)

Boogie Woogie pianist and singer from Greymouth, New Zealand.

Although Jerry Lee Lewis chose to go for a contemporary Rock ('n' Roll) arrangement of 'Honky Tonk Women', he could just as easily have cut a Boogie Woogie version instead. Well *that's* exactly what renowned New Zealand pianist Jan Preston does with her wonderful cover. Featuring light Jazzy vocals, pumpin' piano and brushed drum work, it can be heard on her album 2013 'My Life As A Piano'. Ian and Charlie would be smiling!

Whose idea was it to record this song?

"It was my idea to record 'Honky Tonk Women'. Why? Because I am that person, the Honky Tonk Woman. The Honky Tonks were small houses where piano players such as myself pounded it out (often for drinks and tips) all night. Most piano players these days are in the classical or jazz scene, and we are quite rare in blues, even now. So I greatly relate to that song and wanted to sing it in the first person."

Do you perform this or any other Stones songs live?

"The only one they wrote that I play is 'Honky Tonk Women' at the moment, but I play other boogie/blues covers the Stones did such as 'Down The Road Apiece' and 'Dust My Broom'."

Were the Rolling Stones an influence on your own music?

"The Stones were an influence in that I listened to them a lot in my youth, but more than anything it was their piano players I was mad on. I had a vinyl record I used to play over and over called 'Jamming With Edward' (Edward refers to Nicky Hopkins' nickname). I love the grooves on this record, Keith's not playing so it's driven more by the piano playing and Nicky Hopkins was brilliant. Of course Billy Preston often played with the Stones and he was phenomenal as well."

[150] HOT STUFF - The Mighty Mocambos with Afrika Bambaataa, Charlie Funk and Deejay Snoop (2014)

(Jagger-Richards)

Rolling Stones original: Black and Blue (1976) + US A-side (1976)

Funk band from Germany, with Lance Taylor (b. 1957), DJ and Rapper from New York City, USA; Charles Andre Glenn (b. 1967), DJ from USA; and Hebil Houdaifa, DJ from Belgium.

The Stones' original of 'Hot Stuff' had a funk guitar riff inspired by James Brown, and this is retained on The Mighty Mocambos' single version. It also has lots of rapping by the guest DJs, which either greatly enhances or totally ruins it, depending entirely on one's point of view.

[151] I AM WAITING - The Quiet Five (1966)

(Jagger-Richards)

Rolling Stones original: Aftermath (1966)

Kris Ife (d. 2013 - vocals and guitar), Roger McKew (guitar), John Howell (organ, guitar and vocals), Richard Barnes (b. 1944 - bass and vocals), Ray Hailey (drums) and John 'Satch' Goswell (saxophone). Beat and Pop group from London (and yes, there were 6 of 'em!).

'I Am Waiting' is a song from 'Aftermath' with an unusual quiet / loud arrangement, a trick everyone would be using 30 years later. The Quiet Five live up to their name with a slower and less loud cover. It was issued as a single within weeks of the Stones' album release.

[152] I AM WAITING - Jennifer Warnes (1968)

(Jagger-Richards)

Rolling Stones original: Aftermath (1966)

Jennifer Jean Warnes (b. 1947), Country Rock and Pop singer from Seattle, Washington, USA.

Before she found major fame, Jennifer Warnes sometimes released records under different names, including (just) Jennifer, and Jennifer Warren. Her orchestrated cover of 'I Am Waiting' was issued as a 1968 single, and is also on her album 'I Remember Everything'.

[153] I AM WAITING - Them (1969)

(Jagger-Richards)

Rolling Stones original: Aftermath (1966)

Jerry Cole (Jerald Edward Kolbrak, b. 1939 - d. 2008 - vocals, guitar and drums) and Alan Henderson (b. 1944 - d. 2017 - bass). Psychedelic Rock and Folk Rock duo from Green Bay, Wisconsin, USA/Belfast, Northern Ireland.

Under Van Morrison's guidance, Them issued Rhythm 'n' Blues styled records that rivalled The Rolling Stones for both their intensity and authenticity. By the end of the '60s however, they were reduced to a duo, with American musician Jerry Cole the main contributor. With distorted guitar, piano, pounding drums and harmonies, Them's version of 'I Am Waiting' is a criminally-overlooked gem. It is on their imaginatively-titled 1969 album 'Them'.

[154] **I AM WAITING - Ollabelle** (2004)

(Jagger-Richards)

Rolling Stones original: Aftermath (1966)

Amy Helm (Amy Louise Helm - b. 1970 - vocals and mandola), Jimi Zhivago (guitar and vocals), Fiona McBain (Fiona Mary McBain - vocals, guitar and bass), Byron Isaacs (Byron David Isaacs - vocals, bass, guitar and dobro), Tony Leone (Anthony Leone, b. 1969 - vocals, drums, percussion and mandolin) and Glenn Patscha (vocals, keyboards and accordion). Folk, World and Country band from New York, USA.

For a song that is largely unknown to the general public, 'I Am Waiting' has inspired a number of excellent covers. Ollabelle's stunning modern Folk arrangement is up there with the best, and is on their 2004 debut album 'Ollabelle'.

[155] **I AM WAITING - Lindsey Buckingham** (2006)

(Jagger-Richards)

Rolling Stones original: Aftermath (1966)

Lindsey Adams Buckingham (b. 1949). Rock and Rock-Pop singer and guitarist from Palo Alto, California, USA.

Best-known as a sometimes member of Fleetwood Mac, Lindsey Buckingham's relaxed version features just him and his impressively finger-picked guitar, and is on his 2006 album 'Under The Skin'.

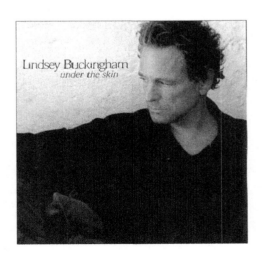

[156] **I AM WAITING - Tomo Nakayama feat. Jesse Sykes** (2014)

(Jagger-Richards)

Rolling Stones original: Aftermath (1966)

Folk Rock Multi-instrumentalist, born in Japan and raised in Seattle, Washington, USA, with Jesse Sykes (b. 1967). Folk, Blues, Country, Orchestral Pop singer and guitarist from Mount Kisco, New York, USA.

Gently played with just widescreen acoustic guitars and a little percussion, Tomo Nakayama and Jesse Sykes' exquisite duet is a highlight of the 2014 various artists album 'I Saved Latin - A Tribute To Wes Anderson'. [Interviews are with both Tomo Nakayama and Jesse Sykes]

'I Am Waiting' isn't the only Rolling Stones song on 'I Saved Latin!'.

How did your collaboration come about?

Tomo: "My cover of 'I Am Waiting' was recorded for a tribute album to the movies of Wes Anderson. 'Rushmore' is one of my favourite of his films, and I always loved the montage he set to the song, a kind of nadir in Max's character arc before he finds his redemption. I was a long time fan of Jesse Sykes, whose mystical spirit and lyrical songwriting reminded me of the mystery inherent in 'I Am Waiting'. Her voice kept coming to mind while I was recording the song, especially the ominous bridge. We had mutual friends through the Seattle music scene, but I was still shocked and delighted when she agreed to sing on it. I think she delivered a beautiful, timeless performance. It's one of my favourite recordings I've ever been a part of."

Jesse: "I've had the pleasure of knowing Tomo for many years, as we both lived, or live in Seattle, and play in bands from Seattle. I believe he was asked by the folks putting together that Wes Anderson tribute compilation to participate, and I suppose he wanted a different voice along with his own, to add some nuance... I was very flattered when he invited me to sing on the song!"

Have you ever performed this song (or any other Stones songs) live?

Tomo: "Jesse and I only performed the song live once, in a tiny old speakeasy owned by one of our friends. It had dirt floors and exposed wiring and bales of hay for seating, and a vintage bar from the turn of the century."

Jesse: "Many musical incarnations I've been involved in over the years have covered the Stones. My band in more recent times did a cool rendition of 'Paint It Black', but never recorded it sadly."

Were the Rolling Stones an influence on you?

Tomo: "I do love The Rolling Stones and respect their incredible body of work, though if I am being honest, when it comes to influence on my own work I am definitely more of a Lennon/McCartney man. I did spend quite a lot of time listening to the audio book of Keith Richards' memoir during one tour, and I always think of him when I'm on the road. What a life."

Jesse: "Yes. The stones have always been one of my top bands since childhood, to the point where they are deeply enmeshed in my soul's cosmic Braille, my DNA. When I need to reconnect or recalibrate emotionally, I listen to them, and I am transported - remembering myself again. I've viewed much of my life thru the lens and tone of the Stones. The guitar player in my band The Sweet Hereafter, Philip Wandscher, is also hugely influenced by them, and would probably say much of the same."

[157] I GO WILD - Omar Coleman (2018)

(Jagger-Richards)

Rolling Stones original: Voodoo Lounge (1994) + UK/US A-side (1995)

(b. 1973). Blues singer and harmonicist from Chicago, Illinois, USA.

A fair typical Stones Rock song from 'Voodoo Lounge', in Omar Coleman's hands it becomes a tough Chicago Blues that the late great Muddy Waters would've been proud of. This fabulous track is yet another highlight of 'Chicago Plays The Stones'.

[158] I GOT THE BLUES - Solomon Burke (2005)

(Jagger-Richards)

Rolling Stones original: Sticky Fingers (1971)

Solomon Vincent McDonald Burke (b. 1940 - d. 2010). Soul, Rhythm 'n' Blues, Blues and Gospel singer from Philadelphia, Pennsylvania, USA.

A fabulous soulful Blues song from the album 'Sticky Fingers', it could've been tailor-made for Solomon Burke. Someone who was influential on the Stones themselves, he retained his powerhouse vocals, despite being in less than stellar health at the time. It is on his 2005 album 'Make Do With What You Got'.

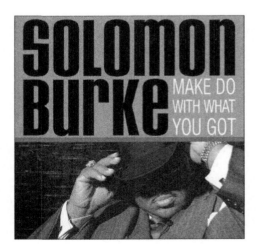

[159] I GOT THE BLUES - Aloe Blacc and Joel Van Dijk (2011)

(Jagger-Richards)

Rolling Stones original: Sticky Fingers (1971)

Egbert Nathaniel Dawkins III (b. 1979). Hip Hop, Soul, R&B and Reggae singer from Laguna Hills, California, USA, and Joel Van Dijk, Blues and Rock guitarist from Los Angeles, California, USA.

Featuring Aloe Blacc solely backed by Joel Van Dijk's arpeggio electric guitar picking, the end result is awe-inspiring. It's a highlight of 'Sticky Soul Fingers: A Rolling Stones Tribute'. [Interview is with Joel Van Dijk]

How did your collaboration with Aloe Blacc come about?

"We were in the rise of Aloe Blacc's fame and the 2 ½ year long 'I Need A Dollar Tour' for the hit song and his 'Good Things' album. I had been playing guitar and musical directing for Aloe on the road, when he was asked to make a cover for the Mojo Magazine 'Sticky Fingers' Tribute, he asked me to produce it for him. In particular he suggested that I run his vocal tracks through guitar amps to give it a nice vintage tone. To be honest this is one of my favourite vocal recordings to date that I have heard from Aloe, he really nailed it, he must have had some real blues that day!"

Do you perform this (or any other Stones songs) live?

"We once performed a version of 'Paint It Black' for the French TV Show Taratata live in Belgium in the Capital Square."

Were the Rolling Stones an influence on you?

"My mom was a big Rolling Stones fan and had all the CDs around the house. It was in the water at my house you could say. I definitely loved some of their songs, 'Satisfaction', 'Paint it Black' and 'Time Is On My Side' are some of my favourites."

[160] I JUST WANT TO SEE HIS FACE - The Blind Boys of Alabama (2001)

(Jagger-Richards)

Rolling Stones original: Exile On Main St. (1972)

Clarence Fountain (b. 1929 - d. 2018), George Scott (b. 1929 - d. 2005), Jimmy Carter (b. 1932), Ricky McKinnie (b. 1952) and Bishop Billy Bowers (b. 1942 - d. 2013). Gospel group from Talladega, Alabama, USA.

A somewhat murky and poorly-mixed recording on 'Exile On Main St.', 'I Just Want To See His Face' was allegedly based on an old spiritual song. Whatever its origins, The Blind Boys of Alabama's incredible Gospel performance has even the strongest doubters believing! It can be found on their 2001 album 'Spirit Of The Century'. [Interview is with the group's manager Charles Driebe]

Whose idea was it to record this song?

"The idea to cover 'I Just Wanna See His Face' originated with the late John Chelew, who produced the album. He also had the idea to cover 'Down In The Hole' by Tom Waits, which later became the theme song to the first season of The Wire."

Do you perform this (or any other Stones songs) live, and were the Rolling Stones an influence on you?

"The band does not perform this song live, and they were not influenced by The Rolling Stones - in fact, the opposite is true. The Blind Boys recorded the song 'This May Be The Last Time' in the 1950s on the Specialty Records album 'The Sermon'. This song was the basis of the song by 'The Last Time' by the Rolling Stones! The Blind Boys recorded the song a year before The Staple Singers did."

[161] **I WANNA BE YOUR MAN - The Beatles** (1963)

(Lennon-McCartney)

Rolling Stones original: UK A-side (1963) and US B-side (1964)

John Lennon (John Winston Lennon, b. 1940 - d. 1980 - vocals, guitar and harmonica), Paul McCartney (James Paul McCartney, b. 1942 - vocals and bass), George Harrison (b. 1943 - d. 2001 - guitar and vocals) and Ringo Starr (Richard Starkey, b. 1940 - drums and occasional vocals). Beat Group from Liverpool, UK.

OK, this is a bit of a cheeky one… The song was mainly written by Paul McCartney, and then famously finished by John and Paul in the corner of a Richmond club while The Rolling Stones chatted - something that impressed Mick and Keith no end. With Mick's assured vocal, Brian's blistering solo and Bill's frantic bass playing, the Stones' version deservedly became their first Top 20 UK hit. So, how does The Beatles' own version, released on 'With The Beatles', compare? Well, it is faster and in a higher key, Ringo's double-tracked vocal is enthusiastic, and George's solo is nice. But really, there *is* no comparison.

The Beatles performing 'I Wanna Be Your Man' on 'Big Night Out', 1964 [UK TV]

[162] I'D MUCH RATHER BE WITH THE BOYS - The Toggery Five (1965)
(Oldham-Richards)

Rolling Stones original: 1965 Demo: Metamorphosis (1975)

Paul Young (b. 1947 - d. 2000 - vocals), Frank Renshaw (b. 1943 - vocals and guitar), Alan Doyle (guitar), Ken Mills (bass) and Graham Smith (drums). Beat and Rhythm 'n' Blues band from Manchester, UK.

A slightly awkward-sounding song in its original demo form (as heard on 1975's endlessly fascinating 'Metamorphosis' compilation), The Toggery Five saw the potential of the song, and came up with a single that fellow Mancunian's The Hollies would've been proud of. [Interview is with Frank Renshaw]

How did you end up recording an exclusive Oldham-Richards song?

"Well, I don't know who arranged it, and I didn't know then that Andrew Loog Oldham was a Photographer, but that's what we went to his offices for. On the roof actually, where we had a photo session with him. I never did get to see the pictures. Whilst generally chatting with him, he asked what we had in the pipeline. He just happened to mention that he had this song he had written with Keith. We liked it and quickly recorded it at Abbey Road.

It's me singing the single. When we recorded our first record, we went in to record a completely different song that our Producer (who was also The Hollies' Producer) had chosen for us. As it wasn't our cup of tea, and it wasn't working out too well, he asked if we had anything else. As sessions were in 3 hour slots in those days, time was at a premium. I had this song that I had written, and as Paul has only been with us less than a month and didn't know it, I sang it. So when it came to the Stones song, Ron Richards wanted the continuity of voice, therefore I sang that also.

Everybody had great expectations for the song, but then some silly tarts at some Girlie Magazines decided it was sexist, and slagged it off. So that was the end of that. In 1966, I was guitar player for Wayne Fontana, and we supported the Rolling Stones at Paris Olympia Theatre. I spoke with Andrew backstage after the show, about the song, and he was as dismayed as us. It seems that the Woke Society actually started around that time."

Did you perform this or any other Stones songs live?

"No, but we did perform other R&B songs that the Stones also performed."

Were the Rolling Stones an influence on the band's own music?

"No. I think we were all influenced by the same black R&B Artistes, performing mostly the same songs."

Frank Renshaw: "Due to the negativity, we quickly arranged a photo session in Hyde Park with five of the popular Models of the day, just to prove that we actually did like girls! (I'm in the middle by the way)"

[163] I'D MUCH RATHER BE WITH THE GIRLS - Donna Lynn (1965)
(Oldham-Richards)

Rolling Stones original: 1965 Demo: Metamorphosis (1975)

Camille Donna Albano (b. 1950). Pop singer from Canada.

A lovely Girl Group-styled Pop record that is similar to Lesley Gore's better hits, 'I'd Much Rather Be With The Girls' was released as a single.

[164] I'D MUCH RATHER BE WITH THE BOYS - Johnny Thunders (1983)
(Oldham-Richards)

Rolling Stones original: 1965 Demo: Metamorphosis (1975)

John Anthony Genzale (b. 1952 - d. 1991). Rock, Punk Rock and Glam Rock singer and guitarist from Queens, New York, USA. Ex-New York Dolls and The Heartbreakers.

His voice was a bit of an acquired taste, but there's no doubting that Johnny Thunders meant every word he sung, and such is the case with this simple vocals plus guitar cover. It was on his 1983 album 'Hurt Me'.

[165] I'D MUCH RATHER BE WITH THE GIRLS - Ronnie Spector (2016)
(Oldham-Richards)

Rolling Stones original: 1965 Demo: Metamorphosis (1975)

Veronica Yvette Bennett (b. 1943 - d. 2022). Pop and Rock singer from New York City, USA.

The late, great, legendary lead singer from Girl Group The Ronettes, Ronnie Spector's unique vibrato sounds as great as ever on this inspired cover. It is the highlight of her 2016 album 'English Heart'.

[166] I'M FREE - Chris Farlowe (1966)
(Jagger-Richards)

Rolling Stones original: Out Of Our Heads [UK version] (1965) + December's Children (and Everybody's) (1965) + US B-side (1965)

Chris Farlowe (John Henry Dighton, b. 1940). Rhythm 'n' Blues, Soul and Pop singer from Islington, London.

A strong candidate for The Rolling Stones' (and anyone else's) greatest B-side ever, Chris Farlowe's version loses the Folk-Rock feel of the original in favour of a faster, brass-led, Soul arrangement. It was on 1966's 'The Art of Chris Farlowe', an album that also included three other Jagger-Richards songs.

[167] I'M FREE - Wilmer and The Dukes (1969)
(Jagger-Richards)

Rolling Stones original: Out Of Our Heads [UK version] (1965) + December's Children (and Everybody's) (1965) + US B-side (1965)

Wilmer Alexander Jr. (b. 1943 - vocals and saxophone), Ralph 'Duke' Gillotte (keyboards and vocals), Doug Brown (guitar), Monte Alberts (bass) and Ron Alberts (drums). Rhythm 'n' Blues band from Geneva, New York, USA. Disbanded in 1974.

With the song given a full Stax/Atlantic-styled Southern Soul makeover, Wilmer and The Dukes' cover is on their eponymous 1969 album.

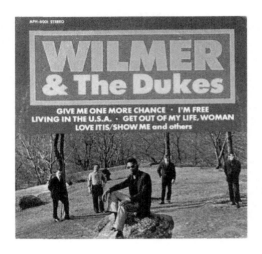

[168] I'M FREE - The Soup Dragons (1989)
(Jagger-Richards)

Rolling Stones original: Out Of Our Heads [UK version] (1965) + December's Children (and Everybody's) (1965) + US B-side (1965)

Sean Dickson (vocals and guitar), Jim McCulloch (guitar and vocals), Sushil K. Dade (bass) and Paul Quinn (drums). Indie Pop and Alternative Dance band from Bellshill, Lanarkshire, Scotland. Disbanded in 1995.

With a modern Dance beat, wah-wah guitar, and Reggae "toasting" from guest Junior Reid, The Soup Dragons' radical update of 'I'm Free' got to No. 5 in the UK charts when released as a 1989 single, bringing the song to a whole new generation. [Note: A former member responded to my questions, but wanted his comments to be kept strictly off-the-record]

[169] I'M NOT SIGNIFYING (I AIN'T SIGNIFYING) - Greg 'Stackhouse' Prevost (2012)

(Jagger-Richards)

Rolling Stones original: Exile On Main St. - Expanded Reissue Bonus Disc (2010) (recorded in 1971)

Greg Prevost (b. 1959). Garage Rock and Psychedelic Rock singer and multi-instrumentalist from Rochester, New York, USA. Former member of The Chesterfield Kings.

In 2010, the expanded CD reissue of 'Exile On Main St.' added a few bonus tracks, including a slow piano blues entitled 'I'm Not Signifying', complete with harmonica and brass that was added in 2009. Keen collectors of RS bootlegs however, would've been familiar with a mid-paced version under the title 'I Ain't Signifying' *without* the overdubs and piano, but instead with blistering Mick Taylor guitar. It is *this* version that inspired ex-The Chesterfields front man Greg 'Stackhouse' Prevost's version. Kicking off with an acoustic guitar and Greg's powerful Jagger-esque voice, some very Stones-like harmonies and slide guitar soon kick in. This excellent cover is on his 2002 album 'Mississippi Murderer'. *See [54] for interview!*

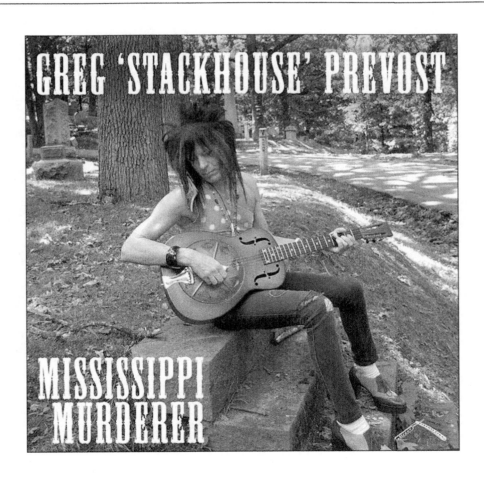

[170] **IN ANOTHER LAND - 57** (2013)
(Wyman)

Rolling Stones original: Their Satanic Majesties Request (1967) + US A-side (1967)

Unknown band, probably studio musicians from Italy.

'In Another Land' was Bill Wyman's first and best released song with The Rolling Stones, and every bit as crucial to 'Their Satanic Majesties Request' as George's and Ringo's contributions are to 'Sgt. Pepper'. This very different and strange Grunge cover was issued on an Italian Stones Tribute album entitled 'Stoned Town'.

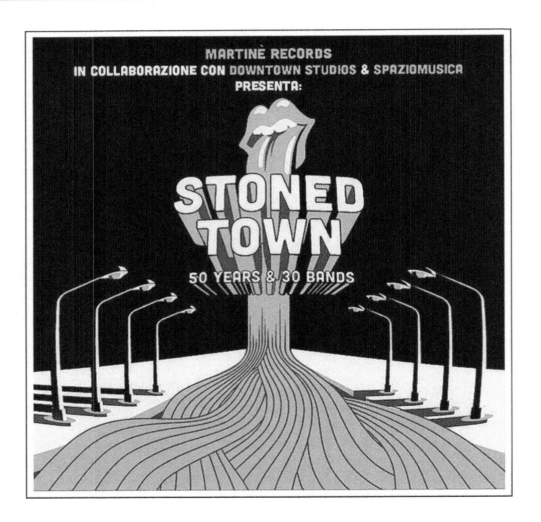

[171] **IT SHOULD BE YOU** - George Bean (1964)

(Jagger-Richards)

Rolling Stones original: 1963 Demo: Bootleg only

(d. 1970). Folk and Pop singer from the UK.

According to Mick Jagger, this is the first song he and Keith wrote together, and if true, it is an acceptable enough attempt at lightweight Mersey-styled Pop. A friend of Mick and Keith's flat mate James Phelge, George Bean's version sticks closely to the Stones' well-known demo, and, backed by another mediocre Jagger-Richards song 'Will You Be My Lover Tonight?', it's January 1964 release makes it almost certainly the earliest available record to feature Jagger-Richards songs.

[172] **IT'S NOT EASY** - Blue Öyster Cult (1980) *(Not released until 2012)*

(Jagger-Richards)

Rolling Stones original: Aftermath (1966)

Eric Bloom (Eric Jay Bloom, b. 1944 - vocals, guitar and keyboards), Buck Dharma (Donald Roeser, b. 1947 - guitar and vocals), Allen Lanier (Allen Glover Lanier, b. 1946, d. 2013 - keyboards, guitar and vocals), Joe Bouchard (Joseph J. Bouchard, b. 1948 - bass and vocals) and Albert Bouchard (Albert Thomas Bouchard, b. 1947 - drums and vocals). Hard Rock and Prog-Rock band from Stony Brook, New York, USA.

An excellent rock 'n' roll song from 'Aftermath', Blue Öyster Cult's live version initially sticks closely to the Stones' original, until a 3 minute drum solo(!), and then a double speed finale. It is on 'The Columbia Albums Collection' box set.

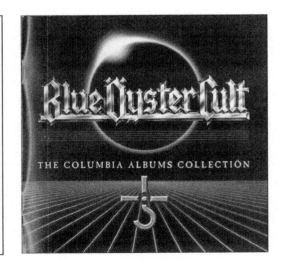

[173] **IT'S ONLY ROCK 'N' ROLL - Rita Lee** (1992)
(Jagger-Richards)

Rolling Stones original: It's Only Rock 'N' Roll (1974) + UK/US A-side (1974)

Rita Lee Jones (b. 1947). Rock, Pop and Tropicália singer and guitarist from São Paulo, Brazil.

The ever-popular 'It's Only Rock 'n' Roll' was The Rolling Stones only real musical nod to the early 70s UK Glam Rock phenomenon. Not that you'd know it here, with this relaxed cover performed solely on acoustic guitar. Rita Lee's version is on her 1992 album 'Rita Lee em Bossa 'n Roll'.

[174] **IT'S ONLY ROCK 'N' ROLL - Rebecca Lynn Howard** (2008)
(Jagger-Richards)

Rolling Stones original: It's Only Rock 'N' Roll (1974) + UK/US A-side (1974)

(b. 1979). Country, Pop and Rock singer and guitarist from Salyersville, Kentucky, USA.

Similar in arrangement to the original, Rebecca Lynn Howard's 'Country Rock' version is far more Rock than Country. It is on the various artists 'Gone Country '70s Rock' CD.

[175] JE SUIS UN ROCK STAR (JE SUIS UNE DOLLY) - Dolly Rockers (2009)
(Wyman)

Rolling Stones original: UK/US A-Side (1981) + Bill Wyman [Bill Wyman solo single & album] (1982)

Brooke Challinor, Lucie Kay and Sophie King. Pop, Electropop and Dance trio from the UK.

Bill Wyman's 1981 single 'Je Suis Rock Star' has the distinction of being the biggest ever UK hit by a solo Rolling Stone, peaking at No. 14. Dolly Rockers' 'Je Suis Une Dolly' has an additional 7 composer credits and features mostly different lyrics, but the melody and backing are basically the same as Bill's hit, and it's even sung in the same "Cockney French" as the original. The end result - and the accompanying video - is a lot of fun!

[176] JIGSAW PUZZLE - Melanie (1972)
(Jagger-Richards)

Rolling Stones original: Beggars Banquet (1968)

Melanie Anne Safka (b. 1947). Folk and Pop singer and guitarist from Queens, New York, USA.

Songs as legendary as 'Sympathy For The Devil', 'Street Fighting Man', 'No Expectations' and 'Stray Cat Blues' are inevitably going to overshadow others, and that's exactly what they do on 'Beggars Banquet' with the largely overlooked 'Jigsaw Puzzle'. Perhaps it's the lack of a proper chorus and the involved, Dylan-inspired lyrics that make it a little less appealing? Fortunately, there *are* a couple of great covers. Melanie's passionately-sung and impeccably-played version of 'Jigsaw Puzzle' with its unobtrusive bass, drums and fiddle, is one of her very best interpretations of other people's songs. It is on her 1972 album 'Garden In The City'.

[177] **JIGSAW PUZZLE - Billy Goodman** (2011)

(Jagger-Richards)

Rolling Stones original: Beggars Banquet (1968)

(b. 1954). Blues, Folk, World and Country singer and guitarist from Yonkers, New York, USA. Based in Berlin, Germany.

Featuring just his clear, strong vocals and open-tuned guitar (complete with occasional slide), Billy Goodman's excellent cover is well worth checking out. It can be found on his 2011 'Walk The Street Alone' album.

Whose idea was it to record this song?

"It was my idea to perform or record these old Stones songs. I always loved 'Jigsaw Puzzle'".

Do you perform this or any other Stones songs live?

"I play it live, 'Sister Morphine' too."

Were the Rolling Stones an influence on your own music?

"I was a huge fan of the Stones up till 'Sticky Fingers', they had a huge influence on me. I plan on doing 'Child Of The Moon' on my next album."

[178] **JIVING SISTER FANNY - Izzy Stradlin** (1993)
(Jagger-Richards)

Rolling Stones original: Metamorphosis (1975) (recorded in 1969)

Jeffrey Dean Isbell (b. 1962). Hard Rock and Blues-Rock singer and guitarist from Lafayette, Indiana, USA. Best known as a member of Guns 'n' Roses.

A straight ahead rocker that first saw the light of day on 1975's 'Metamorphosis' album, Izzy Stradlin's live recording is harder and heavier, with frantic lead guitar work. It is on the 1993 'Izzy Stradlin and The Ju Ju Hounds Live' EP.

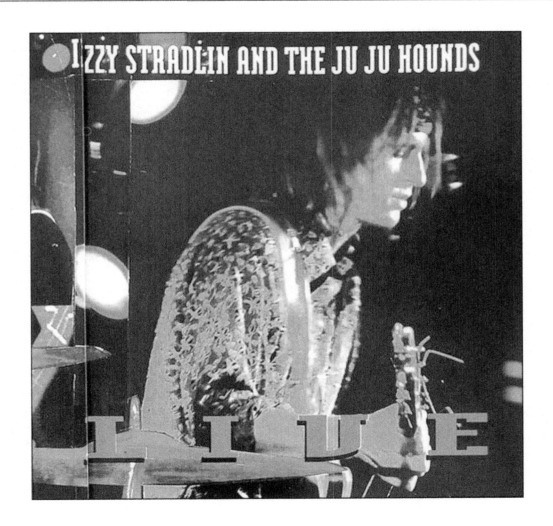

[179] JUMPIN' JACK FLASH - Thelma Houston (1969)

(Jagger-Richards)

Rolling Stones original: UK/US A-side (1968)

Thelma Jackson (b. 1946). Soul and Disco singer from Leland, Mississippi, USA.

Tiring of the Baroque Pop and Psychedelia of recent singles and albums (there would be no more songs like 'Ruby Tuesday' and 'She's A Rainbow'), 'Jumpin' Jack Flash' saw the band return to their Blues roots, albeit with a new-found Rock sensibility. It very quickly became a much-covered standard, and Thelma Houston's version was one of the first of real note. Proving herself to be one of the greatest Soul singers of her generation, Thelma's exciting Soul-Rock cover was released on her 1969 debut album 'Sunshower', as well as on a single.

Whose idea was it to record this song?

"Well it was Jimmy Webb's idea as he loved 'Jumpin' Jack Flash'. I was reluctant at first but gave in as Jimmy had written such beautiful songs for my debut album called 'Sunshower', so I decided to record the song."

Do you perform this (or any other Stones songs) live?

"Yes I sometimes perform 'Jumpin' Jack Flash' within my 'Thelma Houston: My Motown Memories and More' band show. I also do the song 'Ruby Tuesday' as well."

Were the Rolling Stones an influence on you?

"I'm personally influenced by Mick Jagger's inclusion of exercise and his longevity in the business as a terrific performer."

[180] JUMPIN' JACK FLASH - Alex Harvey (1969)

(Jagger-Richards)

Rolling Stones original: UK/US A-side (1968)

Alexander James Harvey (b. 1935 - d. 1982). Rock, Blues and Soul singer and guitarist from Glasgow, Scotland.

Best remembered for the aptly-named The Sensational Alex Harvey Band in the 70s, the not-quite-yet sensational Alex Harvey's cover of 'Jumpin' Jack Flash' found him backed by a weird combination of over-driven guitars and brassy orchestration. It is on Alex's 1969 'Roman Wall Blues' album.

[181] JUMPIN' JACK FLASH - Johnny Winter (1971)

(Jagger-Richards)

Rolling Stones original: UK/US A-side (1968)

John Dawson Winter III (b. 1944 - d. 2014). Blues-Rock singer and guitarist from Beaumont, Texas, USA.

Johnny Winter was never known for his subtlety, and such is the case with his Hard Rock live cover of 'Jumpin' Jack Flash', which can be found on the 1971 album 'Live'.

[182] JUMPIN' JACK FLASH - YOUNGBLOOD - Leon Russell (1972)

(Jagger-Richards/Leiber-Stoller)

Rolling Stones original: UK/US A-side (1968)

Claude Russell Bridges (b. 1942 - d. 2016). Rock, Country and Gospel singer, pianist, guitarist and bassist from Lawton, Oklahoma, USA.

For all its big names there - George Harrison, Ringo Starr, Billy Preston, Bob Dylan - arguably the most exciting moment at The Concert For Bangladesh was Leon Russell's medley of 'Jumpin' Jack Flash' with The Coasters' 'Youngblood'. It is on the box set 'The Concert For Bangladesh', as well as in the movie of the same name.

[183] JUMPIN' JACK FLASH - Peter Frampton (1972)

(Jagger-Richards)

Rolling Stones original: UK/US A-side (1968)

Peter Kenneth Frampton (b. 1950). Rock singer and guitarist from Beckenham, Kent, UK.

Previously a member of The Herd and Humble Pie, Peter Frampton included a somewhat relaxed cover of 'Jumpin' Jack Flash' on his debut solo album 'Wind Of Change'.

[184] **JUMPIN' JACK FLASH - Marcia Hines** (1975)

(Jagger-Richards)

Rolling Stones original: UK/US A-side (1968)

Marcia Elaine Hines (b. 1953). Australia-based Pop, Disco, Jazz and Funk singer, originally from Boston, Massachusetts, USA.

A raucous combination of Soul, Disco and Rock, Marcia Hines cover of 'Jumpin' Jack Flash' first appeared on her 1975 debut album 'Marcia Shines', as well as on 1978's 'Marcia Hines Live Across Australia'.

Whose idea was it to record this song?

"It was my decision to record after performing it live with my band to great audience response, and the natural progression was to take it into the studio, exactly as we performed it. It forms an important part of the 'Live Across Australia Album' and was pivotal to the live performances in the eighties."

Do you perform this (or any other Stones songs) live?

"'Jumpin' Jack Flash' is the only Rolling Stones song that I have ever recorded or performed."

Were the Rolling Stones an influence on you?

"The Rolling Stones influenced most musicians when I was growing up. Even in Boston the influence of British music in general was perceived as both very cool and extremely progressive. As a young black woman in North America, to me the Stones were a seminal part of my musical growth. I loved them."

[185] JUMPIN' JACK FLASH - Aretha Franklin [with Keith Richards and Ronnie Wood] (1986)

(Jagger-Richards)

Rolling Stones original: UK/US A-side (1968)

Aretha Louise Franklin (b. 1942 - d. 2018). Soul, Gospel, Jazz and Pop singer and pianist from Memphis, Tennessee, USA.

Recorded for the 1986 Whoopi Goldberg comedy movie of the same name, Aretha Franklin's great Soul-Rock version of 'Jumpin' Jack Flash' was recorded with Keith Richards and Ronnie Wood during a time when Mick Jagger was otherwise enhaged with solo projects. Released as a single, it peaked at No. 21 in the US Billboard charts, though in the UK it stalled at No. 58.

Aretha Franklin (with Keith Richards) performing 'Jumpin' Jack Flash' (Promo Video, 1986)

[186] **JUMPIN' JACK FLASH - Guns N' Roses** (1986) *(Not released until 2018)*

(Jagger-Richards)

Rolling Stones original: UK/US A-side (1968)

Axl Rose (William Bruce Rose Jr., b. 1962 - vocals and occasional keyboards), Slash (Saul Hudson, b. 1965 - guitar and vocals), Izzy Stradlin (Jeffrey Dean Isbell, b. 1962 - guitar and vocals), Duff McKagan (Michael Andrew McKagan, b. 1964 - bass and vocals) and Steven Adler (Michael Coletti, b. 1965 - drums and vocals). Hard Rock band from Los Angeles, California, USA.

Guns N' Roses finally included their fast Hard Rock run-through of 'Jumpin' Jack Flash' on 2018's 'Appetite For Destruction - Super Deluxe Edition', though it had been available on bootlegs for decades.

[187] **JUMPIN' JACK FLASH - Motörhead** (1993) *(Not released until 2001)*

(Jagger-Richards)

Rolling Stones original: UK/US A-side (1968)

Lemmy Kilmister (Ian Fraser Kilmister, b. 1945 - d. 2015 - vocals and bass), Michael 'Würzel' Burston (Michael Richard Burston, b. 1949 - d. 2011 - guitar and vocals), Phil 'Wizzö' Campbell (Philip Anthony Campbell[1] (b. 1961 - guitar and vocals) and Mikkey Dee (Micael Kiriakos Delaoglou, b. 1963 - drums). Heavy Metal, Hard Rock and Speed Metal band from London, UK.

Another cover that wasn't released until later, Motörhead's version of 'Jumpin' Jack Flash' sticks closely to the Stones' original tempo, despite being harder and noisier. It was released as a bonus track on the 2001 reissue of 1993's 'Bastards' album.

[188] JUMPIN' JACK FLASH - Rodney Crowell (1997)

(Jagger-Richards)

Rolling Stones original: UK/US A-side (1968)

(b. 1950). Country, Folk and Americana singer and guitarist from Houston, Texas, USA.

With an arpeggio guitar intro and prominent fiddle throughout, Rodney Crowell's fine Country-Rock version of 'Jumpin' Jack Flash' is on the various artists 'Stone Country' CD.

Whose idea was it to record this song?

"If I remember correctly I was asked to be part of a Rolling Stones tribute from Nashville and I jumped on 'Jumpin' Jack Flash'. I produced a very cool version of 'The Last Time' with Ronnie Milsap singing, that for some strange reason didn't make the album. I thought it was better than mine."

Do you perform this (or any other Stones songs) live?

"On occasion I've been known to perform, 'The Last Time,' 'It's All Over Now', 'Honky Tonk Women' and 'Wild Horses.' Usually when we've been out on tour for a while and need a shot in the arm."

Were the Rolling Stones an influence on your own songwriting?

"Since I place 'Honky Tonk Women' and 'Brown Sugar' among my all time favourite rock and roll recordings, it's safe to say The Stones have influenced my songwriting in ways I may not even be aware of."

[189] **LADY JANE - Glynt Johns** (1966)

(Jagger-Richards)

Rolling Stones original: Aftermath (1966) + US B-side (1966)

Glyn Thomas Johns (b. 1942). Rock and Pop Producer, Audio Engineer and occasional singer from Epsom, Surrey, UK.

Glyn Johns engineered every Rolling Stones release from 1965's 'December's Children (And Everybody's)' to the 1976's 'Black and Blue', as well as working with The Beatles, The Who, Led Zeppelin, The Faces, Bob Dylan and countless others. He also released a handful of singles in the mid-'60s as a vocalist, with 'Lady Jane' released exclusively for the Spanish market under the name Glynt Johns. The Stones' original of their ground-breaking Baroque Pop ballad was enhanced considerably by Brian Jones' use of the Dulcimer, something that cannot be beaten, right? Well, Glyn(t) Johns' version features *Brian Jones on sitar!* Vocally Glyn is nothing special, but wouldn't it be wonderful if a Stones' outtake existed with the sitar arrangement?

Glynt Johns performing 'Lady Jane' on 'Tele-Ritmo', 1966 [Spanish TV]

[190] **LADY JANE - David Garrick** (1966)

(Jagger-Richards)

Rolling Stones original: Aftermath (1966) + US B-side (1966)

Philip Darrell Core (b. 1945 - d. 2013). Pop and Rock singer from Liverpool, UK.

Although his voice sounds closer to Peter Noone than it does Mick Jagger, David Garrick's cover of 'Lady Jane' was otherwise a carbon copy. Released as a single, it peaked at just No. 28 in the UK but got as high as No. 5 in The Netherlands.

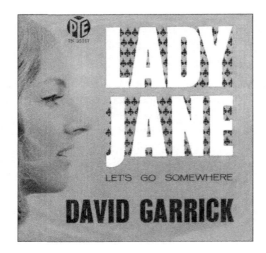

[191] **LADY JANE - Trini Lopez** (1967)

(Jagger-Richards)

Rolling Stones original: Aftermath (1966) + US B-side (1966)

Trinidad López III (b. 1937 - d. 2020). Pop and Folk singer and guitarist from Dallas, Texas, USA.

Best known for faster songs like 'If I Had A Hammer' and 'Lemon Tree', Trini Lopez included a gently crooned version of 'Lady Jane' on his 1967 'Trini Lopez in London' album.

[192] **LADY JANE - Jane Duboc** (2003)
(Jagger-Richards)

Rolling Stones original: Aftermath (1966) + US B-side (1966)

Jane Duboc Vaquer (b. 1950). MPB, Jazz, Bossa Nova and Pop singer, guitarist and pianist from Belém, Brazil.

Jane's beautifully-sung cover of 'Lady Jane' features gentle acoustic guitar with orchestration, and can be found on her 2003 album 'Sweet Lady Jane'.

Whose idea was it to record this song?

"Ivan Lins had the idea to record the song."

Do you perform this (or any other Stones songs) live?

"I perform the song every now and then. I play it on my guitar."

Were the Rolling Stones an influence on you?

"I think that the Rolling Stones influenced musicians, young people in the sixties, and they continue to be a great example for the whole world. They are beautiful. Great energy, great attitude. I will never forget the day I saw and heard Mick Jagger singing with Muddy Waters."

[193] **THE LANTERN - Mac Rybell** (1968)

(Jagger-Richards)

Rolling Stones original: Their Satanic Majesties Request (1967) + US B-side (1967)

Psych-Folk band from Sao Paulo, Brazil.

One of the weaker songs on 'Their Satanic Majesties Request', Brazilian band Mac Rybell's version has a more adventurous arrangement but is otherwise similar. It was released as a single in the band's homeland. .

[194] **THE LAST TIME - The Andrew Oldham Orchestra** (1966)

(Jagger-Richards)

Rolling Stones original: Out Of Our Heads [US version] (1965) + UK/US A-side (1965)

Andrew Loog Oldham (b. 1944). Producer, Manager and Band Leader from London, UK.

Loosely inspired by an old Gospel number called 'This May Be the Last Time', 'The Last Time' was notable for being the first song Jagger and Richards released as a UK A-side. Andrew Oldham's imaginative re-arrangement earned him a co-writing credit, but it was otherwise largely forgotten for over 30 years. Then in 1997, lead vocalist and songwriter for Brit-Pop band The Verve used a sample from Andrew's version in their song 'Bitter Sweet Symphony'. Released as a single, it got to No. 2 in the UK charts, and also did well around the globe, including a No. 11 US hit. Sadly though, there was a major and lengthy dispute over composer credits, which was not fully resolved until as recently as 2019, when Richard Ashcroft was finally handed over full rights to the song.

[195] **THE LAST TIME - The Who** (1967)

(Jagger-Richards)

Rolling Stones original: Out Of Our Heads [US version] (1965) + UK/US A-side (1965)

Roger Daltrey (Roger Harry Daltrey, b. 1944 - vocals and harmonica), Pete Townshend (Peter Dennis Blandford Townshend, b. 1945 - guitar and vocals), John Entwistle (John Alec Entwistle (b. 1944 - d. 2002 - bass and vocals) and Keith Moon (Keith John Moon, b. 1946 - d. 1978 - drums and vocals). Rhythm 'n' Blues and Rock band from London, UK.

After the 1967 imprisonment of Mick and Keith on drugs charges, the Who recorded 'The Last Time' and 'Under My Thumb' for a single, and announced in an advertisement: "The Who consider Mick Jagger and Keith Richards have been treated as scapegoats for the drug problem and as a protest against the savage imposed on them at Chichester yesterday, The Who are issuing today the first of a series of Jagger/Richard songs to keep their work before the public until they are again free to record themselves." However, by the time the record was released, they had been freed on appeal. Whatever, The Who's versions are wonderful, despite the bass being a little weaker usual, probably because it was overdubbed by Pete Townshend due to John Entwistle being away on honeymoon.

[196] **THE LAST TIME - Dada** (1970)

(Jagger-Richards)

Rolling Stones original: Out Of Our Heads [US version] (1965) + UK/US A-side (1965)

Elkie Brooks (Elaine Bookbinder, b. 1945 - vocals), Robert Palmer (Robert Allan Palmer, b. 1949 - d. 2003 - vocals), Paul Korda (Paul Kunstler, b. 1948 - d. 2020 - vocals), Jimmy Chambers (vocals and percussion), Pete Gage (b. 1947 - guitar and bass), Don Shinn (Donald Shinn, b. 1945 - keyboards, bass and vibes), Martyn Harryman (drums and percussion), Barry Duggan (b. 1958 - saxophone and flute), Malcolm Capewell (saxophone and flute) and Ernie Luchlan (trumpet and flugelhorn). Blues-Rock and Jazz-Rock band from London, UK. Later evolved into Vinegar Joe.

Dada's overblown, complex arrangement of 'The Last Time' was released on their 1970 eponymous album.

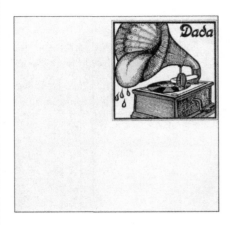

[197] **THE LAST TIME - Bobby Bare** (1978)

(Jagger-Richards)

Rolling Stones original: Out Of Our Heads [US version] (1965) + UK/US A-side (1965)

Robert Joseph Bare (b. 1935). Country singer and guitarist from Ironton, Ohio, USA.

A Country music legend, Bobby Bare's version of 'The Last Time' is given a very modern (at the time) 'Outlaw' Country makeover, with a relaxed rhythm and a prominent electric lead guitar.

[198] **THE LAST TIME - Transvision Vamp** (1989)

(Jagger-Richards)

Rolling Stones original: Out Of Our Heads [US version] (1965) + UK/US A-side (1965)

Wendy James (b. 1966 - vocals), Nick Christian Sayer (guitar and vocals), Dave Parsons (David Richard Parsons, b. 1964 - bass and vocals), Tex Axile (Anthony Doughty, b. 1963 - keyboards, sequencer, drums, guitar and vocals) and Martin 'Mallet' Hallett (drums and vocals). Pop-Punk and Pop-Rock band from Putney, London, UK.

Transvision Vamp's powerful live revamp was a bonus track on their 1989 'Born To Be Sold' single. [Interview is with Wendy James]

Whose idea was it to perform this song?

"The whole band's idea!"

Did you perform any other Stones songs live?

"No other RS Songs (Dylan x 2, Gary Glitter x 1)."

Were the Rolling Stones an influence on you?

"Enormously for their songs, sound, look, intelligence, attitude, style, talent and the culture which surrounded them, especially late sixties early seventies. Enormously in all ways."

[199] **THE LAST TIME - Dwight Yoakam** (1997)
(Jagger-Richards)

Rolling Stones original: Out Of Our Heads [US version] (1965) + UK/US A-side (1965)

Dwight David Yoakam (b. 1956). Country, Bluegrass and Rockabilly singer and guitarist from Pikeville, Kentucky, USA.

Dwight Yoakam's very fast Country-Rockabilly version of 'The Last Time' is on his 1997 album 'Under The Covers'.

[200] **THE LAST TIME - The Tractors** (1997)
(Jagger-Richards)

Rolling Stones original: Out Of Our Heads [US version] (1965) + UK/US A-side (1965)

Steve Ripley (Paul Steven Ripley, b. 1950 - d. 2019 - vocals and guitar), Ron Getman (d. 2021 - guitar, dobro, mandolin and vocals), Walt Richmond (keyboards, piano and vocals), Casey van Beek (b. 1942 - bass and vocals) and Jamie Oldaker (b. 1951 - d. 2020 - drums). Country Rock band from Tulsa, Oklahoma, USA. Disbanded in 2018.

The Tractors' surprisingly straight-forward Country-Rock cover was released on the various artists 'Stone Country' CD.

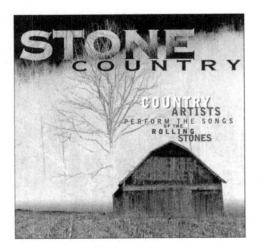

[201] THE LAST TIME (BITTER SWEET SYMPHONY) - The Andrew Oldham Orchestra and Vashti Bunyan (2013)
(Jagger-Richards-Oldham-Ashcroft)

Rolling Stones original: Out Of Our Heads [US version] (1965) + UK/US A-side (1965)

Andrew Loog Oldham (b. 1944). Producer, Manager and Band Leader from London, UK, with Jennifer Vashti Bunyan (b. 1945). Folk and Pop singer from Newcastle-upon-Tyne, UK.

Although Mick and Keith for a long time did their best to distance themselves from the 'Bitter Sweet Symphony' row between ABKCO and The Verve's Richard Ashcroft, Andrew Loog Oldham had very little sympathy with him (he allegedly declared "Fair cop! Absolute total pinch!" when he heard it). Cheekilly, he then included the song on his own album 'Play The Rolling Stones Songbook Volume 2', bringing everything full circle by featuring the legendary Vashti Bunyan on vocals - the singer he first worked with nearly half a century earlier. The end result is wonderful, with the now-famous riff played on an acoustic guitar, and Vashti's youthful-sounding vocals retaining the same fragile and dreamy qualities that they had all those years earlier. *See [387] for Vashti Bunyan interview, and see [194] for more on the 'Bitter Sweet Symphony' saga!*

[202] **THE LAST TIME - Chatham County Line (2019)**

(Jagger-Richards)

Rolling Stones original: Out Of Our Heads [US version] (1965) + UK/US A-side (1965)

Dave Wilson (vocals, guitar and harmonica), John Teer (mandolin, fiddle and vocals), Greg Readling (bass, pedal steel, piano and vocals) and Chandler Holt (banjo). Americana band from Raleigh, North Carolina, USA.

Played in stripped down Bluegrass style complete with harmonies, mandolin and banjo, Chatham Country Line's wonderful version is on their 2019 album 'Sharing The Covers'. [Interview is with Dave Wilson]

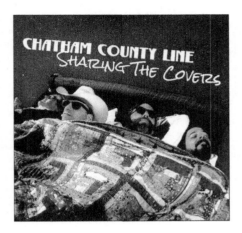

Whose idea was it to record this song?

"I had seen The Grateful Dead do this song at RFK stadium years ago. It was the 'last time' I saw them live and it was quite a night. We have fooled around with Stones tunes for many years having been rock and roll kids trying to play some form of Bluegrass. 'Let It Bleed' was a personal favourite to do through the years. Once Chandler hit that classic Last Time riff on the banjo and John and I started harmonizing we knew the song could work. Obviously a huge debt is owed to one of my favourite bands of all time The Staple Singers, where Keith nicked the tune to begin with."

Do you perform this (or any other Stones songs) live?

"This last December we did 'Monkey Man' during our special run of Electric Holiday shows. That one got the crowd moving!"

Were the Rolling Stones an influence on you?

"The Stones are a huge influence on us as a band. I believe very early on, Keith and Mick realized they could be a moderately successful blues cover band or they could succeed by writing their own material. The same scenario applied to our little band from North Carolina. We excelled in the world because we stuck to our guns of writing our own material.

In the latest incarnation of CCL, after the retirement of our banjo player, I have begun to play a good deal of open G on a Stratocaster. Originally I started doing it merely to continue playing the song 'Chip Of A Star' that features a great banjo figure running throughout. Banjo is most likely tuned to open G in the real world. The power of that open tuning on an electric guitar really opened a whole new world for me, as I am sure it did for Keith all those years ago. I use it onstage every night and our latest album will feature a good deal of it. I owe a huge debt to Keith but also Ry Cooder (who showed it to Keith), Bonnie Raitt and Lowell George, who all found that open G on an electric as quite a muse."

[203] **THE LAST TIME - The U.K. Subs** (2019)

(Jagger-Richards)

Rolling Stones original: Out Of Our Heads [US version] (1965) + UK/US A-side (1965)

Charlie Harper (David Charles Perez, b. 1944 - vocals and harmonica), Steve Straughan (guitar), Alvin Gibbs (bass) and Jamie Oliver (drums). Punk Rock band from London, UK.

Probably owing as much to The Who's cover as it does the Stones' original, Punk legends The U.K. Subs' fine revival is on their 2019 album 'Subversions II'. [Interview is with Charlie Harper]

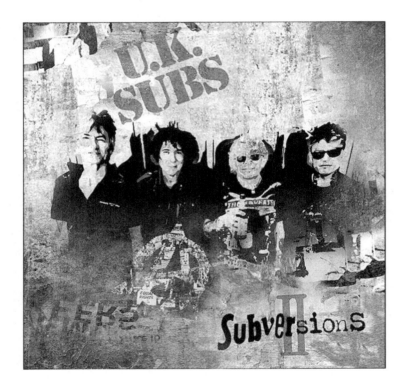

Whose idea was it to record this song?

"It was me, Charlie."

Do you perform this (or any other Stones songs) live?

"We are planning to."

Were the Rolling Stones an influence on you?

"Big time!"

[204] **LET IT BLEED - Johnny Winter** (1973)

(Jagger-Richards)

Rolling Stones original: Let It Bleed (1969)

John Dawson Winter III (b. 1944 - d. 2014). Blues-Rock singer and guitarist from Beaumont, Texas, USA.

The title track of the Stones' darkest and in many ways most impressive album, Johnny Winter's subtle as a sledge hammer boogie is on his 1973 album 'Still Alive and Well'.

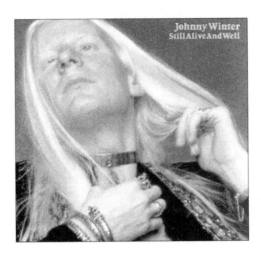

[205] **LET IT BLEED - Joan Jett and The Blackhearts** (1990)

(Jagger-Richards)

Rolling Stones original: Let It Bleed (1969)

Joan Jett (Joan Marie Larkin, b. 1958 - vocals and guitar), Ricky Byrd (Richard Scott Bird, b. 1956 - guitar and vocals), Kasim Sultan (b. 1955 - bass and keyboards) and Thommy Price (b. 1956 - drums). Hard Rock band from USA.

Featuring a tough but simple guitar riff that sounds more like 'Honky Tonk Women', Joan Jett's cover of 'Let It Bleed' is on her 1990 single 'Dirty Deeds'.

[206] LET IT BLEED - John Primer (2018)
(Jagger-Richards)

Rolling Stones original: Let It Bleed (1969)

(b. 1945). Blues singer and guitarist from Camden, Mississippi, USA.

The brilliant 'Chicago Plays The Stones' CD gets mentioned quite a few times in this book, and here it is again. John Primer's mid-paced Blues shuffle is notable for his soulful vocals and some prominent harmonica.

Whose idea was it to record this song?

"Larry Skollar with Raisin Music was the producer of that Rolling Stones Tribute album 'Chicago Plays the Stones', and he picked 'Let it Bleed' for me to do. I am not sure why, but he thought my voice would fit the song."

Do you perform any other Stones songs live?

"I do perform this song live from time to time. I get people requesting it actually."

Were the Rolling Stones an influence on your own music?

"The Rolling Stones were a big influence on me. I met them when I played in Muddy Waters Band. They were and still are larger than life guys. They were a lot of fun to hang with and to play with. They took what we were doing with the blues and turned it into rock n roll. Really amazing times back then. I would love to hang with them again someday. I wonder if they remember me? It would be cool to play with Keith again. He was such a cool cat!"

[207] LET'S SPEND THE NIGHT TOGETHER - Muddy Waters (1968)

(Jagger-Richards)

Rolling Stones original: Between The Buttons [US version] (1967) + Flowers (1967) + UK A-side (1967)
+ US B-side (1967)

McKinley Morganfield (b. 1913 - d. 1983). Blues singer and guitarist from Issaquena County, Mississippi, USA.

With its controversial lyrics (famously changed to "Let's spend *some time* together" when performed on 'The Ed Sullivan Show'), 'Let's Spend The Night Together' was a move away from the Stones' mid-'60s 'Wall of Noise' sound exemplified by the previous single 'Have You Seen Your Mother, Baby, Standing In The Shadow?'. Muddy Waters' 'Electric Mud' album saw Chess compromising his original sound in an attempt to gain him more commercial success, but he sounds ill-at-ease on 'Let's Spend The Night Together' with its Cream-inspired heavy backing.

[208] **LET'S SPEND THE NIGHT TOGETHER - David Bowie** (1973)

(Jagger-Richards)

Rolling Stones original: Between The Buttons [US version] (1967) + Flowers (1967) + UK A-side (1967) + US B-side (1967)

David Robert Jones (b. 1947 - d. 2016). Glam Rock, Art Rock, Electronic and Pop singer, guitarist, keyboardist and saxophonist from London, UK.

David Bowie's 100 mph Glam-fest with its discordant piano and excellent guitar appeared on his 1973 'Aladdin Sane' album, though it would've perhaps suited Bowie's 'Pin Ups' album of '60s cover versions a lot better.

[209] **LET'S SPEND THE NIGHT TOGETHER - Fanny** (1974)

(Jagger-Richards)

Rolling Stones original: Between The Buttons [US version] (1967) + Flowers (1967) + UK A-side (1967) + US B-side (1967)

Patti Quatro (b. 1948 - guitar and vocals), Jean Millington (b. 1949 - bass and vocals), Nickey Barclay (b. 1951 - keyboards and vocals) and Cam Davis (drums). Rock band from Los Angeles, California, USA. Disbanded in 1975.

A ground-breaking all-female Rock group that at this point included Suzi Quatro's sister Patti, their otherwise fine piano-dominated cover of 'Let's Spend The Night Together' is marred a little by the somewhat plodding tempo. It is on their 1974 'Rock and Roll Survivors' album.

[210] **LET'S SPEND THE NIGHT TOGETHER - Hello** (1975)

(Jagger-Richards)

Rolling Stones original: Between The Buttons [US version] (1967) + Flowers (1967) + UK A-side (1967) + US B-side (1967)

Bob Bradbury (Robert Bradbury, b. 1956 - vocals and guitar), Keith Marshall (b. 1956 - guitar, harmonica and vocals), Vic Faulkner (Victor Faulkner, b. 1956 - bass) and Jeff Allen (Jeffrey Leon Allen, b. 1956 - drums). Glam Rock band from London, UK.

David Bowie wasn't the only UK Glam act to take a fancy to 'Let's Spend The Night Together'. Hello's great foot-stomping version sounds just like (Bell label mates) The Glitter Band, and is on their debut album 1975's 'Keep Us Off The Streets'. [Interview is with Bob Bradbury]

Whose idea was it to record this song?

"It was my idea to record 'Let's Spend the Night Together' for the' Keeps Us Off The Streets' album. It was one of my favourite Stones tracks."

Do you perform this (or any other Stones songs) live?

"Yes we still play it live."

Were the Rolling Stones an influence on you?

"I loved the Stones, I liked their raw energy. I used to listen to them quite a lot when I was first starting out. We used to play 'Brown Sugar' when we were doing the working men's clubs as 'The Age' before we got signed and changed our name to 'Hello'. In fact we covered The Stones' cover of Chuck Berry's 'Carol' on 'Keeps Us Off The Streets' too."

[211] **LET'S SPEND THE NIGHT TOGETHER** - Melanie Harrold (1978)

(Jagger-Richards)

Rolling Stones original: Between The Buttons [US version] (1967) + Flowers (1967) + UK A-side (1967) + US B-side (1967)

(b. 1951). Folk and Country singer and guitarist from Cornwall, UK.

An excellent slow boogie with electric slide guitar and prominent saxophone, Melanie Harrold's cover of 'Let's Spend The Night Together' was released as a 1978 single.

Whose idea was it to record this song?

"The idea for the song came from my producer at the time Hugh Murphy as something to work on in between albums. I liked the way we reworked the song."

Did you perform this (or any other Stones songs) live?

"I didn't do any other versions of Rolling Stones music."

Were the Rolling Stones an influence on you?

"I think I appreciate the influence of The Rolling Stones now more than I did back then (I was more of a Beatles girl). However their songs were a backdrop to my growing up. I really appreciate now how they opened a doorway for all the Blues artists in America to come to England and perform and be appreciated and to get work and create new audiences for their music. I am thinking of B.B. King for example."

[212] **LET'S SPEND THE NIGHT TOGETHER - Roger Chapman** (1979)

(Jagger-Richards)

Rolling Stones original: Between The Buttons [US version] (1967) + Flowers (1967) + UK A-side (1967) + US B-side (1967)

Roger Maxwell Chapman (b. 1942). Blues-Rock and Prog-Rock singer from Leicester, UK.

The former vocalist for the band Family, Roger Chapman's 1979 single release of 'Let's Spend The Night Together' sticks closely to the Stones' original arrangement, though of course his distinctive voice is very different from Mick Jagger's.

Whose idea was it to record this song?

"It was recorded for a hotel franchise, then people liked it so much released it as a single."

Do you still perform this (or any other Stones songs) live?

"Only 'Spend', as people like to hear you play your hits and this was a hit for me in Germany, Austria, etc, though have played many Stones songs live along the way because most musicians know them. So easy and fun to play off the cuff on live gigs."

Were the Rolling Stones an influence on you?

"Yes right from the start."

[213] **LITTLE BY LITTLE - The Bintangs** (1969)
(Nanker-Phelge-Spector-Stewart)

Rolling Stones original: The Rolling Stones (1964) + England's Newest Hit Makers (1964) + UK B-side (1964)

Rhythm 'n' Blues band from Beverwijk, The Netherlands, led by Frank Kraaijeveld (vocals and bass).

An early Stones original that has more than a passing resemblance to Jimmy Reed's 'Shame, Shame, Shame', The Bintangs slower-paced Blues shuffle with powerful harmonica could easily pass for Canned Heat. It was released on their 1969 album 'Blues On The Ceiling'.

[214] **LITTLE BY LITTLE - The Count Bishops** (1977)
(Nanker-Phelge-Spector-Stewart)

Rolling Stones original: The Rolling Stones (1964) + England's Newest Hit Makers (1964) + UK B-side (1964)

Johnny Guitar (John Crippen - vocals and guitar), Zenon de Fleur (Zenon Hierowski, b. 1951, d. 1979 - vocals and guitar), Steve Lewins (bass) and Paul Balbi (drums). Pub Rock and Rhythm 'n' Blues band from London, UK.

The Count Bishops included an unsubtle, rough 'n' ready, Pub Rock cover on their debut album in 1977.

[215] **LIVE WITH ME - Girlschool** (1982)

(Jagger-Richards)

Rolling Stones original: Let It Bleed (1969)

Kim McAuliffe (b. 1959 - guitar and vocals), Kelly Johnson (Bernadette Jean Johnson, b. 1958 - d. 2007 - guitar and vocals), Ghislaine 'Gil' Weston (b. 1958 - bass and vocals) and Denise Dufort (b. 1958 - drums). Hard Rock and Heavy Metal band from London, UK.

Kicking off with a bass introduction just like the Stones' studio version, Girlschool's cover of 'Live With Me' is much faster, with thrashing chords and Punky, attitude-filled vocals. It was released on the band's 1982 album 'Screaming Blue Murder'.

[216] **LIVE WITH ME - Sheryl Crow [with Mick Jagger]** (2022)

(Jagger-Richards)

Rolling Stones original: Let It Bleed (1969)

Sheryl Suzanne Crow (b. 1962). Rock, Pop and Country singer and guitarist from Kennett, Missouri, USA.

Just as Dave Grohl does with The Beatles/Paul McCartney, Sheryl Crow has consistently stated her love of The Rolling Stones, recording and performing their songs (sometimes with the Stones) many times. A little slower than the original, Sheryl Crow's tough, Grungy version of 'Live With Me' includes a fabulous harmonica solo from Mick Jagger. It is on her 2022 album 'Sheryl: Music From The Feature Documentary'.

[217] **LOCKED AWAY - Robert Forster** (1995)
(Richards-Jordan)

Rolling Stones original: Talk Is Cheap [Keith Richards solo album] (1988)

Robert Derwent Garth Forster (b. 1957). Pop, Country and Indie Rock singer and guitarist from Brisbane, Queensland, Australia.

A ballad from Keith Richards' acclaimed 'Talk Is Cheap' album (recorded at a time when Mick Jagger was concentrating on his own solo career in preference to the Stones), Robert Forster's cover is similar in arrangement to the original, and is on his 1995 album 'I Had A New Girlfriend'.

Whose idea was it to record this song?

"It was my idea."

Do you perform this or any other Stones songs live?

"No I don't."

Were the Rolling Stones an influence on your own music?

"Yes they were. Jagger and Richards are strong songwriters. And the Stones are a great band. I'd love to write a song like 'Ruby Tuesday'."

[218] **LONG, LONG WHILE - The Idols** (1968)
(Jagger-Richards)

Rolling Stones original: UK B-side (1966)

Vasilis Papavassiliou (vocals and bass), Notis Lalaitis (vocals and organ), Anthony Youlis (guitar), Vasilis Konstantinidis (drums and vocals) and George Pentzikis (piano, flute and vocals). Rock and Pop band from Athens, Greece. Disbanded in 1972.

The UK B-side to 1966's 'Paint It Black', this soulful ballad was covered by Greek band The Idols for a sound-alike single 2 years later.

[219] **LOVING CUP - Nanette Workman with Peter Frampton (1977)**

(Jagger-Richards)

Rolling Stones original: Exile On Main St. (1972)

Nanette Joan Workman (b. 1945). Rock singer from Brooklyn, New York, USA, with Peter Kenneth Frampton (b. 1950). Rock singer and guitarist from Beckenham, Kent, UK.

A song that dates back to 1969 (and was even performed at that year's Hyde Park concert), 'Loving Cup' was later reworked for 'Exile On Main St.'. Nanette Workman's lively Country-tinged performance includes some nice Peter Frampton guitar work, and is on 1977's 'Grits and Cornbread'.

[220] **LOVING CUP - The Bittersweets (2011)**

(Jagger-Richards)

Rolling Stones original: Exile On Main St. (1972)

Chris Meyers (guitar, keyboards and vocals) and Hannah Prater (vocals and guitar). Alt-Country and Folk duo from San Francisco, California, USA.

With its slow tempo, clearly enunciated female vocals and reverberating guitar, The Bittersweets' revival of 'Loving Cup' is a real highlight of 'Paint It Black: An Alt Country Tribute To The Rolling Stones'.

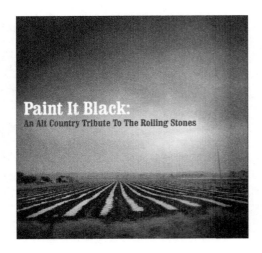

[221] **LUXURY - The Hammersmith Gorillas** (1974) *(Not released until 1999)*

(Jagger-Richards)

Rolling Stones original: It's Only Rock 'N' Roll (1974)

Jesse Hector (vocals and guitar), Alan Butler (bass) and Gary Anderson (drums). Rhythm 'n' Blues, Punk Rock and Hard Rock band from Hammersmith, London, UK. Also known as The Gorillas. Disbanded in 1981.

One of the weaker tracks from the admittedly patchy 'It's Only Rock 'N' Roll' album, The Hammersmith Gorillas' demo-like recording is a bit hesitant in nature, but is lifted enormously by Jesse Hector's raw vocals. It finally surfaced on the 1999 'Gorilla Got Me' compilation.

[222] **MAKE NO MISTAKE - Kat Kramer** (2001)

(Jagger-Jordan)

Rolling Stones original: Talk Is Cheap [Keith Richards solo album] (1988) + UK/US A-side (1988)

Katherine Kramer. Actress, producer, activist, and Pop and Country singer from USA.

A slow-ish soulful song from Keith's first solo album, Kat Kramer's cover sticks closely to the original's arrangement, though of course her country-tinged voice gives it a very different feel compared to Keith's gravelly crooning. It is from her 'Gemstone' project. *See [40] for interview!*

[223] MELODY - Bill Wyman and The Rhythm Kings (1997)
(Jagger-Richards)

Rolling Stones original: Black and Blue (1976)

William George Perks (b. 1936). Rock and Pop singer, bassist and keyboardist (with band) from London, UK, with Georgie Fame (Clive Powell, b. 1943 - vocals and keyboards), Beverley Skeete (vocals), Eric Clapton (Eric Patrick Clapton, b. 1945 - guitar), Terry Taylor (Terence Martin Taylor, b. 1948 - guitar), Graham Broad (drums), Dave Hartley (piano), Frank Mead (horns), Nick Payn (horns) and Martin Drover (horns) [The line-up above applies to 'Melody' only, *not* the whole album or the live band]. Rhythm 'n' Blues and Rock 'n' Roll band with ever-changing membership, from London, UK.

Bill Wyman was always someone who had keen interests outside the band, but when he finally quit (officially in early 1993, but effectively a couple of years before that), few expected to hear much more from him musically. Yet, he has turned out to be far more prolific than pretty much all the other Stones, particularly with his group Bill Wyman and The Rhythm Kings. A previously overlooked song from the consistently good 'Black and Blue' album, the original is effectively a duet between Mick Jagger and Billy Preston. That duet arrangement is retained here, this time with Georgie Fame and Beverley Skeete.

 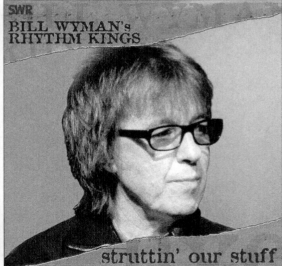

Bill Wyman struts his stuff: The 1997 release of 'Struttin' Our Stuff', and the 2004 reissue.

[224] **MEMO FROM TURNER - The Nighthawks (1974)**

(Jagger-Richards)

Rolling Stones original: Performance [Mick Jagger solo version] (1970) + Metamorphosis [Rolling Stones version] (1975) (Note: both versions were taped in 1968)

Mark Wenner (vocals and harmonica), Jimmy Thackery (b. 1953 - guitar and vocals), Jan Zukowski (bass and vocals) and Pete Ragusa (drums). Rhythm 'n' Blues band from Washington, D.C., USA.

There were actually two released versions of 'Memo From Turner'; one credited to Mick Jagger (famously heard in the notorious 'Performance' movie), and a faster, looser, Rolling Stones version that was issued on 1975's 'Metamorphosis'. Predating the release of the latter, The Nighthawks' powerful cover with excellent harmonica is clearly based on Mick's solo version, and was released on their debut album 'Rock 'n' Roll' in 1974. [Interview is with Mark Wenner]

Whose idea was it to record this song?

"I had not even seen the movie ('Performance') when I learned the song. It was a perfect vehicle for Jimmy Thackery's slide guitar. We were doing a lot of Little Feat at the time and did a whole set in an open A guitar tuning. We relied on Stones, Geils, and Allman Brothers material to sneak into the Top 40 rooms that asked for set lists. They didn't want Muddy Waters or Howlin' Wolf!"

Do you perform this (or any other Stones songs) live?

"We are not currently doing any Stones material. We did also record their version of 'Stop Breaking Down'."

Were the Rolling Stones an influence on you?

"Of course they were an influence. Their first couple of albums were very much an exploration of American Roots music beyond just Blues but included a lot of R&B. We brought in more rockabilly being east coast rednecks! We also had a relationship with Muddy that included a birthday phone call."

[225] **MEMO FROM TURNER - Dramarama (1991)**
(Jagger-Richards)

Rolling Stones original: Performance + A-side [Mick Jagger solo version] (1970) + Metamorphosis [Rolling Stones version] (1975) (Note: both versions were taped in 1968)

John Easdale (b. 1961 - vocals), Mr. E. (Mark Englert - guitar), Peter Wood (guitar), Chris Carter (Chris Paul Carter, b. 1959 - bass) and Brian MacLeod (b. 1962 - drums). Alternative Rock and Power Pop band from Wayne, New Jersey, USA.

Similar in both looseness and tempo to the 'Metamorphosis' version, though with a more 90s Grungy feel, Dramarama's fine cover is on their 1991 album 'Vinyl'. [Interview is with John Easedale]

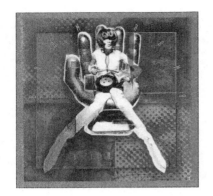

Whose idea was it to record this song?

"If memory serves, it was Chris Carter (bass) who suggested we record 'Memo From Turner'; we all worshipped the Stones, though perhaps none more than guitarist Peter Wood. Our version owed a lot more to the Stones' version on side two of 'Metamorphosis' than the one from the soundtrack of 'Performance' with Ry Cooder on guitar. 'Vinyl' is my favorite of our LPs, thanks to the exceptional contributions of producer/engineer Don Smith (Keith Richards, Traveling Wilburys, Tom Petty). And Don brought Mick Taylor in to add some of his trademark brilliance to some songs on the album - though not 'Memo from Turner'! Mick's presence in the studio was a highlight for all of us!"

Do you perform this (or any other Stones songs) live?

"We haven't played 'Memo From Turner' live for quite some time, probably not since the shows just after 'Vinyl' was released. Over the years, we have played lots of Stones songs in the rehearsal room (including but not limited to 'The Last Time', '19th Nervous Breakdown', 'Sway' and 'Can't You Hear Me Knocking'), although we did record a killer rip-off of the Stones' arrangement of another favorite from Metamorphosis, 'I Don't Know Why', with our "secret band", The Bent Backed Tulips, which we've played live. You have to be careful playing Stones songs live, though; most, if not all, require the kind of swagger that only Mick can pull off."

Were the Rolling Stones an influence on you?

"They weren't the very first rock and roll band I remember, but they were probably the third (1. Monkees, 2. Beatles, 3. Rolling Stones). I recall hearing 'Satisfaction', 'Mother's Little Helper', 'Paint It Black' and 'Jumping Jack Flash' on top 40 radio, but 'Honky Tonk Woman' led to my purchase of 'Through the Past Darkly' at the age of 8 and I have never looked back. They have always been and continue to be one of the most important influences on me, and pretty much every rock band that has come after them."

[226] **MEMORY MOTEL - Ian McNabb** (2016)

(Jagger-Richards)

Rolling Stones original: Black and Blue (1976)

Robert Ian McNabb (b. 1960). Alternative Rock and New Wave singer, guitarist and keyboardist from Liverpool, UK. Former front man of The Icicle Works.

A long-time fan favourite, the Stones' original of 'Memory Motel' is a touching Mick and Keith duet featuring lots of piano. Ian McNabb's cover is a little slower, and with more acoustic guitar and less keyboards, but it's a lovely version, and can be found on his 2016 album 'Respectfully Yours'.

Whose idea was it to record this song?

"It was my idea to record the song, for my covers album 'Respectfully Yours'."

Do you perform this (or any other Stones songs) live?

"No."

Were the Rolling Stones an influence on your own music?

"Yes. I love The Rolling Stones."

[227] **MIDNIGHT RAMBLER - Larry McCray** (1997)

(Jagger-Richards)

Rolling Stones original: Let It Bleed (1969)

Larry McCray (b. 1960). Blues singer and guitarist from Magnolia, Arkansas, USA.

A song that quickly acquired mythical status, 'Midnight Rambler' was often greatly extended and improvised on stage, and remains a concert highlight to this day. Surprisingly, there have been very few cover versions, with Larry McCray's being the most interesting. Performed as a very different funky mid-tempo Blues, it is on the various artists 'Paint It, Blue: Songs of The Rolling Stones' album.

[228] **MISS AMANDA JONES - The March Violets** (1986)

(Jagger-Richards)

Rolling Stones original: Between The Buttons (1967)

Cleo Murray (Elizabeth Jean Murray - vocals), Tom Ashton (Thomas Gordon Ashton - guitar), Loz Elliot (Laurence Hugh Elliott - bass) and Andy Tolson (drums). Post-Punk and Gothic Rock band from Leeds, UK.

A largely ignored but rather wonderful track from the criminally-underrated 'Between The Buttons', the song was unexpectedly revived for the 1987 Hollywood blockbuster 'Some Kind Of Wonderful'. And the main character's name? Amanda Jones! The key song on the movie's soundtrack is The March Violets' revival of 'Miss Amanda Jones'. With a drastic re-arrangement, U2-meets-The Cult guitar and an excellent vocal from Cleo Murray, this is one of the best Stones covers of the '80s.

[229] **MISS YOU - Ann Peebles** (1982)

(Jagger-Richards)

Rolling Stones original: Some Girls (1978) + UK/US A-side (1978)

Ann Lee Peebles (b. 1947). Soul and Rhythm 'n' Blues singer from St. Louis, Missouri, USA.

Although criticised by some for the Stones supposedly "Going Disco", 'Miss You' owes a great deal to the Blues, and has an integrity that is missing from such songs as Rod Stewart's 'Da Ya Think I'm Sexy' and Wings' 'Goodnight Tonight'. Ann Peebles' cover was recommended to me by musician Dani Wilde (someone who cut a mean version of 'Miss You' herself), and with her soulful vocals and solid, unfussy backing, it is indeed superb. Re-titled 'I Miss You', it is on Ann's 1982 album 'Full Time Love'.

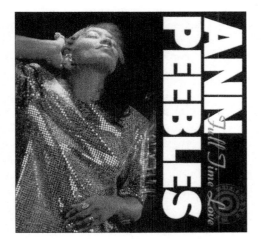

[230] **MISS YOU - Sugar Blue** (1994)

(Jagger-Richards)

Rolling Stones original: Some Girls (1978) + UK/US A-side (1978)

James Joshua Whiting (b. 1949). Blues-Rock harmonicist and singer from Harlem, New York City, USA.

The harmonica on the Stones' original of 'Miss You' was not played by Mick, but instead by Sugar Blue, someone Jagger apparently discovered busking on the streets of New York. He's a far better harmonica player than he is a singer, but Sugar Blue's own, more funky version, is on his 1994 album 'Blue Blazes'.

[231] **MISS YOU - Etta James** (2000)

(Jagger-Richards)

Rolling Stones original: Some Girls (1978) + UK/US A-side (1978)

Jamesetta Hawkins (b. 1938 - d. 2012). Rhythm 'n' Blues and Soul singer from Los Angeles, California, USA.

A legendary Soul and Blues pioneer, Etta James' relaxed version of 'Miss You' is on 2000's 'Matriarch Of The Blues'. Etta supported The Rolling Stones on some shows of their 1978 US Tour, so if she hung around afterwards to check out the headline act, then she would've been very familiar with this song.

[232] **MISS YOU - Dani Wilde** (2010)

(Jagger-Richards)

Rolling Stones original: Some Girls (1978) + UK/US A-side (1978)

(b. 1985). Electric Blues singer and guitarist from Hullavington, Wiltshire, UK.

As The Rolling Stones and a handful of contemporaries first proved over 60 years ago, you don't have to be old, black and American to have a genuine feel for the Blues. Someone who keeps up this British Blues tradition is Dani Wilde, who (also like the Stones) fuses Country, Soul and Gospel into her music. Dani's excellent version of 'Miss You' has a guitar riff reminiscent of Albert King's 'Oh, Pretty Woman', along with passionately sung vocals and inspired guitar and harmonica solos. It is on her 2nd album, 2010's 'Shine'. *See [38] for interview!*

[233] **MONKEY MAN - Crazy Baldhead** (2008)

(Jagger-Richards)

Rolling Stones original: Let It Bleed (1969)

Jayson Nugent (b. 1972 - guitar and vocals), Victor Rice (b. 1967 - bass), Eddie Ocampo (drums), Victor Ruggiero (keyboards) and Rob Jost (French horn). Ska and Reggae band from New York, USA.

A song written in Italy that may or may not be about Italian artist Mario Schifano, 'Monkey Man' was oddly over-looked by the band themselves for many years, finally being performed live for the first time in 1994. Crazy Baldhead's cover has a slight Reggae rhythm, but otherwise largely sticks to the Stones' original arrangement. It is on their 2009 album 'The Sound of '69'.

[234] **MONKEY MAN - Gov't Mule** (2014)

(Jagger-Richards)

Rolling Stones original: Let It Bleed (1969)

Warren Haynes (b. 1960 - guitar and vocals), Jorgen Carlsson (bass guitar), Matt Abts (b. 1953 - drums and vocals) and Danny Louis (Daniel Louis Schliftman - keyboards, guitar, trumpet and vocals). Southern Rock band from Atlanta, Georgia, USA. Initially a side project of the Allman Brothers Band.

A live recording with a Southern Rock feel, this fine cover was released on 'Stoned Side of the Mule Vol. 1', a limited edition vinyl LP featuring 6 live Stones covers.

[235] **MONKEY MAN - The Lords Of Altamont** (2014)

(Jagger-Richards)

Rolling Stones original: Let It Bleed (1969)

Garage Rock and Psychedelic Rock band from Los Angeles, California, USA, led by Jake 'The Preacher' Cavaliere (Jacob William Cavaliere, b. 1950 - vocals and organ).

Crazy Baldhead's 'The Sound of '69' album consists entirely of songs first released by a wide variety of artists in 1969; The Lords of Altamont went one better, and recorded an album of songs only by acts that were at the ill-fated Altamont Free Concert in 1969. 'Monkey Man' wasn't actually performed by the Stones at that concert, but it doesn't matter: it's a brilliant, inspired and energetic performance, and can be heard on their 2014 album 'Lords Take Altamont'. [Interview is with Jake Cavaliere]

Whose idea was it to record this song?

"We really dig this era of Rolling Stones, 'Monkey Man' suited us. The band decided to record this song. We shelved it till a few years ago, and made it a bonus track on 'Lords Take Altamont', our tribute to the bands that performed at Altamont Speedway on Dec. 6th 1969. We could never truly give it justice being it was a recorded masterpiece."

Do you perform this or any other Stones songs live?

"We've recorded 'Gimme Shelter', 'Sympathy For The Devil', and Robert Johnson's 'Love In Vain'. All for the tribute to Altamont album."

Were the Rolling Stones an influence on your own music?

"We named our band after the infamous day at Altamont Speedway. I think The Rolling Stones have influenced most musicians at some point in their careers."

[236] MOONLIGHT MILE - The 5th Dimension (1975)

(Jagger-Richards)

Rolling Stones original: Sticky Fingers (1971)

Marilyn McCoo (b. 1943), Florence LaRue (b. 1944), Billy Davis Jr. (b. 1938), LaMonte McLemore (b. 1939) and Ronald L. Townson (b. 1933 - d. 2001). Pop and Soul vocal group from Los Angeles, California, USA.

A ballad from 'Sticky Fingers' that was somewhat under-appreciated for many years, it has only recently received quite a few cover versions, as well as the occasional live outing from the band themselves. One '70s act that did cover it was The 5th Dimension, in a version perhaps best described as M.O.R. Soul, and it can be found on their 1975 album 'Earthbound'.

[237] MOONLIGHT MILE - Alvin Youngblood Hart (1997)

(Jagger-Richards)

Rolling Stones original: Sticky Fingers (1971)

Gregory Edward Hart (b. 1963). Blues singer and guitarist from Oakland, California, USA.

Featuring just his vocals and acoustic guitar plus a distant electric slide, Alvin Youngblood Hart's excellent Blues is on the various artists 'Paint It, Blue: Songs of The Rolling Stones' album.

[238] **MOONLIGHT MILE - Turin Brakes** (2004)

(Jagger-Richards)

Rolling Stones original: Sticky Fingers (1971)

Gale Paridjanian (Stephan Gale Paridjanian - vocals and guitar), Olly Knights (Oliver Howard Knights - vocals and guitar), Eddie Myer (bass) and Rob Allum (drums). Folk Rock and Indie Rock band from Balham, London, UK.

Turin Brakes' gorgeous cover features two weaving acoustics (one of them slide) and some lovely harmonies, and is on their 2004 album 'Late Night Tales'. [Interview is with Gale Paridjanian]

Whose idea was it to record this song?

"Me and Olly decided to record this when we were asked for a cover version for the Another Late Nights series. 'Sticky Fingers' was a mainstay of my music and Rolling Stones education. For me it had so many formative songs on - not just the big ones like 'Brown Sugar' or 'Wild Horses', but amazing nuggets like 'Sway'.

But 'Moonlight Mile' is by far the best ending song ever. It starts off at the sunset and rides through a long languid night. Which is what you could do with that album if you were 15 and getting into playing guitars and drinking after school! I thought we could do a decent lo-fi version of the strings and there were lots of themes that we shared with the song - 'I got silence in my radio, let the airwaves flow ...' Its influence was so complete it even appears in Turin Brakes hit 'Fishing For A Dream: 'let's put on Moonlight Mile and feel those radio waves flow'."

Do you perform this (or any other Stones songs) live?

"No we do not. I think we have tried in the past when our version was first available but our sets are already overpopulated with Turin Brakes favourites."

Were the Rolling Stones an influence on your own music?

"Very much so. At the time anyone learning guitar as far as I could tell would be listening to music from this era - Pink Floyd, Hendrix, Muddy Waters etc. They were an extension of the blues and they were taking something from a tradition and making it their own as others had before. That was very appealing to us, we have very little interest in repeating a tradition note for note. Far more interesting to start with a form and put yourself and your feels through that form to get something new. The Stones had internalised the blues so much that it wasn't a homage but more an expression through the means of, and in turn we had internalised the Stones and were putting our colour on it. 'Sticky Fingers' and 'Let It Bleed' were the big ones for me."

[239] **MOONLIGHT MILE - Lee Fields and The Expressions** (2011)
(Jagger-Richards)

Rolling Stones original: Sticky Fingers (1971)

Elmer Lee Fields (b. 1950). Soul, Funk and Rhythm 'n' Blues singer from Wilson, North Carolina, USA.

With its soaring, soulful vocals, prominent organ and relaxed horns, Lee Fields and The Expressions' stunning cover could be mistaken for a lost Al Green classic. It is on the various artists 'Sticky Soul Fingers: A Rolling Stones Tribute' CD.

Whose idea was it to record this song?

"A famous magazine was doing a story on The Stones and asked us to do a cover, and we obliged."

Do you perform this or any other Stones song live?

"Yes we do, occasionally."

Were the Rolling Stones an influence on your own music?

"Yes of course."

[240] **MOONLIGHT MILE - Cowboy Junkies** (2011)
(Jagger-Richards)

Rolling Stones original: Sticky Fingers (1971)

Margo Timmins (b. 1961 - vocals), Michael Timmins (guitar), Alan Anton (bass) and Peter Timmins (drums). Americana, Alt-Country and Folk Rock band from Toronto, Ontario, Canada.

Featuring Margo Timmins' relaxed vocals and an unusual wah-wah electric slide, Cowboy Junkies fine cover is on 'Paint It Black: An Alt Country Tribute To The Rolling Stones'.

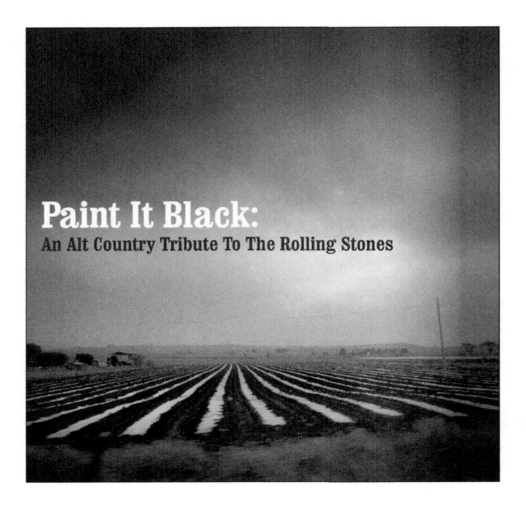

[241] **MOONLIGHT MILE - Kimmie Rhodes** (2013)
(Jagger-Richards)

Rolling Stones original: Sticky Fingers (1971)

Kimmie Ray Willingham (b. 1954). Americana, Country, Pop and Folk singer and guitarist from Wichita Falls, Texas, USA.

With her beautiful Country-tinged vocals, Kimmie Rhodes' excellent cover gradually builds to a near-crescendo before coming down again. It is on her 2013 album 'Covers'.

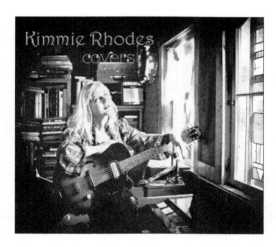

Whose idea was it to record this song?

"I was having dinner (on the Delbert McClinton Sandy Beaches Cruise) with my friends Colin Linden and Janice Powers and mentioned that I was going to indulge myself in recording a covers album. Because choosing ten songs to cover from a sea of great music is a very daunting task, I decided to perhaps take requests. Janice suggested Moonlight Mile and it was just off the wall enough to keep my attention. Keyboard player, Michael Thompson (The Eagle) was in Austin for the sessions and staying at my house and we stayed up until the wee hours playing with different tunings and ways to cut the song and recorded it the next day."

Do you perform this (or any other Stones songs) live?

"I performed the songs a lot when I toured with the album and still do from time to time, yes."

Were the Rolling Stones an influence on your own music?

"The Stones were a HUGE influence on my music. Like many others, the Beatles gave me the harmonic melodic quirky sense, and the Stones made sure my writing and productions keep 'the cool'... the edge."

[242] MOONLIGHT MILE - Lucinda Williams (2020)
(Jagger-Richards)

Rolling Stones original: Sticky Fingers (1971)

Lucinda Gayle Williams (b. 1953). Americana, Folk and Country singer and guitarist from Lake Charles, Louisiana, USA.

Lucinda Williams 2020 'It's Only Rock and Roll - A Tribute to The Rolling Stones' album features no less than 15 Jagger-Richards songs, as well as Fred McDowell's 'You Gotta Move'. The best of these is probably 'Moonlight Mile', which is highly suited to her world-weary vocals.

[243] **MOTHER'S LITTLE HELPER - Gene Latter** (1966)
(Jagger-Richards)

Rolling Stones original: Aftermath [UK version] (1966) + US A-side (1966) + Flowers (1967)

Arthur Ford (d. 2004). Rhythm 'n' Blues and Psych-Pop singer and guitarist from Caerdydd, Wales.

At a time when everyone wa sneaking in little pro-drug references, The Rolling Stones bucked the trend with this tale warning about the dangers of addiction. Gene Latter's hasty single release, though impressive enough, failed to chart.

[244] **MOTHER'S LITTLE HELPER - Liz Phair** (2005)
(Jagger-Richards)

Rolling Stones original: Aftermath [UK version] (1966) + US A-side (1966) + Flowers (1967)

Elizabeth Clark Phair (b. 1967). Indie Rock and Rock Pop singer, guitarist and pianist from New Haven, Connecticut, USA.

Liz Phair's contemporary and modern update appeared on the various artists album 'Music From and Inspired by Desperate Housewives'.

[245] **MOTHER'S LITTLE HELPER - Linda Draper** (2009)

(Jagger-Richards)

Rolling Stones original: Aftermath [UK version] (1966) + US A-side (1966) + Flowers (1967)

Folk, World and Country singer and guitarist from New York City, USA.

An acclaimed Americana musician, Linda Draper's remarkable cover of 'Mother's Little Helper' features just her vocals and a little light percussion. It is on her 2009 album 'Bridge and Tunnel'.

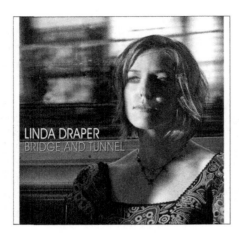

Whose idea was it to record this song?

"It was my idea. I like to include a different cover song for each album I record, and this song kept on getting stuck in my head (I've always loved singing out that oddly catchy guitar riff that Keith Richards did... only he could make a 12-string slide guitar sound like a sitar). After experimenting with some different instrumentation in the studio, with nothing really quite gelling, Brad Albetta (who produced the album) had the brilliant idea of stripping away all the other elements and it morphed into this kind of strange, but pretty cool A cappella version (with a couple tracks of egg shakers and occasional tambourine 'jangle', courtesy of my bass player Robert Woodcock and me, just to add a in subtle hint of percussion)."

Do you perform this or any other Stones songs live?

"I played this song live, years ago, around the time that album came out. I haven't performed any other Stones songs live... yet!"

Were the Rolling Stones an influence on your own music?

"Yes! Even though my genre of music may not fall in the same genre as theirs, it's their lyrics, their delivery, and their genuine love and passion for the music that is contagious. As a songwriter, when I sit down with an aim to write something, a band like the Stones will always make me want to aim a little higher."

[246] **MY OBSESSION - Hooyoosay** (2012)

(Jagger-Richards)

Rolling Stones original: Between The Buttons (1967)

International music recording project, featuring a variety of loose and unnamed contributors.

'Between The Buttons' features several excellent but largely ignored songs, and Hooyousay have covered six of 'em: 'Connection', 'All Sold Out', 'Please Go Home', 'Who's Been Sleeping Here' (featured elsewhere in this book), 'Complicated' and this one, 'My Obsession'. The Stones' original of 'My Obsession' had a palpable air of menace - so much so, that a visibly agitated Brian Wilson had to be escorted from the studio. Hooyoosay's version lacks that menace, but it's still a good, modern sounding cover. As with their other songs, it is available via download and streaming sites. [Interview is with 'Rudy']

Whose idea was it to record this song?

"Hooyoosay is not really a band, but rather a project of recording and releasing music. The project came into existence by mere coincidence, some session players having to wait in a recording studio for the artist who had hired them, and starting to play some cover songs to while away time. These cover songs happened to be sixties Rolling Stones songs, as they all seemed to know these songs without needing much rehearsal. When later on, they finally decided to elaborate and release those spontaneous recordings, it seemed that some of the players had their reasons for remaining uncredited, so then the concept of anonymous participants and the name 'hooyoosay' arose. Next the project was carried on and extended with many more collaborators, even from all over the globe, contributing over the internet, but all of them accepting and severely respecting the core original principle of anonymity."

Do you perform this or any other Stones song live?

"All this implies that there can never be any live performances."

Were the Rolling Stones an influence on your own music?

"As for the influence of The Rolling Stones on hooyoosay's self-penned material, it depends on who were the contributors. Songs by the founding members of hooyoosay indeed may show Rolling Stones influences, whereas this might be totally absent in material by collaborators who only joined in later. So far, hooyoosay have released 72 titles, these being 38 originals and 34 titles also recorded by The Rolling Stones during the sixties.

[247] 19TH NERVOUS BREAKDOWN - The Standells (1966)

(Jagger-Richards)

Rolling Stones original: UK/US A-side

Larry Tamblyn (vocals, guitar and keyboards), Tony Valentino (Emilio Tony Belilissimo - guitar), Gary Lane (Gary McMillan, b. 1938 - d. 2014 - bass) and Dick Dodd (d. 2013 - vocals and drums). Pop and Garage band from Los Angeles, California, USA.

Retaining the attitude of the original, The Standells' cover includes a guitar riff straight out of The Sir Douglas Quintet's 'She's About A Mover'. It is on their 1966 album 'Dirty Water'. [Interview is with Larry Tamblyn]

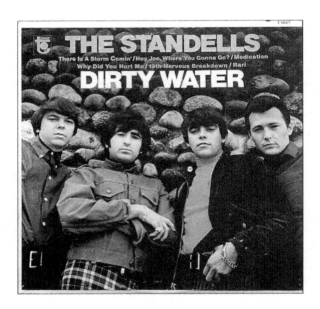

Whose idea was it to record this song?

"During that time period, we played in nightclubs, mostly doing covers. '19th Nervous Breakdown' was a normal part of our set. The decision to record it was made by our producer Ed Cobb."

Do you perform this (or any other Stones songs) live?

"No. I perform all Standells songs these days."

Were the Rolling Stones an influence on your own music?

"Of course, as well as the Beatles, Yardbirds, and many other U.K. groups."

[248] 19TH NERVOUS BREAKDOWN - Jason and The Scorchers (1986)

(Jagger-Richards)

Rolling Stones original: UK/US A-side

Jason Ringenberg (b. 1958 - vocals and harmonica), Warner Hodges (guitar and vocals), Jeff Johnson (bass) and Perry Baggs (Perry Armand Baggs III, b. 1962 - d. 2012 - drums and vocals). Cowpunk, Alt-Country and Americana band from Nashville, Tennessee, USA.

Although slower, Jason and The Scorchers' cover has a more contemporary Punk/New Wave feel, and can be found on their 1986 album 'Still Standing'.

[249] 19TH NERVOUS BREAKDOWN - Teresa James (2008)

(Jagger-Richards)

Rolling Stones original: UK/US A-side

Blues, Folk, World and Country singer and keyboardist from Houston, Texas, USA.

Sounding like Dolly Parton meets The Buckaroos, Teresa James hot up-tempo Country version of '19th Nervous Breakdown' is on her 2008 album 'Sing Some Country By Request'.

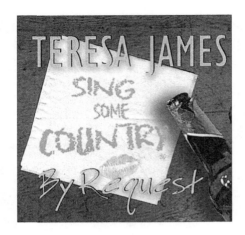

Whose idea was it to record this song?

"It was definitely my idea to record this song. I always felt like it would be really fun to hear this song done in a Bakersfield country style with a kind of yodel on the bridge. So when we decided to make an actual country record, this was the first song that I thought of for it. I live in Los Angeles where we recorded half of the record, but we went to Nashville and recorded with some friends for a bunch of the songs. And I was lucky enough to get our friend big Al Anderson, formerly of NRBQ, to record with us. He did his best to talk me out of doing this song (not sure why - probably because he is such a great writer of country songs), but I insisted. And I'm so glad I did. And, of course, his guitar playing on it is perfect."

Have you performed this (or any other Stones songs) live?

"We have not been playing this live with my original band that I have been working with for years and do the bluesier stuff with (the band that got nominated for a Grammy in 2019), but I am planning on performing it with another band in the LA area that I also play with and we will be working it up, for sure. I think it will be really fun to do live, it just doesn't quite go with the original material of my other band."

Were the Rolling Stones an influence on your own music?

"I have always loved the Stones. I remember as a kid playing outside and singing, 'HEY YOU, get off of my cloud' at the top of my lungs, and I wore out my brother's copy of 'Out Of Our Heads'. It wasn't until later that I realized that so many of those songs were covers of such great old R&B songs. The Stones were my first exposure to that style of music."

[250] 19TH NERVOUS BREAKDOWN - Chris Norman (2011)

(Jagger-Richards)

Rolling Stones original: UK/US A-side

Christopher Ward Norman (b. 1950). Rock and Pop singer and guitarist from Redcar, Yorkshire, UK. Best known as the former lead vocalist for Smokie.

Sounding considerably less gravelly than on Smokie's hits, Chris Norman's fine '19th Nervous Breakdown' update is on his 2011 album 'Time Traveller'.

Whose idea was it to record this song?

"It was my idea, when I chose the songs for that 'Time Traveller' album I wanted to include a Stones song. We used to do '19th Nervous Breakdown' when we first started as a group and it was always a favourite."

Do you perform this (or any other Stones songs) live?

"No not these days. In the early days when we were starting out we played some, like 'Jumping jack Flash', 'Honky Tonk Woman', 'Satisfaction'."

Were the Rolling Stones an influence on your own music?

"Yes to an extent. I think a lot of 60s groups were."

[251] 19TH NERVOUS BREAKDOWN - Sarah Menescal (2019)

(Jagger-Richards)

Rolling Stones original: UK/US A-side

Jazz and Bossa Nova singer from Argentina.

With its radical, relaxed, Electro-Bossa makeover, Sarah Menescal's cover is on her 2019 album 'My World'.

Whose idea was it to record this song?

"Mine, love this song since ever and also the company had no version of it until the moment I recorded it. I personally select all songs from albums."

Do you perform this or any other Stones songs live?

"I will include it in my next live session. Don't have confirmed date yet. Probably in Buenos Aires."

Were the Rolling Stones an influence on your own music?

"Yes, a lot. I listen to them since I was 15 years old. I had the opportunity of see them live in Los Angeles last year, front row (see above pic)"

[252] **NO EXPECTATIONS - Joan Baez** (1970)

(Jagger-Richards)

Rolling Stones original: Beggars Banquet (1968) + US B-side (1968)

Joan Chandos Baez (b. 1941). Folk singer and guitarist from Staten Island, New York, USA.

Brian Jones' contribution to the band peaked around the time of 'Aftermath'/'Between The Buttons', and the same era's singles, when his creativity and use of exotic instrumentation knew no bounds. By 'Beggar's Banquet' however, he was increasingly sidelined, with his final contribution of any significance being the poignant slide guitar on 'No Expectations'. Joan Baez's pure-voiced cover is on her 1970 'One Day At A Time' album.

[253] **NO EXPECTATIONS - Odetta** (1970)

(Jagger-Richards)

Rolling Stones original: Beggars Banquet (1968) + US B-side (1968)

Odetta Holmes (b. 1930 - d. 2008). Folk, Blues and Gospel singer from Birmingham, Alabama, USA.

Sung at a funeral-like pace, with a near-mumbled voice full of despair, Odetta really does sound like she has no expectations to pass this way again. It is on her 1970 album 'Odetta Sings'.

[254] **NO EXPECTATIONS - Johnny Cash** (1978)
(Jagger-Richards)

Rolling Stones original: Beggars Banquet (1968) + US B-side (1968)

John R. Cash (b. 1932 - d. 2003). Country, Rockabilly and Folk singer and guitarist from Kingsland, Arkansas, USA.

With his trademark 'chugga-chugga' rhythm and a harmonica solo, Johnny Cash makes the song his own. It is on his 1978 album 'Gone Girl'.

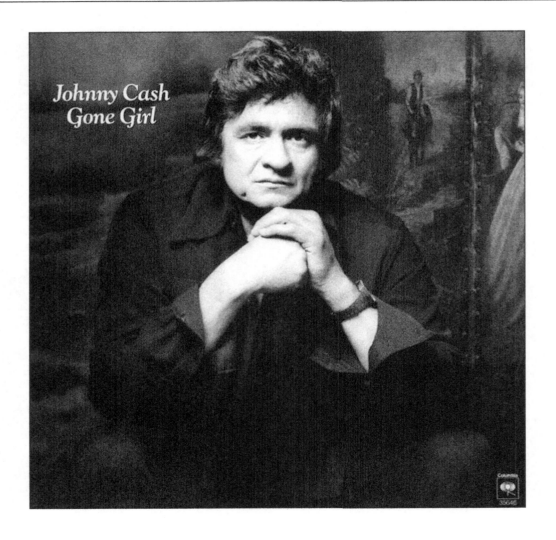

[255] **NO EXPECTATIONS - No Expectations - Anita Livs** (1995)

(Jagger-Richards)

Rolling Stones original: Beggars Banquet (1968) + US B-side (1968)

Anita Livstrand (Ingrid Anita Livstrand, b. 1953 - vocals, saz, tamboura, viola and percussion), Lise-Lotte Norelius (b. 1961 - drums, percussion and sampler) and Monica Åslund (percussion, kalimba and vocals). Nordic Folk, World and Country trio from Stockholm, Sweden.

Anita Livs' remarkable version of 'No Expectations' combines Folky vocals with percussive African-influenced backing. It is on their 1995 album 'Wild World Web'. [Interview is with Anita Livstrand]

Whose idea was it to record this song?

"It was my idea to play and record this song."

Do you perform this or any other Stones songs live?

"I played it with guitar in the early 70s as a street singer. My band Anitas Livs have not been playing on stages since 2006 I believe."

[256] **NO EXPECTATIONS - Nanci Griffith** (1997)

(Jagger-Richards)

Rolling Stones original: Beggars Banquet (1968) + US B-side (1968)

Nanci Caroline Griffith (b. 1953 - d. 2021). Country, Folk and Americana singer and guitarist from Seguin, Texas, USA.

Complete with a Country-Folk-Bluegrass arrangement and a dramatic organ solo, the late great Nanci Griffith's cover of 'No Expectations' is particularly good. It is on the various artists 'Stone Country' collection.

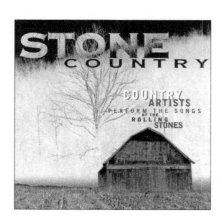

[257] **NO EXPECTATIONS - Chris Spedding** (2002)

(Jagger-Richards)

Rolling Stones original: Beggars Banquet (1968) + US B-side (1968)

Peter Robinson (b. 1944). Rock and Pop singer and guitarist from Staveley, Derbyshire, UK.

A much-respected session guitarist, Chris Spedding's cover of 'No Expectations' features some notably great electric slide, and is on his 2002 album 'One Step Ahead of the Blues'.

Whose idea was it to record this song?

"The song was on an album of mine called 'One Step Ahead Of The Blues', produced by Philippe Rault. There was a bluesy theme to the album. I think we chose 'No Expectations' as a good example of a Jagger-Richards song that wasn't too well known or covered."

Do you perform this (or any other Stones songs) live?

"I never performed 'No Expectations' or any other Stones song live."

Were the Rolling Stones an influence on your own music?

"Not really. It would be more true to say that the Stones and I shared many similar influences."

Have you ever worked with any Stones members?

"I worked with both Mick and Keith on a session for John Phillips of the Mamas and Papas around 1978. I think Ronnie Wood may also have been on the session."

[258] **NO EXPECTATIONS - George Thorogood** (2017)

(Jagger-Richards)

Rolling Stones original: Beggars Banquet (1968) + US B-side (1968)

George Lawrence Thorogood (b. 1950). Blues-Rock and Rock 'n' Roll singer, guitarist and harmonicist from Wilmington, Delaware, USA.

A true solo record, the Destroyers-less George Thorogood's cover features just him and his acoustic slide guitar. It is on the 2017 album 'Party Of One'.

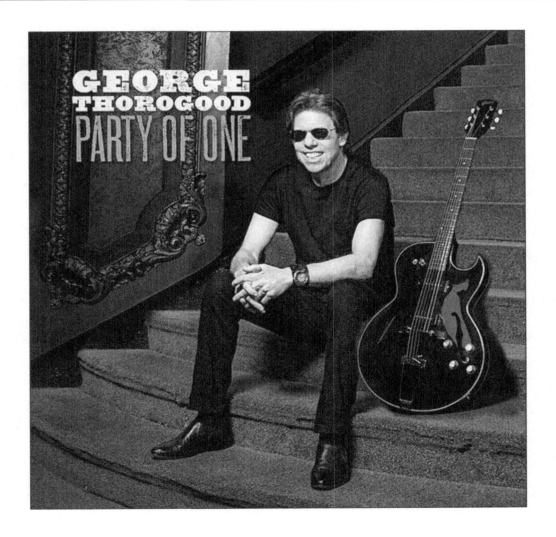

[259] **NO EXPECTATIONS - Tiffany Pollack and Eric Johanson (2019)**
(Jagger-Richards)

Rolling Stones original: Beggars Banquet (1968) + US B-side (1968)

Jazz and Blues singer from New Orleans, Louisiana, USA, with Blues and Rock guitarist and singer from New Orleans, Louisiana, USA.

A stunning duet featuring tasteful and nicely restrained electric slide guitar, Tiffany Pollack and Eric Johanson's cover of 'No Expectations' is on their 2019 album 'Blues In My Blood'. [Interview is with Tiffany Pollack]

How did the collaboration with Eric Johanson some about?

"I ended up making an album with my first cousin Eric Johanson because my record label heard some live recording from a show we put on for our family. They loved us and wanted us to do a duet album together."

Do you ever perform this (or any other Stones songs) live?

"I don't regularly perform this one cause I like it as a duet, and Eric and I don't regularly play together and I sing the songs by myself in my own band. I'd like to revisit it though. My sax player is a good singer. I've been meaning to get him to do a duet with me. I don't currently cover any more Stones songs, but I'd love to cover 'Paint it Black' or 'Gimme Shelter'. I've sung 'Gimme Shelter' with a different band I'm in and it was a hella fun to sing."

Were the Rolling Stones an influence on your own music?

"I can't say that the Rolling Stones influenced my music specifically. I love the Rolling Stones, but I think I like them because they're just doing what I do. Writing songs inspired by old American blues and country singers from the late teen, twenties and thirties."

[260] **NO EXPECTATIONS - Icarus Peel's Acid Reign** (2022)

(Jagger-Richards)

Rolling Stones original: Beggars Banquet (1968) + US B-side (1968)

Icarus Peel (vocals and guitar), Andy Budge (bass) and Jay Robertson (drums). Psychedelic Rock band from Devon, UK.

With a bass intro, appealing vocals and imaginative guitar, Icarus Peel's Acid Reign's version of 'No Expectations' is one of the most original. It is on their 2022 album 'No Choir, No Cowbell'. [Interview is with Icarus Peel]

Whose idea was it to record this song?

"We were in Howard's Barn, our jamming space, when Andy Budge proceeded with a bass line which Jay joined in on drums with. It nagged at me that the root chords were familiar and once the penny had dropped I gave it the first line. As a Stones nut Mr. Budge recognized it straight away and was astonished, he had no idea he had re-written the song. We added the intro bit later, it is, of course, a nod to '2000 Light Years From Home'."

Do you perform this or any other Stones songs live?

"We play 'No Expectations' at every gig we do, it always goes down very well. No-one has accused us of blasphemy yet and most people are just very pleased to hear it in whatever form."

Were the Rolling Stones an influence on your own music?

"The Rolling Stones were a huge influence on me in every way, My Obsession if you will. I learnt song structure from constantly listening to the classic stuff. I learnt that sometimes the sound and intonation of a word can be more important than the meaning from Jagger. I learnt that 2 acoustic guitars can be way heavier than the biggest fuzz pedal from Keef. I learnt about relentless basic rhythms from Bill and Charlie and Brian taught me that bottleneck can be beautiful and colour can be obtained from diverse surprising instrumentation. And Mick Taylor taught me that virtuosity has its place even in the Rock and Rollingest situations.

They also influenced what I wear on stage. The first thing I think is would Keef wear it in the 70's (good), would Mick wear it in the 80's (bad), would Brian wear it in the 60's (I should be so lucky!). We tend to forget just how influential Mick was back then. Serious interviews in the high brow press as well as the music weeklies, and on television, about his position on current affairs etc were poured over. And of course, we were all trying to look elegantly wasted... and you didn't get there by drinking brown and mild!"

[261] **NOW I'VE GOT A WITNESS - Lyres** (1993)

(Nanker-Phelge)

Rolling Stones original: The Rolling Stones (1964) + England's Newest Hit Makers (1964)

Jeff Conolly (Jeffrey Lynn Conolly - vocals, keyboards, harmonica and tambourine), Richard Carmel Jr. (guitar), Rick Coraccio (bass) and Paul Murphy (drums). Garage Rock band from Boston, Massachusetts, USA.

The most disposable track on The Rolling Stones' first album was probably 'Now I've Got A Witness', which is basically an instrumental jam of Marvin Gaye's 'Can I Get A Witness' - a song also on the album of course. So it is surprising to hear a cover version of the song. The Lyres' cover is a bit faster and the guitars are a little more prominent, but otherwise it stays loyal to the original. It is on their 1992 album 'Happy Now', as well as on a Norton single b/w 'Stoned'.

[262] **OFF THE HOOK - The Pete Best Combo** (1965) *(Not released until 1981)*

(Jagger-Richards)

Rolling Stones original: UK B-side (1964) + The Rolling Stones No. 2 (1965) + The Rolling Stones, Now! (1965)

Pete Best (Randolph Peter Best, b. 1941 - drums and occasional vocals), Tony Waddington (Anthony Brendon Joseph Waddington, b. 1943 - vocals and guitar), Tommy McGurk (guitar), Wayne Bickerton (Arthur Ronald Bickerton, b. 1941 - d. 2015 - vocals and bass) and Bill Burton (saxophone). Beat Group from Liverpool.

The Beatles' original drummer, Pete Best never covered a Lennon-McCartney song in the 60s - but he did record a Jagger-Richards song! The vocals are more Ringo than Jagger and there's a rather incongruous honking sax, but otherwise this sticks fairly closely to the Stones' original arrangement. It first appeared on 1981's 'Rebirth / Resurrection' compilation LP.

[263] **OFF THE HOOK - Tommy Vance** (1966)

(Jagger-Richards)

Rolling Stones original: UK B-side (1964) + The Rolling Stones No. 2 (1965) + The Rolling Stones, Now! (1965)

Richard Anthony Crispian Francis Prew Hope-Weston (b. 1940 - d. 2005). DJ and Pop and Rhythm 'n' Blues singer from Eynsham, Oxfordshire, UK.

As well as a lengthy career as a much-respected DJ, Tommy Vance issued a few Rhythm 'n' Blues-inflected Pop singles. Though OK vocally, 'Off The Hook' features some excitable horns that couldn't sound more out of place.

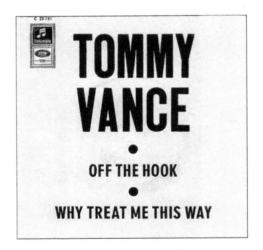

[264] **OFF THE HOOK - The Cash Box Kings** (2011)
(Jagger-Richards)

Rolling Stones original: UK B-side (1964) + The Rolling Stones No. 2 (1965) + The Rolling Stones, Now! (1965)

Joe Nosek (vocals and harmonica), Oscar Wilson (vocals), Joel Patterson (guitar and vocals), Billy Flynn (b. 1956 - guitar and mandolin), Jimmy Sutton (bass and vocals), Kenny 'Beedy Eyes' Smith (drums) and Barrelhouse Chuck (Harvey Charles Goering, b. 1958 - d. 2016 - piano). Blues band from Chicago, Illinois, USA.

With that wonderfully loose, swinging, slightly distorted sound heard so frequently on Chess records, The Cash Box Kings' version of 'Off The Hook' sounds just like a genuine late 50s/early 60s original rather than a cover. [Interview is with Joe Nosek]

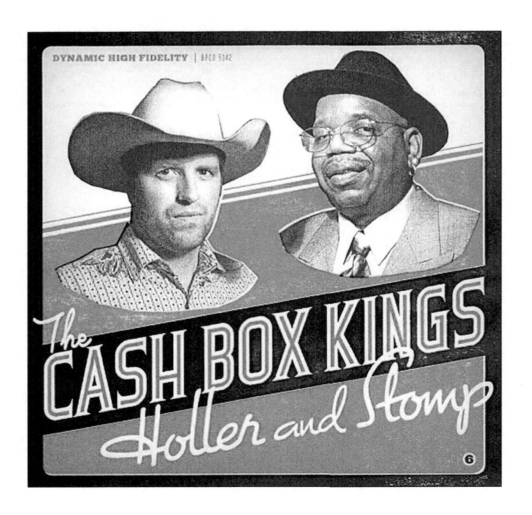

Whose idea was it to record this song?

"It was my idea to record the song. I remember hearing it on my dad's Stones records as a kid and liking it. My main impetus for recording it was because I wanted to pull a switcheroo on the Stones. So much of their early work is either covers or variations of African American blues and R&B music. I really wanted a Chicago Blues band with a traditional Blues Man singing the song. Our lead singer Oscar Wilson grew up on the south side of Chicago. People like Honey Boy Edwards, Elmore James, Junior Wells and Big Smokey Smothers were regular house guests for Friday night fish fries at his family's home. Oscar was familiar with the Stones but did not know their sound catalog very well especially more obscure sounds like 'Off The Hook'. He really dug the tune and jumped right into recording it with us.

An interesting side note about the recording: One of our guitarists Billy Flynn and our piano / organ player Barrelhouse Chuck, who passed away a few years ago, have performed with Keith Richards at a number of times at tribute shows for American Blues icons like Hubert Sumlin. I know Keith was a big fan of Chuck's playing and his encyclopedic knowledge of blues music."

Do you perform this (or any other Stones songs) live?

"We don't usually perform any Stones songs live other than 'Off The Hook.' Occasionally I sing 'Midnight Rambler'."

Were the Rolling Stones an influence on your own music?

"Oscar Wilson and I are the principal songwriters for the band. The Stones were not an influence on Oscar at all. However, the musicians who influenced Oscar were major influences on the Rolling Stones. Oscar's father was a blues man and Oscar grew up on the same street as Muddy Waters. As I mentioned before he was family friends with people like Elmore James, Junior Wells, and Big Smokey Smothers.

I was a middle class white kid who started listening to my dad's Stone's records when I was about six or seven years old. I loved the stones. At a young age I started to look at the songwriting credits and realized that not all the songs were written by Jagger and Richards. I went down to my local library to try and find out who Chester Burnett and McKinley Morganfield were. I soon found out that they were the Howlin' Wolf and Muddy Waters. I started digging deeper into the blues music that the Stones were influenced by. As much as I loved the Stones, as soon as I heard Muddy Waters, Little Walter, and the Howlin' Wolf, I stopped wanting to play in a rock band and decided to start my own blues band."

[265] **ON WITH THE SHOW - The Prisoner Of Mars** (2011)
(Jagger-Richards)

Rolling Stones original: Their Satanic Majesties Request (1967)

Bryan Shore. Psychedelic Rock, Acid Rock and Indie Rock singer and multi-instrumentalist from Cambridge, Cambridgeshire, UK.

A strong candidate for the most unlikely Rolling Stones song ever to inspire covers, this is part of Bryan Shore's 'The Prisoner of Mars Performs Their Satanic Majesties Request' album. *See [123] for interview, including more details on this song!*

[266] **ONE HIT (TO THE BODY) - The Stone Coyotes** (2017)

(Jagger-Richards)

Rolling Stones original: Dirty Work (1986) + UK/US A-side (1986)

Barbara Keith (Barbara Allen Keith - vocals and guitar), John Tibbles (bass) and Doug Tibbles (drums). Garage Rock and Country Rock band from Massachusetts, USA.

Generally regarded by both critics and fans as The Rolling Stones' worst album, cover versions of songs from 1986's 'Dirty Work' are very thin on the ground. So, The Stone Coyotes' 2017 cover of 'One Hit (To The Body)' is a nice surprise. The guitar riff is simplified a little compared to the original, but Barbara Keith's superb vocal (sounding like a female Michael Stipe) more than makes up for it. It is on their 2017 album 'Sally In The Doorway'.

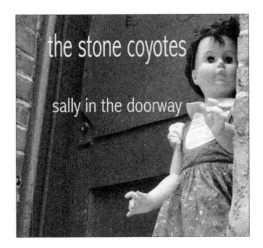

[267] **100 YEARS AGO - Head Of Femur** (2007)

(Jagger-Richards)

Rolling Stones original: Goats Head Soup (1973)

Matt Focht (vocals, guitar and drums), Michael Elsener (guitar and vocals), Ben Armstrong (keyboards, drums and vocals), Darryl Rivers (bass and vocals) and James Cuato Ballarin (keyboards and saxophone). Indie Rock band from Chicago, Illinois, USA.

A piano-led song from 'Goats Head Soup' known for its particularly good Mick Taylor guitar, Head Of Femur's nicely understated cover sticks largely to the same arrangement. It is on their 2007 'Leader and The Falcon' EP.

[268] **ONE MORE TRY - The Silks** (2013)

(Jagger-Richards)

Rolling Stones original: Out Of Our Heads [US version] (1965)

Tyler James Kelly (vocals and guitar), Jonas Parmelee (bass and vocals) and Matt Donnelly (drums and vocals). Roots Rock band from Providence, Rhode Island, USA.

An up-tempo Rhythm 'n' Blues song that wasn't released in the UK until the '70s, The Silks' cover is slower but otherwise similar, with an exciting live-in-the-studio feel. It was issued on the B-side of their 'Down At The Heel' single.

[269] **OUT OF CONTROL - Carlos Johnson** (2018)

(Jagger-Richards)

Rolling Stones original: Bridges To Babylon (1997) + UK A-side (1998)

(b. 1953). Blues singer and guitarist from Chicago, Illinois, USA.

A popular live favourite from 'Bridges To Babylon', Carlos Johnson's very different cover is reinvented as a frantically fast Rhythm 'n' Blues song with prominent harmonica. It is yet another great track from the 'Chicago Plays The Stones' CD.

[270] **OUT OF TIME - Chris Farlowe** (1966)
(Jagger-Richards)

Rolling Stones original: Aftermath [UK version] (1966) + Flowers [1967]; 1966 Demo: Metamorphosis (1975)

Chris Farlowe (John Henry Dighton, b. 1940). Rhythm 'n' Blues, Soul and Pop singer from Islington, London.

The Rolling Stones released two, very different, versions of 'Out Of Time'. The first one, featuring prominent marimbas from Brian Jones, was issued on the UK version of 'Aftermath' and (in edited form) on the following year's 'Flowers'; while a 2nd version, with heavy orchestration, was used as the basis for Chris Farlowe's Jagger-produced version, and eventually released (with a prominent overdub from vocalist Christine Ohlman) on 1975's 'Metamorphosis'. Chris' version is wonderful of course, and will always be *the* version that others are compared to. A UK chart-topper, it was also by far the most successful song the Stones "gave away". In 2022, the Rolling Stones played the song live for the first time ever on their European Tour, with both Mick and the crowd clearly having a ball.

Chris Farlowe performing 'Out Of Time' on 'Beat! Beat! Beat!', 1966 [German TV]

UNDERCOVER

[271] **OUT OF TIME - P.J. Proby** (1967)
(Jagger-Richards)

Rolling Stones original: Aftermath [UK version] (1966) + Flowers [1967]; 1966 Demo: Metamorphosis (1975)

James Marcus Smith (b. 1938). Rhythm 'n' Blues, Rock, Pop, Soul and Easy Listening singer from Houston, Texas, USA.

A amazingly versatile artist, P.J. Proby can effortlessly switch from crooning Billy Eckstine ballads one minute to out-screaming James Brown the next (any doubters should check out his debut album 'I Am P.J. Proby' for an insight into his vocal capabilities). Marginally faster than Chris Farlowe's version and putting his own distinctive stamp on it, P.J. Proby's cover of 'Out Of Time' is on his 1967 album 'Enigma'.

Whose version inspired you to record the song, The Rolling Stones' or Chris Farlowe's?

"Chris Farlowe's. I'd never heard the Rolling Stones' version or maybe once. I thought their version was terrible. Chris Farlowe's version was the only one that was any good. I knew that Chris's girlfriend would not let him fly to The States to promote the number, so I did the number!"

Did you ever perform any Stones songs live? I think you sang 'Satisfaction'...

"I may have. I can't remember."

Have you ever worked with members of the Stones?

"Only on television shows like 'Top Of The Pops' and 'Ready Steady Go!'. Never on any stage shows. In 1964 I was supposed to do a tour with them for Robert Stigwood. While he was away, he left Stephen Komlosy in charge to do the contract with me. I took him out to dinner, he had quite a lot to drink and I got him to get me a great contract, where I was paid more than the Rolling Stones. When Stigwood got back he went berserk, but I refused to change it. So Stigwood cancelled the whole tour!"

[272] **OUT OF TIME - Arthur Brown** (1974)
(Jagger-Richards)

Rolling Stones original: Aftermath [UK version] (1966) + Flowers [1967]; 1966 Demo: Metamorphosis (1975)

Arthur Wilton Brown (b. 1942). Rock, Rhythm 'n' Blues and Psychedelic Rock singer from Whitby, Yorkshire, UK.

A little slower than most versions, and with prominent piano and saxophone, the not-so-crazy sounding Arthur Brown's cover is on his 1975 'Dance with Arthur Brown' album.

[273] **OUT OF TIME - Dan McCafferty** (1975)
(Jagger-Richards)

Rolling Stones original: Aftermath [UK version] (1966) + Flowers [1967]; 1966 Demo: Metamorphosis (1975)

William Daniel McCafferty (b. 1946). Rock singer from Dunfermline, Scotland. Best known as the lead vocalist for Nazareth.

With power-house vocals and an O.T.T. orchestration that makes Chris Farlowe's version sound sparse, the Nazareth front man's cover was a minor UK hit single, getting to No. 41 in the charts. For a short period in late 1975 there were *three* different versions of 'Out Of Time' in the UK charts at the same time: Dan McCafferty's, Chris Farlowe's reissued single, and The Rolling Stones 'Metamorphosis' version.

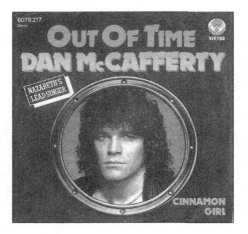

Dan McCafferty performing 'Out Of Time' on 'Top Of The Pops', 1975 [UK TV]

[274] **OUT OF TIME - Del Shannon** (1981)
(Jagger-Richards)

Rolling Stones original: Aftermath [UK version] (1966) + Flowers [1967]; 1966 Demo: Metamorphosis (1975)

Charles Weedon Westover (b. 1934 - d. 1990). Rock 'n' Roll and Pop singer and guitarist from Grand Rapids, Michigan, USA.

With just guitar, bass and drums supporting his occasionally double-tracked voice, Del Shannon's excellent update is on his 1981 album 'Drop Down and Get Me'.

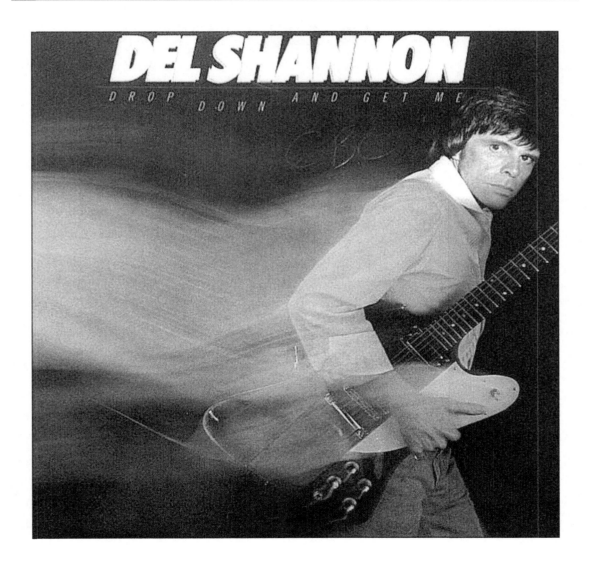

[275] **OUT OF TIME - Andrew Strong** (2000)

(Jagger-Richards)

Rolling Stones original: Aftermath [UK version] (1966) + Flowers [1967]; 1966 Demo: Metamorphosis (1975)

(b. 1973). Soul, Pop and Rock singer from Dublin, Ireland.

Perhaps best known as the singer in the 1991 movie 'The Commitments', Andrew Strong's powerful and soulful cover of 'Out Of Time' is on his 2000 album of the same name.

Whose idea was it to record this song?

"First time I heard 'Out Of Time' was Chris Farlowe's version, and I think my agent sent me the track."

Do you perform this (or any other Stones songs) live?

"No, I don't perform any other Stones songs."

Were the Rolling Stones an influence on your own music?

"Although I was fortunate enough to support them for 6 shows around Europe on their 'Voodoo Lounge' tour, no not really, I was more into Rock and Soul music. Don't get me wrong, I love the Stones but there are other artists and bands who have influenced me more."

[276] **OUT OF TIME - Elvis Costello and The Imposters** (2012)
(Jagger-Richards)

Rolling Stones original: Aftermath [UK version] (1966) + Flowers [1967]; 1966 Demo: Metamorphosis (1975)

Declan Patrick MacManus (b. 1954 - vocals and guitar), Steve Nieve (Stephen John Nason, b. 1958 - keyboards), David Allen Faragher (b. 1957 - bass and vocals) and Pete Thomas (Peter Michael Thomas, b. 1954 - drums). New Wave and Power Pop band from London.

Elvis Costello and The Imposters' rather good live cover is on the Super-Deluxe Limited Edition of Elvis' 2012 'The Return of the Spectacular Spinning Songbook!!!' album.

[277] **OUT OF TIME - Steve Harley** (2020)
(Jagger-Richards)

Rolling Stones original: Aftermath [UK version] (1966) + Flowers [1967]; 1966 Demo: Metamorphosis (1975)

Stephen Malcolm Ronald Nice (b. 1951). Glam Rock and Art Rock singer and guitarist from Deptford, London, UK.

Rather cleverly, Steve Harley's version amalgamates an acoustic instrumental arrangement of 'Honky Tonk Women', with the lyrics, melody and chords of 'Out Of Time'! It is on his 2020 'Uncovered' album.

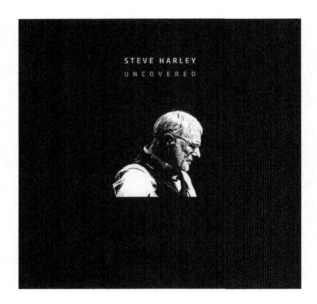

Whose idea was it to record this song?

"Mine. It's on my CD, 'Uncovered'. I am the Producer."

Have you performed this (or any other Stones songs) live?

"We play my interpretation at every Acoustic Band show. We have played 50 already this year. The audience loves it. The whole place sings the chorus when I encourage them at the end of the song. Very uplifting. A real Communion is created in the theatres."

Were the Rolling Stones an influence on your own music?

"I wasn't really influenced by The Stones musically. But I bought every single they released in the 60s. And every album."

[278] **PAINT IT BLACK - The Standells** (1966)

(Jagger-Richards)

Rolling Stones original: Aftermath [US version] (1966) + A-side (1966)

Larry Tamblyn (vocals, guitar and keyboards), Tony Valentino (Emilio Tony Belilissimo - guitar), Gary Lane (Gary McMillan, b. 1938 - d. 2014 - bass) and Dick Dodd (d. 2013 - vocals and drums). Pop and Garage band from Los Angeles, California, USA.

Even in the fast-changing sixties, it was one hell of a leap from '19th Nervous Breakdown' to 'Paint It Black' just 3 months later. Sure, The Beatles used a sitar first, on 'Norwegian Wood', but no-one before or since has come up with such a perfect combination of East meets West as 'Paint It Black'. The Standells' enthusiastic and fun version is on their 1966 'Why Pick On Me - Sometimes Good Guys Don't Wear White' album. *See [247] for interview!*

[279] **PAINT IT BLACK - Chris Farlowe** (1966)

(Jagger-Richards)

Rolling Stones original: Aftermath [US version] (1966) + A-side (1966)

Chris Farlowe (John Henry Dighton, b. 1940). Rhythm 'n' Blues, Soul and Pop singer from Islington, London.

Chris Farlowe covered no less than seven Jagger-Richards songs in the 60s, every one of them excellent. 'Paint It Black' features a prominent violin with orchestration and a speeded up ending, and was released both on his 1966 'The Art of Chris Farlowe' album and (in slightly different form) as a flop 1968 single.

[280] PAINT IT BLACK - Eric Burdon and The Animals (1967)
(Jagger-Richards)

Rolling Stones original: Aftermath [US version] (1966) + A-side (1966)

Eric Burdon (Eric Victor Burdon, b. 1941 - vocals), Vic Briggs (Victor Harvey Briggs III, 1945 - d. 2021 - guitar), John Weider (b. 1947 - guitar and violin), Danny McCulloch (Daniel Joseph McCulloch, b. 1945 - d. 2015 - bass) and Barry Jenkins (Colin Ernest Jenkins, b. 1944 - drums). Rock, Rhythm 'n' Blues and Psychedelia band who originated in Newcastle-upon-Tyne, UK.

With Eastern-sounding guitar and violin, a powerful rhythm section, and of course Eric's powerful and expressive vocals, Eric Burdon and The Animals' cover of 'Paint It Black' manages to straddle that fine line between structure and improvisation. Memorably performed live at The Monterey Pop festival, the studio version is on 1967's 'Winds of Change'.

 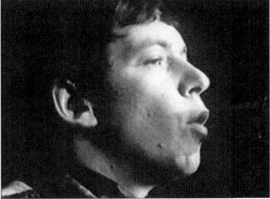

Eric Burdon and The Animals performing 'Paint It Black' at the Monterey Pop Festival, 1967 [USA]

[281] **PAINT IT BLACK - Eric Burdon and War** (1970)
(Jagger-Richards)

Rolling Stones original: Aftermath [US version] (1966) + A-side (1966)

Eric Victor Burdon (b. 1941). Rock and Rhythm 'n' Blues singer from Newcastle-upon-Tyne, UK, with Howard E. Scott (b. 1946 - guitar and vocals), Lee Oskar (b. 1948 - harmonica and vocals), Thomas 'Papa Dee' Allen (Thomas Sylvester Allen, b. 1931 - d. 1988 - percussion and vocals), Charles Miller (Charles William Miller, b. 1939 - d. 1980 - saxophone and vocals), B.B. Dickerson (b. 1949 - d. 2021 - bass and vocals), Leroy 'Lonnie' Jordan (b. 1948 - keyboards and vocals) and Harold Ray Brown (b. 1946 - drums and vocals). Funk-Rock band from Long Beach, California, USA.

Improvised, jammed and ad-libbed, this sometimes uneasy combination of Rock, Jazz, Funk and World is on 1970's 'The Black-Man's Burdon' album.

Eric Burdon and War performing 'Paint It Black' on 'Beat Club', 1970 [German TV]

[282] **PAINT IT BLACK - Ian A. Anderson** (1970)
(Jagger-Richards)

Rolling Stones original: Aftermath [US version] (1966) + A-side (1966)

> (b. 1947). Folk-Blues, Psych-Folk and World singer and guitarist from Weston-super-Mare, Somerset, UK.
>
> A very different Psych-Folk arrangement (with the emphasise more on Folk than Psych), Ian A. Anderson's foot-tapper is on his 1970 album 'Singer Sleeps On As Blaze Rages'.

Whose idea was it to record this song?

"Mine entirely. There were two versions of 'Paint It Black' that I recorded - firstly in 1972 for my LP 'Singer Sleeps On As Blaze Rages' (Village Thing). I also revisited it in 2013 in my duo The False Beards with Ben Mandelson on our CD 'Ankle' (Ghosts From The Basement)."

Have you performed this (or any other Stones songs) live?

"Yes, 'Paint It Black' was regularly gigged. Briefly used to do 'Honky Tonk Women' live in the '70s, never recorded."

Were the Rolling Stones an influence on your own music?

"Not really - it's more that we shared some of the same influences/heroes (Muddy Waters, Bo Diddley, Fred McDowell etc)."

[283] PAINT IT BLACK - The Mo-Dettes (1980)
(Jagger-Richards)

Rolling Stones original: Aftermath [US version] (1966) + A-side (1966)

Ramona Carlier (vocals), Kate Korris (Kate Corris - guitar), Jane Crockford (Jane Perry Crockford - bass) and June Miles-Kingston (June Patricia Miles-Kingston - drums). Post-Punk band from the UK. Disbanded in 1982.

Sounding like a marginally more conventional The Slits, The Mo-Dettes' percussive arrangement of 'Paint It Black' was released as a single in 1980, when it got to No. 42 in the UK charts.

[284] **PAINT IT BLACK - Anvil** (1981)

(Jagger-Richards)

Rolling Stones original: Aftermath [US version] (1966) + A-side (1966)

> Steve 'Lips' Kudlow (Steven Barry Kudlow, b. 1956 - vocals and guitar), Dave 'Squirrely' Allison (guitar and vocals), Ian 'Dix' Dickson (bass) and Robb 'Robbo' Reiner (Robb Géza Reiner - drums). Speed Metal and Heavy Metal band from Toronto, Ontario, Canada.
>
> Fortunately, not the Speed Metal thrash one might expect, Anvil's powerful and enjoyable Heavy Rock cover is on 1981's 'Hard'n'Heavy' album. [Interview is with Steve 'Lips' Kudlow]

Whose idea was it to record this song?

"It was my idea to do a version of 'Paint it Black' with a galloping feel, similar to 'Diamonds and Rust' by Judas Priest, which is also a cover, of a Joan Baez song."

Have you performed this (or any other Stones songs) live?

"Yes we did play this as well as a version of 'Jumpin' Jack Flash'."

Were the Rolling Stones an influence on your own music?

"Absolutely! They influenced everything that came after them. The first heavy metal distorted guitar riff ever is 'Satisfaction'... the rock world is in tremendous debt to the Stones. They virtually invented the genre!"

[285] **PAINT IT BLACK - Echo and The Bunnymen** (1988)

(Jagger-Richards)

Rolling Stones original: Aftermath [US version] (1966) + A-side (1966)

Ian McCulloch (Ian Stephen McCulloch, b. 1959 - vocals and guitar), Will Sergeant (William Alfred Sergeant, b. 1958 - guitar), Les Pattinson (Leslie Thomas Pattinson, b. 1958 - bass) and Pete de Freitas (Peter Louis Vincent de Freitas, b. 1961 - d. 1989 - drums). Post-Punk band from Liverpool, UK.

Recorded live, Echo and The Bunnymen's powerful and surprisingly straight cover was released as a bonus track on their 1988 'People Are Strange' single.

[286] **PAINT IT BLACK - The Meteors** (1991)

(Jagger-Richards)

Rolling Stones original: Aftermath [US version] (1966) + A-side (1966)

P. Paul Fenech (vocals and guitar), Strange Lee Brown (bass and vocals) and 'Rubber' Mark Howe (drums and vocals). Psychobilly band from London.

Sounding like hillbillies from hell, the Hank Williams-meets-Johnny Rotten vocals, reverberating tremolo guitar and pounding drums make this one of the most original and exciting covers of 'Paint It Black'. It is on The Meteors' 1991 album 'Madman Roll'.

[287] **PAINT IT BLACK - U2** (1992)
(Jagger-Richards)

Rolling Stones original: Aftermath [US version] (1966) + A-side (1966)

Bono (Paul David Hewson, b. 1960 - vocals), The Edge (David Howell Evans, b. 1961 - guitar, keyboards and vocals), Adam Clayton (Adam Charles Clayton, b. 1960 - bass) and Larry Mullen Jr. (Lawrence Joseph Mullen Jr., b. 1961 - drums). Post-Punk and Rock band from Dublin, Ireland.

Featuring U2's usual trademark vocal and guitar sound, 'Paint It Black' was on their 1992 'Who's Gonna Ride Your Wild Horses' single.

[288] **PAINT IT BLACK - David Essex** (1993)
(Jagger-Richards)

Rolling Stones original: Aftermath [US version] (1966) + A-side (1966)

David Albert Cook (b. 1947). Pop and Rock singer from Plaistow, Essex, UK.

David Essex's very dramatic version of 'Paint It Black', comes complete with Wagnerian strings, and is on his 1993 'Cover Shot' album.

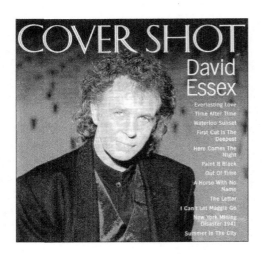

[289] **PAINT IT BLACK - Marc Almond** (1998)

(Jagger-Richards)

Rolling Stones original: Aftermath [US version] (1966) + A-side (1966)

Marc Almond (Peter Mark Sinclair Almond, b. 1956). Synth-Pop, Cabaret and Pop singer from Southport, Lancashire, UK.

With imaginatively-arranged orchestration and his usual excellent voice, Marc Almond's cover is on 1998's various artists 'Philharmania - Vol. 1' album.

Whose version inspired your recording, Chris Farlowe or The Rolling Stones?

"The Rolling Stones version without a doubt."

Have you performed this (or any other Stones songs) live?

"None."

Were the Rolling Stones an influence on your own music?

"I think they were an influence on some many people's music. It is all but impossible to discount their influence."

[290] **PAINT IT BLACK - Thee Headcoatees** (2002)
(Jagger-Richards)

Rolling Stones original: Aftermath [US version] (1966) + A-side (1966)

Holly Golightly (Holly Golightly Smith, b. 1966), Kyra LaRubia, Ludella Black and Debbie Green. Garage band from Chatham, Kent, UK. Disbanded in 1999.

Thee Headcoatees' version is a fairly straight cover, albeit with the low fidelity and distortion of an early Bo Diddley record. It is on 2002's various artists 'Standing in the Shadows - A Tribute to the Golden Days of The Rolling Stones 1963-1967'.

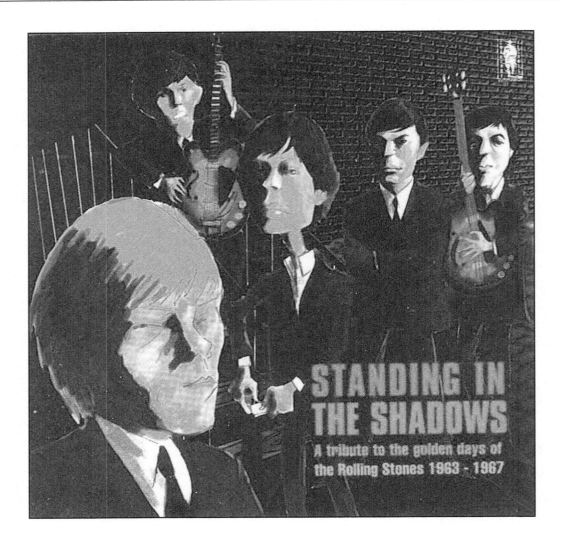

[291] **PAINT IT BLACK - Vanessa Carlton** (2002)

(Jagger-Richards)

Rolling Stones original: Aftermath [US version] (1966) + A-side (1966)

Vanessa Lee Carlton (b. 1980). Pop and Rock singer and pianist from Milford, Pennsylvania, USA.

Probably owing as much to Eric Burdon and The Animals' version as it does the Stones' original, Vanessa Carlton's interesting quiet/loud cover includes a droning sitar, organ and powerful drums, and can be found on her 2002 album 'Be Not Nobody'.

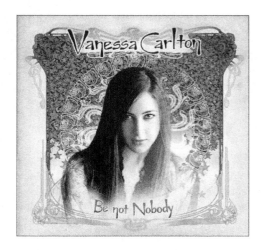

[292] **PAINT IT BLACK - Chalice** (2002)

(Jagger-Richards)

Rolling Stones original: Aftermath [US version] (1966) + A-side (1966)

Reggae band with ever-changing line-up from St. Mary, Jamaica.

Chalice's unusual Reggae arrangement features a very different guitar riff, and is on the various artists 'Paint It Black: A Reggae Tribute To The Rolling Stones' CD.

[293] **PAINT IT BLACK - Hayseed Dixie** (2007)

(Jagger-Richards)

Rolling Stones original: Aftermath [US version] (1966) + A-side (1966)

Rockgrass (Rock and Bluegrass) band from Nashville, Tennessee, USA, led by John Wheeler (John Christopher Wheeler, b. 1970 - vocals, guitar, piano and violin).

Featuring a medium tempo Country Bluegrass arrangement complete with mandolin and fiddle, Hayseed Dixie's unique cover is on 2007's 'Weapons Of Grass Destruction' album. [Interview is with John Wheeler]

Whose idea was it to record these songs?

"I pick the songs we do."

Have you performed these (or any other Stones songs) live?

"We've played 'Paint It Black' live on a couple of tours but never done 'Street Fighting Man' live."

Were the Rolling Stones an influence on your own music?

"As I'm 52 I reckon the Stones have been an influence in some way on every musician of my generation. The Stones are honestly not one of my favourite bands, though I do like a few of their songs, among those being the two we've covered. I probably like the Mick Taylor period best overall, as I quite dig his guitar vibe. There is a distinct mixing of blues-rock and country in Richards' chord voicings and rhythmic swing which I think is pretty unique and which is one of many cross-genre bridges that inspired me to try to develop a band sound that didn't neatly fit into the generally-recognised boundaries of any particular genre. Of course, after all these years, a record like 'Beggar's Banquet' or 'Let It Bleed' doesn't sound especially radical because we've been hearing these and everything they influenced for our entire lives, but I reckon they sounded pretty different when they were released."

[294] **PAINT IT BLACK - Ali Campbell** (2010)
(Jagger-Richards)

Rolling Stones original: Aftermath [US version] (1966) + A-side (1966)

Alistair Ian Campbell (b. 1959). Reggae singer and guitarist from Birmingham, UK.

Just like most of his former group UB40's covers, Ali Campbell's Reggae version of 'Paint It Black' is highly distinctive, very well sung - and utterly predictable. It is on Ali Campbell's 2010 album 'Great British Songs'.

[295] **PAINT IT BLACK - Robyn Adele Anderson** (2020)
(Jagger-Richards)

Rolling Stones original: Aftermath [US version] (1966) + A-side (1966)

(b. 1989). Jazz and Pop singer from Albany, New York, USA.

Robyn Adele Anderson's remarkable version features the song's usual lyrics sung over a mash-up of 'Paint It Black' and Amy Winehouse's 'Back To Black'. It was issued as a 2020 single, as well on the following year's 'Robyn Adele Vol. 6' album.

Whose idea was it to combine 'Paint It Black' with 'Back To Black'?

"It was my idea to combine 'Paint It Black' with 'Back To Black.' I like creating mash-ups that have some element of irony or wordplay. These songs also had similar enough chord progressions that they could be combined and you could still hear each individual song."

Do you perform this (or any other Stones songs) live?

"I've never actually performed this song live or any other Rolling Stones song. I've also done a cover of '(I Can't Get No) Satisfaction'."

Were the Rolling Stones an influence on you?

"I can't say that the Rolling Stones themselves were an influence, I tend to just gravitate towards music that has had a cultural impact and do my best to put my own spin on it! I never listened to classic rock growing up so I enjoy the challenge of covering songs that I'm not as familiar with because it's always a learning experience."

[296] **PARACHUTE WOMAN - The Piggies** (2013)

(Jagger-Richards)

Rolling Stones original: Beggars Banquet (1968)

Andy Maltz (vocals and guitar), Brad McGee (guitar), Matt Fiveash (bass) and Kris Parrish (drums). Garage Rock band from Brooklyn, New York, USA.

Betraying its cassette recording origins, the Stones' original of 'Parachute Woman' always had a slightly murky sound to it. The Piggies' ragged but good Norton single maintains this lo-fi feel.

[297] **PARTY DOLL - Mary Chapin Carpenter** (1999)

(Jagger)

Rolling Stones original: Primitive Cool [Mick Jagger solo album] (1987)

(b. 1958). Americana, Folk and Country singer and guitarist from Princeton, New Jersey, USA.

One of the better tracks from Mick Jagger's 2nd solo album 'Primitive Cool', the Country song 'Party Doll' has inspired a couple of good covers. Mary Chapin Carter's more gentle, acoustic version is on her 1999 album 'Party Doll and Other Favorites'.

[298] **PARTY DOLL - Kat Kramer with Billy Preston** (2001)

(Jagger)

Rolling Stones original: Primitive Cool [Mick Jagger solo album] (1987)

(b. 1958). Americana, Folk and Country singer and guitarist from Princeton, New Jersey, USA. Katherine Kramer. Actress, producer, activist, and Pop and Country singer from USA, and William Everett Preston (b. 1946 - d. 2006). Rhythm 'n' Blues, Soul and Gospel singer and keyboardist from Houston, Texas, USA.

With a Country-Soul makeover and some excellent guitar (probably played by Waddy Wachtel, a member of Keith Richards' X-Pensive Winos), Kat Kamer's well enunciated vocals contrast nicely with Billy's grittier voice. It is a highlight of her intriguing 'Gemstone' (formerly 'Hang On To Me Tonight') project. *See [40] for interview!*

[299] **PLAY WITH FIRE - Clefs Of Lavender Hill** (1966)

(Jagger-Richards)

Rolling Stones original: Out Of Our Heads [US version] (1965) + UK/US B-side (1965)

Lorraine Ximenes (Coventry Fairchild - vocals and guitar), Joseph Ximenes (Travis Fairchild - vocals and guitar), Bill Moss (bass guitar) and Fred Moss (drums). Folk Rock band from Miami, Florida, USA.

The Rolling Stones recorded some great B-sides - 'Off The Hook', 'I'm Free', 'Child Of The Moon', 'Bitch' - but *none* are so affectionately remembered or as frequently covered as 'Play With Fire'. Clefs Of Lavender Hill's 1966 single successfully combines very Folky (and very British-sounding) vocals with a moody electric guitar riff.

[300] **PLAY WITH FIRE - Twice As Much** (1966)
(Jagger-Richards)

Rolling Stones original: Out Of Our Heads [US version] (1965) + UK/US B-side (1965)

Dave Skinner (David Ferguson Skinner, b. 1946) and Andrew Rose (Andrew Colin Campbell Rose, b. 1946). Pop duo from London.

Played at a rather sprightly tempo, Twice As Much's cover includes prominent harpsichord and orchestration, and can be found on their debut album 'Own Up'.

[301] **PLAY WITH FIRE - The Beau Brummels** (1966)
(Jagger-Richards)

Rolling Stones original: Out Of Our Heads [US version] (1965) + UK/US B-side (1965)

Sal Valentino (Salvatore Spampinato, b. 1942 - vocals and tambourine), Ron Elliott (Ronald Charles Elliott, b. 1943 - guitar and vocals), Donald Jay Irving (b. 1946 - guitar and vocals), Ron Meagher (b. 1941 - bass and vocals) and John Petersen (John Louis Petersen, b. 1942 - d. 2007 - drums and vocals). Folk Rock band from San Francisco, California, USA. Disbanded in 1969, though there was a reunion in 1974-1975.

A nice Folk-Rock cover with Byrds-like guitar and a descending bass line, it is on their album 'Beau Brummels 66'.

[302] **PLAY WITH FIRE - John Fred and His Playboys** (1966)

(Jagger-Richards)

Rolling Stones original: Out Of Our Heads [US version] (1965) + UK/US B-side (1965)

John Fred Gourrier (b. 1941 - d. 2005). Soul, Pop and Rock 'n' Roll singer (and band) from Baton Rouge, Louisiana, USA.

A relaxed cover with an electric guitar riff and organ, John Fred and The Playboys' version of 'Play With Fire' was released on their debut album in 1966.

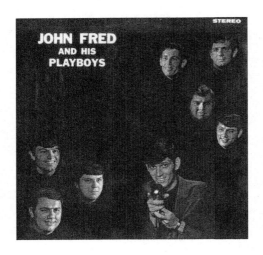

[303] **PLAY WITH FIRE - Ruth Copeland** (1971)

(Jagger-Richards)

Rolling Stones original: Out Of Our Heads [US version] (1965) + UK/US B-side (1965)

Kelly Michaels (b. 1946). Pop, Folk, Soul and Funk singer from Consett, Durham, UK.

Sounding like a smoother Janis Joplin, Ruth Copeland's cover starts with just piano, but then develops into unrestrained Blues Rock. It is on her 1971 album 'I Am What I Am'.

[304] **PLAY WITH FIRE - Dana Valery** (1975)

(Jagger-Richards)

Rolling Stones original: Out Of Our Heads [US version] (1965) + UK/US B-side (1965)

Dana Valery Catalano (Fausta Dana Galli, b. 1944). Pop, Rock and Soul singer from Codogno, Italy.

Dana Valery's version is more subtle than Ruth Copeland's, but only just! Marred only slightly by very heavy handed drumming, her cover is on the 1975 album 'Dana Valery'.

[305] **PLAY WITH FIRE - Manfred Mann's Earth Band** (1996)

(Jagger-Richards)

Rolling Stones original: Out Of Our Heads [US version] (1965) + UK/US B-side (1965)

Manfred Mann (Manfred Sepse Lubowitz, b. 1940 - keyboards and vocals), Chris Thompson (Christopher Hamlet Thompson, b. 1948 - vocals), Noel McCalla (b. 1956 - vocals), Mick Rogers (Michael Oldroyd, b. 1946 - guitar), Steve Kinch (bass) and Clive Bunker (Clive William Bunker, b. 1946 - drums). Rock and Pop band from London.

Almost unrecognisable from the Stones' original, Manfred Mann' Earth Band's cover has a very contemporary A.O.R. arrangement. It is on their 1996 album 'Soft Vengeance'. *See [347] for interview!*

Soft Vengeance
Manfred Mann's Earth Band

[306] PLAY WITH FIRE - The Pretty Things (1999)

(Jagger-Richards)

Rolling Stones original: Out Of Our Heads [US version] (1965) + UK/US B-side (1965)

Phil May (Phillip Arthur Dennis Wadey, b. 1944 - d. 2020 - vocals), Dick Taylor (Richard Clifford Taylor, b. 1943 - guitar), Frank Holland (guitar), Steve Browning (bass), Mark St. John (drums) and [probably] Robert Webb (keyboards). Rhythm 'n' Blues, Psychedelic and Rock band from London, UK. Disbanded in 2018, though they returned to record one more album shortly before Phil May's death in 2020.

Dick Taylor was one on the original members of The Rolling Stones, initially on guitar and then on bass. He left in November 1962 (when he was quickly replaced by Bill Wyman) to return to art college, but fortunately was persuaded by fellow student Phil May to form a new band, The Pretty Things. They soon rivalled (and often surpassed) The Rolling Stones as the most controversial, anti-establishment band of the era. Remaining consistently great throughout their long career, it wasn't until 1999's 'Rage Before Beauty' album that they finally covered a Stones number, and that song was 'Play With Fire'. With Phil's strong vocals, Dick's excellent lead guitar, and some nice piano (reminiscent of The Doors' 'Riders On The Storm'), their cover deserves to be far more widely known. [Interview is with Dick Taylor]

Whose idea was it to record this song?

"It was Mark St. John's idea to record it, which we did in his studio at 145 Wardour Street. It's also him on drums, myself on the tremolo guitar through a vintage Gibson amp, Frank Holland on the other guitar and, I think, Steve Browning on bass I am unfortunately really not sure who played the piano on it, which I really like, as I also do Phil's rather menacing vocal. I remember we recorded the basic track after just a couple of takes one evening at 145 with the brilliant Dave Garland engineering and Mark producing."

Did you ever perform it live?

"Unfortunately we never played it live, much to my disappointment I must say. Maybe Phil didn't want to show Mick up, actually they could have done a great duet on it!"

Have you ever played any other Stones songs live with the Pretty Things or any other (post-Stones) bands?

"Funnily enough I have played it quite often over the last couple of years with my friends JC and Angelina Grimshaw. I also work with a band called the Hillmans on the Isle of Wight where I live and we do a few Stones songs including 'Honky Tonk Women', 'It's All Over Now', 'The Last Time', 'You Can't Always Get What You Want' and 'Not Fade Away', which I also play with JC and Angelina. I like to think we try to put a new slant on all of them, something which Phil always was very insistent on when doing cover versions and I was always in total agreement with."

[307] **PLAY WITH FIRE - Crystal Jacqueline** (2013)
(Jagger-Richards)

Rolling Stones original: Out Of Our Heads [US version] (1965) + UK/US B-side (1965)

Jacqueline Bourne. Psychedelic Rock and Pop singer from Devon, UK.

With an imaginative Psych Folk arrangement, Crystal Jacqueline's excellent cover is on her 'Sun Arise' album from 2013, as well as on the 'A Fairy Tale' EP.

Whose idea was it to record this song?

"Keith Jones of Fruits De Mer hinted that the idea of The Troggs' 'Cousin Jane' sung by a female would make an interesting cover. He also liked 'A Fairy Tale' (we can't remember who did this) and thought the two songs would sit nicely on an EP along with one other. Icarus had always liked 'Play With Fire' and we both thought we could do a good version of the song in the dark, slightly hard-edged style that we were beginning to develop (we'd given the same treatment to 'Cousin Jane'). Keith, as Icarus recalls, didn't particularly like 'Play With Fire' when we presented it to him but agreed to use it for the EP. It then went on to receive a lot of positive reviews, more so than 'Cousin Jane' or 'A Fairy Tale'."

Do you perform this or any other Stones songs live?

"We've never played 'Play With Fire' live. We tend to play our original songs with just a few of the 'must include' covers for a gig. Icarus makes the point that it's actually quite a tricky song to play properly due to its individual picking style."

Were the Rolling Stones an influence on your own music?

"I wouldn't say that The Rolling Stones have particularly influenced me in my music, although I'm sure I must have absorbed some of their incredible songs/sounds at an early age and goodness knows they're played to death whenever Icarus is around! My two older sisters had a wonderful pile of 45s which I used to play on the old, red record player with its white lid. 'As Tears Go By' was a favourite as was 'Satisfaction'. What has probably influenced me more than the music is their fashion. The flamboyant 60's style of Mick Jagger, Brian Jones, and of course Marianne Faithful, Anita Pallenberg and Chrissie Shrimpton screamed a new confidence and disregard for conformity. Brilliant!"

[308] **PLAY WITH FIRE - La La Brooks** (2013)
(Jagger-Richards)

Rolling Stones original: Out Of Our Heads [US version] (1965) + UK/US B-side (1965)

Dolores Brooks (b. 1947). Pop and Soul singer from Brooklyn, New York, USA.

Best known as a former lead vocalist for The Crystals. La La Brooks' fast, retro, Garage Rock version of 'Play With Fire' was released as a Norton single.

[309] **PLAY WITH FIRE - Billy Boy Arnold** (2018)
(Jagger-Richards)

Rolling Stones original: Out Of Our Heads [US version] (1965) + UK/US B-side (1965)

William Arnold (b. 1935). Blues and Rhythm 'n' Blues singer, harmonicist and guitarist from Chicago, Illinois, USA.

Billy Boy Arnold's superb Chicago blues rearrangement is on the consistently brilliant 'Chicago Plays The Stones' various artists CD.

[310] **PLEASE GO HOME - Izzy Stradlin** (2002)
(Jagger-Richards)

Rolling Stones original: Between The Buttons [UK version] (1967) + Flowers (1967)

Jeffrey Dean Isbell (b. 1962). Hard Rock and Blues-Rock singer and guitarist from Lafayette, Indiana, USA. Best known as a member of Guns 'n' Roses.

The Stones original is basically a Psych-tinged update of Bo Diddley, and Izzy Stradlin also utilises that rhythm, albeit at a faster pace and in a lower key. It is on his 2002 album 'On Down The Road'.

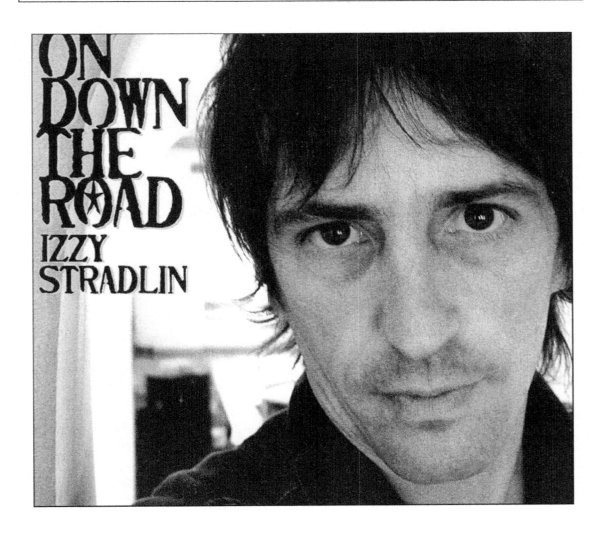

[311] PLEASE GO HOME - The Wildebeests (2003)

(Jagger-Richards)

Rolling Stones original: Between The Buttons [UK version] (1967) + Flowers (1967)

> Russell Wilkins (guitar and vocals), John Gibbs (bass and vocals) and Lenny Helsing (drums and vocals). Garage Rock band from London, UK.
>
> Although rawer and with more prominent guitar, The Wildebeests' cover for Norton retains much of the feel and sound of the original, even down to the weird theremin and echo effects. [Interview is with Lenny Helsing]

Whose idea was it to record this song?

"Well all three of us are fans of that period of the Stones, and given that 'Please Go Home' has a particular Bo Diddley feel about it, we thought it'd be great to cover this. I'd say that I was pretty instrumental in choosing that song as it's also from my fave Stones album 'Between The Buttons'."

Do you perform this or any other Stones songs live?

"Actually, we have also covered loads more mid-sixties Stones songs on a series of split-seven inch vinyl singles released by US label Norton some years back. I think there were six or seven that we were included on but… not using our Wildebeests name, but a host of fictitious names just for fun. These included The Lairds, The Dartford Renegades, The Queensberry Terrors, The Wrecked Angles and The Rotting Stumps - can you guess where that one came from?

On stage we've covered some of them including the likes of 'Citadel', 'Off The Hook', 'My Obsession', '2120 South Michigan Ave' and also 'The Under Assistant West Coast Promo Man'… but not for ages."

[312] **RAIN FALL DOWN** - Ana Popović (2013)
(Jagger-Richards)

Rolling Stones original: A Bigger Bang (2005) + UK/US A-side (2005)

(b. 1976). Blues and Rock singer and guitarist from Belgrade, Yugoslavia (now Serbia).

There aren't many decent cover versions of songs from 2005's 'A Bigger Bang', which is a shame, as there are some genuinely great tracks on it that deserve much further investigation. One rare example is Ana Popović's cover of 'Rain Fall Down', which is both hotter and funkier than the Stones' original, and is (appropriately) on her 2013 album 'Can You Stand The Heat'.

[313] **RESPECTABLE** - The Shop Assistants (1990)
(Jagger-Richards)

Rolling Stones original: Some Girls (1978) + UK A-side (1978)

Sarah Kneale (vocals), David Keegan (guitar), Laura MacPhail (bass) and Margarita Vasquez-Ponte (drums). Indie Pop band from Edinburgh, Scotland. Disbanded in 1990.

Basically, a Punk-inspired update of Chuck Berry, The Shop Assistants' cover has noisier guitars and nonchalant couldn't-care-less vocals. It was released on 'Stoned Again - A Tribute to The Stones'.

[314] **RIDE ON BABY - Chris Farlowe (1966)**
(Jagger-Richards)

Rolling Stones original: Flowers (1967) (recorded in 1965)

Chris Farlowe (John Henry Dighton, b. 1940). Rhythm 'n' Blues, Soul and Pop singer from Islington, London.

Two of the very best songs from the prolific 'Aftermath' sessions (in December 1965 and March 1966) weren't released until the summer of '67 US 'Flowers' compilation. One of these was 'Sittin' On A Fence', a hit for Twice As Much, and the other one was 'Ride On Baby', which was donated to Chris Farlowe. Orchestrated, and sung in a higher key than the Stones', Chris' fine version was the follow-up to his chart-topper 'Out Of Time' (and his third Jagger-Richard A-side in a row), though it sadly stalled at No. 31 in the UK charts.

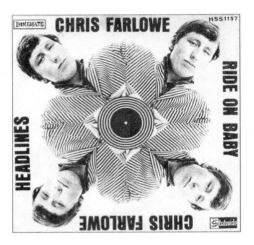

Chris Farlowe performing 'Ride On Baby' on 'Beat! Beat! Beat!', 1966 [German TV]

[315] RIDE ON BABY - Joe Louis Walker (2014)

(Jagger-Richards)

Rolling Stones original: Flowers (1967) (recorded in 1965)

Louis Joseph Walker Jr. (b. 1949). Blues singer and guitarist from San Francisco, California, USA.

Joe's soulful revival of 'Ride On Baby' features some notably excellent piano playing. It is available on his 2014 album 'Hornet's Nest'. *See [136] for interview!*

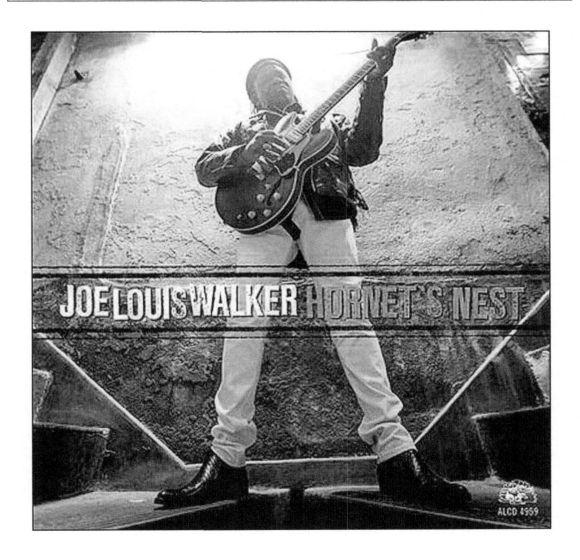

[316] RIP THIS JOINT - Tommy Castro (2003)

(Jagger-Richards)

Rolling Stones original: Exile On Main St. (1972)

(b. 1955). Blues, Soul and Rhythm 'n' Blues singer and guitarist from San Jose, California, USA.

Basically a good old fashioned Little Richard-styled Rock 'n' Roll number with modern lyrics, the beefy saxes on Tommy Castro's storming version, if anything, improve the song further. It is on the various artists 'Exile On Blues St' CD.

Whose idea was it to record this song?

"I was approached by a record label that was doing this Stones tribute by various Blues artists. Can't remember who it was."

Do you perform this or any other Stones songs live?

"Haven't been performing any Stones songs live. But it's on my list. Been thinking about doing 'You Can't Always Get What You Want'. So many great songs to choose from."

Were the Rolling Stones an influence on your own music?

"The Stones have been a big influence on me since I was a teenager. Probably the first Blues I ever hear was the Stones' versions 'Little Red Rooster' or 'Love In Vain'."

[317] **RIP THIS JOINT - Chuck Leavell** (2008)

(Jagger-Richards)

Rolling Stones original: Exile On Main St. (1972)

Charles Alfred Leavell (b. 1952). Blues-Rock and Southern Rock keyboardist and singer from Birmingham, Alabama, USA.

As a Rolling Stones sideman since 1982, Chuck Leavell would've played this song many times, notably on the band's 1995 and 2002-2003 tours. He included his own rockin' version on the 'Live in Germany - Green Leaves & Blue Notes Tour 2007' album.

LIVE IN GERMANY - GREEN LEAVES & BLUE NOTES TOUR 2007

[318] ROCKS OFF - Jimmy Thackery (2003)
(Jagger-Richards)

Rolling Stones original: Exile On Main St. (1972)

James Thackery (b. 1953). Blues and Rock singer and guitarist from Pittsburgh, Pennsylvania, USA.

The opening song from 'Exile On Main St.', Ex-The Nighthawks' Jimmy Thackery's playing on 'Rocks Off' is truly awe-inspiring! It is on the 'Exile On Blues St.' various artists CD.

Whose idea was it to record this song?

"The record label I was with at the time was giving the producer a lot of creative freedom to do pet projects. He came up with several concept records consisting of well known blues artists doing cover versions of things such as an entire CD of 'Beatles Blues' and Rolling Stones, and maybe even something else that I have forgotten about. I think we covered 'Why Don't We Do It In The Road' for the Beatles thing.

'Rocks Off' was always a favourite of mine from 'Exile' and when the idea was presented to do a CD of blues artists doing versions of the songs from that album, I chose one of my favourites. I believe we did another compilation CD where we recorded, 'The Last Time', as well."

Have you performed this (or any other Stones songs) live?

"My first band did a rousing version of 'Jumpin' Jack Flash' years ago. We also did 'Hip Shake', although we were really covering the Slim Harpo version."

Were the Rolling Stones an influence on your own music?

"Beatles, Stones, Animals, Kinks, Yardbirds... all had an early influence on everyone. Me included. However, they simply brought everyone's attention to the music that originated in our own American back yard. Once we youngsters realized that the British bands were simply trying to copy the blues from the Mississippi Delta, Chicago, Detroit and Texas, we just bypassed all that and went straight to the source. For me, personally, it was Peter Greens' Fleetwood Mac that first brought home the real blues sound and made me really dig into where it came from. The Stones were just a better than average English rock 'n' roll band."

[319] **ROCKS OFF - Old 97's** (2010)

(Jagger-Richards)

Rolling Stones original: Exile On Main St. (1972)

Rhett Miller (Stewart Ransom Miller II, b. 1970 - vocals and guitar), Ken Bethea (guitar and vocals), Murry Hammond (bass, guitar and vocals) and Philip Peeples (drums and vocals). Alt-Country and Power Pop band from Dallas, Texas, USA.

The vocals are a little more Country than the Stones' original, but otherwise Old 97's cover is similar in arrangement. It is on their 2010 EP 'Mimeograph'.

[320] **ROCKS OFF - Bason feat. Badflower** (2015)

(Jagger-Richards)

Rolling Stones original: Exile On Main St. (1972)

David Bason (b. 1973), Pop and Rock singer, guitarist and pianist from Los Angeles, California, USA, with Josh Katz (vocals and guitar), Joey Morrow (guitar), Alex Espiritu (bass) and Anthony Sonetti (drums). Hard Rock band from Los Angeles, California, USA.

Reinvented as a slow piano-led ballad, Bason feat. Badflower's cover of 'Rocks Off' is on the 2015 Bason album '100 Floors Above Me'.

[321] **RUBY TUESDAY - Bobby Goldsboro** (1967)
(Jagger-Richards)

Rolling Stones original: Between The Buttons [US version] (1967) + Flowers (1967) + US A-side (1967) + UK B-side (1967)

Robert Charles Goldsboro (b. 1941). Country and Pop singer and guitarist from Marianna, Florida, USA.

Many people assume that Mick wrote the more wordy and melodic songs, while Keith concentrated on the hard-riffing rockers. It was never quite that straight-forward though, and a good example of this is 'Ruby Tuesday', composed almost entirely by Keith. Bobby Goldsboro's pleasant Country Pop version is on his 1967 'The Romantic, Wacky, Soulful, Rockin', Country, Bobby Goldsboro' album. *See [16] for interview!*

[322] **RUBY TUESDAY - Rotary Connection** (1968)
(Jagger-Richards)

Rolling Stones original: Between The Buttons [US version] (1967) + Flowers (1967) + US A-side (1967) + UK B-side (1967)

Mitch Aliotta (Mitchell A. Aliotta, b. 1944 - d. 2015), Minnie Riperton (Minnie Julia Riperton Rudolph, b. 1947 - d. 1979), Sidney Barnes (Sidney Alexander Barnes Jr., b. 1941), Bobby Simms, Kenny Venegas and Judy Hauff. Psychedelic Soul vocal group from Chicago, Illinois, USA. Disbanded in 1974.

Backed by Church-like organ, Rotary Connection's version starts with a solitary female voice singing the song like a slow traditional hymn - until they reach the chorus, which is harmonised and up-tempo. It is on 1968's 'Rotary Connection' album.

[323] **RUBY TUESDAY - Melanie** (1970)

(Jagger-Richards)

Rolling Stones original: Between The Buttons [US version] (1967) + Flowers (1967) + US A-side (1967)
+ UK B-side (1967)

Melanie Anne Safka (b. 1947). Folk and Pop singer and guitarist from Queens, New York, USA.

With her heartfelt and passionately-sung vocals, backed by sympathetic acoustic guitar and strings, Melanie's version is rightly regarded by many as one of *the* Stones covers. Released as a 1970 single (as well as on her album 'Candles In The Rain'), it reached No. 9 in the UK and No. 11 in the US Billboard charts.

[324] **RUBY TUESDAY - Julian Lennon** (1989)

(Jagger-Richards)

Rolling Stones original: Between The Buttons [US version] (1967) + Flowers (1967) + US A-side (1967)
+ UK B-side (1967)

John Charles Julian Lennon (b. 1963). Pop and Rock singer, keyboardist and guitarist from Liverpool, UK. John Lennon's oldest son.

Apart from the typically '80s too-loud drums, Julian Lennon's cover of 'Ruby Tuesday' sticks fairly close to the Stones' original arrangement. It is on 1989's 'The Wonder Years' various artists movie soundtrack album.

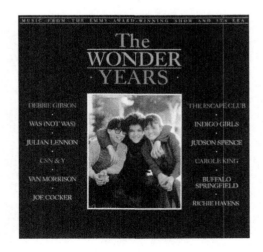

[325] **RUBY TUESDAY - Rod Stewart** (1993)
(Jagger-Richards)

Rolling Stones original: Between The Buttons [US version] (1967) + Flowers (1967) + US A-side (1967)
+ UK B-side (1967)

Roderick David Stewart (b. 1945). Rock singer from Highgate, London, UK.

With a quasi-classical piano intro, strings, and of course his highly distinctive voice, Rod's fine revival was issued as a 1993 single, peaking at No. 11 in the UK charts.

[326] **RUBY TUESDAY - The London Symphony Orchestra feat. Marianne Faithfull** (1994)

(Jagger-Richards)

Rolling Stones original: Between The Buttons [US version] (1967) + Flowers (1967) + US A-side (1967) + UK B-side (1967)

Marianne Evelyn Gabriel Faithfull (b. 1946). Pop, Rock, Folk and Jazz singer from London, UK, with Orchestra from London, UK.

The London Symphony Orchestra's 1994 'Symphonic Music of The Rolling Stones' album features a handful of guest vocalists, and these include no less than Mick Jagger (singing 'Angie') and Marianne Faithfull. Almost a minute and a half of instrumental symphonic music passes before Marianne's vocal starts, but it's well worth the wait. In surprisingly fine voice (she must've laid off the fags for a few days), her cover of 'Ruby Tuesday' is absolutely essential listening.

[327] **RUBY TUESDAY - Deana Carter** (1997)

(Jagger-Richards)

Rolling Stones original: Between The Buttons [US version] (1967) + Flowers (1967) + US A-side (1967) + UK B-side (1967)

Deana Kay Carter (b. 1966). Country singer and guitarist from Nashville, Tennessee, USA.

Clearly based on Melanie's hit version (albeit with a more modern backing and a more Country voice), Deana Carter's cover is on the various artists 'Stone Country' CD.

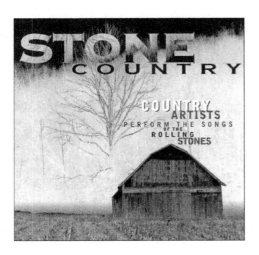

[328] **RUBY TUESDAY - The Corrs feat. Ron Wood** (2002)

(Jagger-Richards)

Rolling Stones original: Between The Buttons [US version] (1967) + Flowers (1967) + US A-side (1967) + UK B-side (1967)

Andrea Corr (Andrea Jane Corr, b. 1974 - vocals, tin whistle, ukulele), Sharon (Sharon Helga Corr, b. 1970 - violin, keyboards and vocals), Caroline (Caroline Georgina Corr, b. 1973 - drums, percussion, piano, bodhrán and vocals) and Jim (James Steven Ignatius Corr, b. 1964 - guitar, piano, keyboards and vocals). Pop Rock, Folk Rock and Celtic Fusion band from Dundalk, County Louth, Ireland.

Although Ronnie Wood is barely featured, The Corrs' sweet harmonies make their live Pop Rock cover of 'Ruby Tuesday' highly enjoyable. It is on the 2002 'Live in Dublin' album.

[329] **RUBY TUESDAY - Twiggy** (2003)

(Jagger-Richards)

Rolling Stones original: Between The Buttons [US version] (1967) + Flowers (1967) + US A-side (1967) + UK B-side (1967)

Lesley Hornby (b. 1949). Pop and Country singer, model and actress from Neasden, Middlesex, UK.

One of the most iconic models of the '60s, Twiggy is also a very good Country-tinged pop singer, and even had a couple of moderate UK hit singles in the '70s. Issued in 2003 but probably recorded in the '80s, Twiggy's cover of 'Ruby Tuesday' is on her album 'Midnight Blue'.

[330] **RUBY TUESDAY - Mary Fahl** (2022)

(Jagger-Richards)

Rolling Stones original: Between The Buttons [US version] (1967) + Flowers (1967) + US A-side (1967) + UK B-side (1967)

Mary Faldermeyer (b. 1958). Folk, World and Chamber Pop singer and guitarist from Rockland County, New York, USA.

With her clear, classy voice, ably supported by backing that includes a string quartet, Mary Fahl's fine cover can be found on her 2022 album 'Can't Get It Out Of My Head'.

Whose version inspired your recording of the song, The Rolling Stones or Melanie?

"It was the Rolling Stones version of 'Ruby Tuesday' that inspired my version. I loved the Brian Jones-era Stones. In fact, 'Ruby Tuesday' was the first single I ever bought. My mother wouldn't let me play the B-Side 'Let's Spend the Night Together'. She didn't want that "dirty talk" in our house!"

Were the Rolling Stones an influence on your own music?

"I'd say the fact that I loved them so early on, they have to be an influence. The early Stones had a chamber-ensemble quality to some of their material that definitely inspires me to this day. They don't call what I do "chamber-pop" for nothing."

[331] SAD DAY - Tan Sleeve (2000)
(Jagger-Richards)

Rolling Stones original: US B-side (1966)

Lane Steinberg (vocals and guitar) and Steven Barry Katz (vocals and piano). Rock and Pop duo from New York City, USA.

A memorable song that was inexplicably only released in the USA during the 60s as the B-side to '19th Nervous Breakdown' (the UK had 'As Tears Go By' instead), Tan Sleeve's cover features just acoustic guitar and piano backing, as well as some nice harmonies. It is on their 2000 album 'White Lie Castle'. [Interview is with Lane Steinberg]

Whose idea was it to record this song?

"Tan Sleeve arose from the ashes of The Wind, who had their fifteen minutes with a feature story in Rolling Stone exactly forty years ago in 1982. Tan Sleeve's 'White Lie Castle' was recorded in 2000. We wanted to do an album of stripped down live acoustic originals and semi-obscure covers. 'Sad Day' was a song we loved."

Have you performed this (or any other Stones songs) live?

"We also did 'Sittin' On A Fence' live."

Were the Rolling Stones an influence on your own music?

"The Stones were a huge influence on us, especially the Brian Jones years."

[332] **SAINT OF ME - Debbie Clarke** (2012)

(Jagger-Richards)

Rolling Stones original: Bridges To Babylon (1997) + UK/US A-side (1998)

(b. 1983). Folk and Pop singer from Herefordshire, Wales.

A contemporary-sounding song from 'Bridges To Babylon', Debbie Clarke's performance retains the original's dance rhythm, but also features Wagnerian strings and an angelic choir. It is on her 2012 'Manhattanhenge' album.

[333] **SAINT OF ME - Nathalie Alvim** (2014)

(Jagger-Richards)

Rolling Stones original: Bridges To Babylon (1997) + UK/US A-side (1998)

Soul, R&B and Funk singer from Brazil.

With a soulful, more retro feel, Nathalie Alvim's fine version of 'Saint Of Me' is on 2014's 'Rockin' Soul' album.

[334] **SALT OF THE EARTH - Rotary Connection** (1969)
(Jagger-Richards)

Rolling Stones original: Beggars Banquet (1968)

Mitch Aliotta (Mitchell A. Aliotta, b. 1944 - d. 2015), Minnie Riperton (Minnie Julia Riperton Rudolph, b. 1947 - d. 1979), Sidney Barnes (Sidney Alexander Barnes Jr., b. 1941), Bobby Simms, Kenny Venegas, John Stocklin and John Jeremiah. Psychedelic Soul vocal group from Chicago, Illinois, USA. Disbanded in 1974.

As well as being the closing track on 'Beggar's Banquet', 'Salt Of The Earth' was the last song performed at Brian Jones' final performance on 'The Rolling Stones Rock and Roll Circus' in 1968, and just as poignantly, by Mick and Keith at 'The Concert for New York City' in 2001. Beautifully harmonised with piano and strings, Rotary Connection's cover is on their 1969 album 'Songs'.

[335] **SALT OF THE EARTH - Joan Baez** (1971)

(Jagger-Richards)

Rolling Stones original: Beggars Banquet (1968)

Joan Chandos Baez (b. 1941). Folk singer and guitarist from Staten Island, New York, USA.

Featuring her usual pure and clear vocals, Joan Baez's cover is a mid-tempo Pop Rock version, complete with horns. It is on her 1971 album 'Blessed Are...'.

[336] **SALT OF THE EARTH - Dandy Livingstone** (1971)

(Jagger-Richards)

Rolling Stones original: Beggars Banquet (1968)

Robert Livingstone Thompson (b. 1943). British-based Reggae, Ska and Rock Steady singer, originally from Kingston, Jamaica.

A relaxed Reggae version complete with strings, Dandy Livingstone's cover of 'Salt Of The Earth' was released as a 1971 single.

[337] **SALT OF THE EARTH - Johnny Adams** (1972)

(Jagger-Richards)

Rolling Stones original: Beggars Banquet (1968)

Laten John Adams Jr. (b. 1932 - d. 1998). Gospel, Rhythm 'n' Blues, Soul and Jazz singer from New Orleans, Louisiana, USA.

A slow, soulfully-sung cover featuring horns and an electric sitar, Johnny Adams' version of 'Salt Of The Earth' was released as a 1972 single.

[338] **SALT OF THE EARTH - Judy Collins** (1975)

(Jagger-Richards)

Rolling Stones original: Beggars Banquet (1968)

Judith Marjorie Collins (b. 1939). Folk and Pop singer and guitarist from Seattle, Washington, USA.

Judy Collins' version has similarities in both tempo and arrangement to Joan Baez's cover, though this one also has an almost danceable beat. It is on her 1975 album 'Judith'.

[339] **SALT OF THE EARTH - Robin Lane** (1993)

(Jagger-Richards)

Rolling Stones original: Beggars Banquet (1968)

Robin Lane (b. 1947). Rock and Pop singer and guitarist from Los Angeles, California, USA.

A largely acoustic and almost unplugged cover with lovely harmonies, Robin Lane's version of 'Salt Of The Earth' was on 1993's various artists 'Boston Gets Stoned' album.

Whose idea was it to record this song?

"I did this song for AJ Wachtel's 1993 project 'Boston Gets Stoned' that was produced by my good friend Jimmy Miller, who produced the original for the Rolling Stones."

Have you performed this (or any other Stones songs) live?

"During the first days of my band Robin Lane and The Chartbusters we performed 'I'm Free'."

Were the Rolling Stones an influence on your own music?

"I listened to the Stones all the time when I was younger, along with Beatles and lots of other music current in the day. I do think they influenced me some, especially Brian Jones."

[340] **SALT OF THE EARTH - Bettye Lavette** (2010)
(Jagger-Richards)

Rolling Stones original: Beggars Banquet (1968)

Betty Jo Haskins (b. 1946). Soul and Rhythm 'n' Blues singer from Muskegon, Michigan, USA.

Bettye Lavette's fabulous, majestical, Gospel-Soul version is on her 2010 album 'Interpretations: The British Rock Songbook'.

[341] (I CAN'T GET NO) SATISFACTION - Otis Redding (1965)

(Jagger-Richards)

Rolling Stones original: Out Of Our Heads [US version] (1965) + UK/US A-side

Otis Ray Redding Jr. (b. 1941 - d. 1967). Soul and Rhythm 'n' Blues singer from Macon, Georgia, USA.

Ask the general public to name one Rolling Stones song, and the chances are that they'll choose '(I Can't Get No) Satisfaction'. Not only was it the song that propelled The Rolling Stones into the big league up there with The Beatles, but it was also, more than any other record, responsible for the transition in music from Rhythm 'n' Blues to ROCK. Otis Redding's cover, with semi-improvised lyrics and horns, is very exciting indeed. Released as a 1965 single, it got to No. 31 on the US Pop charts, No. 4 on the R&B charts, and No. 33 in the UK.

Otis Redding performing '(I Can't Get No) Satisfaction' on 'Ready, Steady, Go!', 1966 [UK TV]

[342] (I CAN'T GET NO) SATISFACTION - Chris Farlowe (1965)

(Jagger-Richards)

Rolling Stones original: Out Of Our Heads [US version] (1965) + UK/US A-side

Chris Farlowe (John Henry Dighton, b. 1940). Rhythm 'n' Blues, Soul and Pop singer from Islington, London.

Unlike the other half-dozen Jagger-Richards song Chris Farlowe cut in the 60s, he doesn't really put his own stamp on '(I Can't Get No) Satisfaction', but instead, closely imitates Otis Redding (albeit impressively). It is on his 1965 'Farlowe In The Midnight Hour' EP.

[343] **(I CAN'T GET NO) SATISFACTION - The Beach Boys** (1965) *(Not released until 2015)*

(Jagger-Richards)

Rolling Stones original: Out Of Our Heads [US version] (1965) + UK/US A-side

Mike Love (Michael Edward Love, b. 1941 - vocals), Carl Wilson (Carl Dean Wilson, b. 1946 - d. 1998 - vocals and guitar), Al Jardine (Alan Charles Jardine, b. 1942 - vocals and guitar), Brian Wilson (Brian Douglas Wilson, b. 1942 - vocals, bass and piano), Bruce Johnston (Benjamin Baldwin, b. 1942 - vocals and bass) and Dennis Wilson (Dennis Carl Wilson, b. 1944 - d. 1983 - vocals and drums). Surf, Pop and Rock band from Hawthorne, California, USA.

During the 1965 sessions for The Beach Boys' 'Beach Boys' Party!' album, the band did a couple of run-throughs of '(I Can't Get No) Satisfaction', one of them featuring harmonica. Unplugged and acoustic, they're ragged and off-key, but they're also Fun! Fun! Fun! They were finally released 50 years later on 'Beach Boys' Party! - Uncovered and Unplugged'.

[344] **(I CAN'T GET NO) SATISFACTION - The Ventures** (1965)

(Jagger-Richards)

Rolling Stones original: Out Of Our Heads [US version] (1965) + UK/US A-side

Nokie Edwards (Nole Edwards, b. 1935 - d. 2018 - guitar), Don Wilson (Donald Lee Wilson, b. 1933 - d. 2022 - guitar), Bob Bogle (Robert Lenard Bogle, b. 1934 - d. 2009 - bass) and Mel Taylor (b. 1933 - d. 1996 - drums). Mainly instrumental Rock 'n' Roll group from Tacoma, Washington, USA.

America's premier Instrumental group in the 60s, The Ventures' cover follows the original arrangement closely, down to the prominent fuzz guitar - the one *big* difference being that the vocals are replaced by a cheesy organ. It is on their 1965 album 'The Ventures à Go-Go'.

[345] **(I CAN'T GET NO) SATISFACTION - Mary Wells** (1966)
(Jagger-Richards)

Rolling Stones original: Out Of Our Heads [US version] (1965) + UK/US A-side

Mary Esther Wells (b. 1943 - d. 1992). Rhythm 'n' Blues and Soul singer from Detroit, Michigan, USA.

Clearly influenced by Otis Redding's version, Mary Wells' slightly messy but well-sung cover is notable for its fine saxophone solo.

[346] **(I CAN'T GET NO) SATISFACTION - The Supremes** (1966) *(Not released until 2008)*
(Jagger-Richards)

Rolling Stones original: Out Of Our Heads [US version] (1965) + UK/US A-side

Diana Ross (b. 1944), Mary Wilson (b. 1944 - d. 2021) and Florence Ballard (Florence Glenda Chapman, b. 1943 - d. 1976). Pop and Soul vocal trio from Detroit, Michigan, USA.

An interesting outtake that was perhaps quite rightly kept in the can, Diana Ross' voice isn't really gritty enough for their cover of the song, and the guitar is *way* too low in the mix. It turned up on 2008's 'Let the Music Play: Supreme Rarities - 1960-1969 - Motown Lost & Found'.

[347] **(I CAN'T GET NO) SATISFACTION - Manfred Mann** (1966)

(Jagger-Richards)

Rolling Stones original: Out Of Our Heads [US version] (1965) + UK/US A-side

---

Manfred Mann (Manfred Sepse Lubowitz, b. 1940 - keyboards), Paul Jones (Paul Pond, b. 1942 - harmonica), Tom McGuinness (Thomas John Patrick McGuinness, b. 1941 - guitar), Jack Bruce (John Symon Asher Bruce, b. 1943 - d. 2014 - bass), Mike Hugg (Michael John Hugg, b. 1942 - drums and vibes), Lyn Dobson (b. 1939 - saxophone) and Henry Lowther (Thomas Henry Lowther, b. 1941 - trumpet and flute). Rhythm 'n' Blues, Jazz and Pop group from London, UK.

An instrumental, Manfred Mann's highly individual version of '(I Can't Get No) Satisfaction' is a contrasting mix of ferocious guitar and pounding drums on the chorus with improvised keyboards and saxophone on the verses. [Interview is with Manfred Mann]

You released a jazzy instrumental version of 'Satisfaction' (along with other songs) for a 1966 EP... whose idea was this?

"I cannot remember clearly but would like to think it was me."

Much, much later, Manfred Mann's Earth Band recorded 'Play With Fire', an unusual choice of cover... is this a song you had long admired?

"No. It was a song I heard long after it was first recorded and I was surprised it was not better known."

Were the Rolling Stones an influence on your own music (particularly in the R&B days)?

"No. We started out at similar times but we were both influenced by black American blues. But in our group there was a jazz influence as well. The Rolling Stones morphed into being great writers as well."

[348] **(I CAN'T GET NO) SATISFACTION - Aretha Franklin** (1967)

(Jagger-Richards)

Rolling Stones original: Out Of Our Heads [US version] (1965) + UK/US A-side

Aretha Louise Franklin (b. 1942 - d. 2018). Soul, Gospel, Jazz and Pop singer and pianist from Memphis, Tennessee, USA.

A minor UK hit single at No. 37, Aretha Franklin's cover is very much in her own, unmistakable, style. It can also be found on her 1967 album 'Aretha Arrives'.

[349] **(I CAN'T GET NO) SATISFACTION - José Feliciano** (1970)

(Jagger-Richards)

Rolling Stones original: Out Of Our Heads [US version] (1965) + UK/US A-side

José Monserrate Feliciano García (b. 1945). Latin Pop singer and guitarist from Lares, Puerto Rico.

In a very fast Bossa Nova arrangement, complete with acoustic guitar, strings and brass, José Feliciano's version of '(I Can't Get No) Satisfaction' is on his 1970 'Fireworks' album.

[350] **(I CAN'T GET NO) SATISFACTION - Ken Boothe** (1970)

(Jagger-Richards)

Rolling Stones original: Out Of Our Heads [US version] (1965) + UK/US A-side

Kenneth George Boothe (b. 1948). Reggae singer from Kingston, Jamaica.

Combining a relaxed Reggae rhythm with remarkably Otis-like vocals, Ken Boothe's impressive cover of '(I Can't Get No) Satisfaction' was released as a 1970 single.

[351] **(I CAN'T GET NO) SATISFACTION - Jerry Lee Lewis** (1973) *(Not released until 1986)*

(Jagger-Richards)

Rolling Stones original: Out Of Our Heads [US version] (1965) + UK/US A-side

(b. 1935 - d. 2022). Rock 'n' Roll and Country singer and pianist from Ferriday, Louisiana, USA.

Played at a lethargically slow pace with prominent Blues-Rock guitar by Rory Gallagher, Jerry Lee Lewis' cover of '(I Can't Get No) Satisfaction' makes a fascinating outtake, but one that was probably deservedly kept in the can for 13 years. More recently, an alternate take has surfaced featuring lead vocals by Rory.

[352] **(I CAN'T GET NO) SATISFACTION - Bubblerock** (1973)

(Jagger-Richards)

Rolling Stones original: Out Of Our Heads [US version] (1965) + UK/US A-side

Jonathan King under a pseudonym (Kenneth George King, b. 1944). Pop singer, producer and music entrepreneur from Marylebone, London.

Throughout much of the '70s, Jonathan King had numerous hits under a variety of different names, including The Weathermen, Sakkarin, Shag, One Hundred Ton and a Feather - and Bubblerock. Jonathan's/Bubblerock's slow, Folk-styled version of '(I Can't Get No) Satisfaction' was A UK hit single at No. 29, as well as a No. 9 hit in the Republic of Ireland.

You had a hit under the name Bubblerock with '(I Can't Get No) Satisfaction'... Have you ever had any feedback or comments from members of The Rolling Stones?

"Indeed! Mick told me, in person (whilst waiting for our cars at the Beverly Wiltshire Hotel) 'The second best version ever'!"

You also recorded 'Get Off Of My Cloud' as a follow-up...

"I actually think Cloud is even better."

Jonathan King performing '(I Can't Get No) Satisfaction' on 'Top Of The Pops', 1974 [UKTV]

[353] **(I CAN'T GET NO) SATISFACTION - The Troggs** (1975)
(Jagger-Richards)

Rolling Stones original: Out Of Our Heads [US version] (1965) + UK/US A-side

Reg Presley (Reginald Maurice Ball, b. 1941, d. 2013 - lead vocals), Richard Moore (Richard Glen Moore, b. 1949 - d. 2016 - guitar and backing vocals), Tony Murray (bass and backing vocals) and Ronnie Bond (Ronald James Bullis, b. 1940, d. 1992 - drums). Rock and Pop Group from Andover, Hampshire, UK.

With snotty, snarled vocals, a distorted guitar on the verge of feedback and pounding drums, The Troggs' cover ain't pretty, but it's very exciting! It was released as a single but failed to chart, despite some TV promotion.

The Troggs performing '(I Can't Get No) Satisfaction' on 'Supersonic', 1975 [UK TV]

[354] **(I CAN'T GET NO) SATISFACTION** - Devo (1977)
(Jagger-Richards)

Rolling Stones original: Out Of Our Heads [US version] (1965) + UK/US A-side

Mark Mothersbaugh (Mark Allen Mothersbaugh, b. 1950 - vocals, keyboards and guitar), Bob Mothersbaugh (Robert Leroy Mothersbaugh, Jr., b. 1952 - guitar and vocals), Bob Casale (Robert Edward Pizzute, Jr., b. 1952 - d. 2014 - guitar, keyboards and vocals), Gerald Casale (Gerald Vincent Pizzute, b. 1948 - bass guitar, bass synthesizer and vocals) and Alan Myers (b. 1954 - d. 2013 - drums). New Wave, Synth-Pop and Art Punk band from Akron, Ohio, USA.

Love it or hate it, there are very few Stones covers that are quite as mind-blowingly original as Devo's version of '(I Can't Get No) Satisfaction'. Sounding and looking like malfunctioning robots, they don't so much cover the song as totally re-invent it. Released as a 1977 single (and getting to No. 41 in the UK charts), it was also on the following year's 'Q: Are We Not Men? A: We Are Devo!' album. [Interview is with Gerald Casale]

Whose idea was it to record this song?

"DEVO was born from collaboration and experimentation. Our seminal, mid-seventies times were pregnant with spontaneous creativity. Our 'cover' of 'Satisfaction' was a prime example. All 5 original members were gathered in an unheated storage space next to a car wash in Mogadore Ohio in the winter of 1976. That was the best facility we could afford at the time. Bob Casale (Bob 2) started improvising on his guitar mostly to warm his frozen fingers. He began playing the robotic figure that defines our cover. Alan sat down at his drums and started playing a very abstract beat to Bob's riff. I laughed and yelled out 'that sounds like backwards reggae!' I proceeded to add the bass part that made it in to the final song minus the chord changes. Mark, who had been setting up his mini-moog, took notice and started playing a pointalistic, 6 note rotating figure over all of it. Bob Mothersbaugh (Bob 1) followed him on guitar picking out the same note pattern but adding a harmonic.

We were 'in the zone' and typical of Devo just kept playing it over and over. At some point Mark started barking out the lyrics to the Stones 'Paint it Black' over the top of the music. It wasn't really working. Bob Casale stopped us and asked Mark to sing 'Satisfaction' lyrics instead. We all thought 'Satisfaction' was the ultimate 1960's rock song. Mark obliged and barked out the cadence that defines the vocal in the version we unleashed upon the world. I added the bass note changes along with Bob 1's chord changes for the chorus 'and I try, and I try'. We smiled, laughed and locked into that groove for at least an hour vowing to play it live as soon as we could find a venue."

Have you performed any other Stones songs live?

"No, we never played any other Stones songs, period."

What did the Rolling Stones think of your version?

"Record companies and music publishers took intellectual property seriously in those pre-digital, pre-sample and mix-tape times. The head of legal affairs at Warner Brothers Records informed our manager, Elliot Roberts, that we would have to get permission from the Rolling Stones to include tour 'Satisfaction' cover on our debut record 'Q: Are We Not Men A: We Are Devo'. He maintained that our cover was legally a 'parody' and without permission we could be sued even if the Stones maintained all the publishing. Elliot set up a meeting with Stones lawyer, Peter Rudge, and the man himself, Mick Jagger, at Peter's NYC office in March of 1978.

Mick arrived looking very sleepy. He had a velour mock turtleneck top, pinwale corduroy bell bottom pants, dark socks and no shoes. I remember wondering where he came from without shoes but of course was afraid to ask. Peter introduced us and Mick grinned and shook our hands before plopping down into one of the plush club chairs. Peter asked Mick if he'd like anything to drink. Mick asked for a glass of Claret. Peter opened a wine cabinet behind his desk and quickly poured a goblet full of red elixir. He handed it to Mick. Mick sniffed and swirled and then set the glass on the floor next to him. He turned and said, 'OK, let's hear it then'.

Mark got up, audio cassette in hand and put it in the boom box sitting on the mantle of the fireplace. He hit play and scampered back to his chair. The volume was loud, but not too loud, and Mick listened with his head down swirling his wine. I felt my stomach drop thinking 'he doesn't like it'. That's when he stood up, put his glass on the mantle, and started dancing in front of the fireplace just like Mick Jagger, sliding moves in his socks on the hardwood floor!!! He declared 'I like it, I like it!'.

After that it was all smiles and niceties with Peter saying he'd talk to Elliot and wrap up the deal. The deal of course was that even though all the music was different from the Stones' 'Satisfaction' they would retain 100% of the publishing on our version. We would control the master. Needless to say then and there in Peter's office Mark and I were doing our best 'we're not worthy' Bill and Ted's Great Adventure' imitation before that even existed.

We returned to LA the next day, a Saturday, and breathlessly told Elliot Roberts the good news on Monday morning. He looked at us kind of rolling his eyes and said, 'ya I already spoke with Peter. In fact I had already told him to tell Mick to say he liked it prior to your meeting because Devo was going to make the Stones a lot of money'. Elliot would periodically give us lessons in business reality throughout our association with him. But that first one still stings."

[355] **(I CAN'T GET NO) SATISFACTION - Sam and Dave** (1982)

(Jagger-Richards)

Rolling Stones original: Out Of Our Heads [US version] (1965) + UK/US A-side

Samuel David Moore (b. 1935) and David Prater Jr., (b. 1937 - d. 1988). Soul and Rhythm 'n' Blues duo from Miami, Florida, USA.

Performed Otis Redding-style, Sam and Dave's version of '(I Can't Get No) Satisfaction' is marred a little by the thin trebly mix. It is on the duo's 1983 'Hold On We're Coming' album.

[356] **(I CAN'T GET NO) SATISFACTION - Junior Wells** (1997)

(Jagger-Richards)

Rolling Stones original: Out Of Our Heads [US version] (1965) + UK/US A-side

Amos Wells Blakemore Jr. (b. 1934 - d. 1998). Blues and Rhythm 'n' Blues singer and harmonicist from West Memphis, Arkansas, USA.

Unbelievably, Junior Wells' audacious cover of '(I Can't Get No) Satisfaction' is sung over a powerful 'Smokestack Lightning' backing - and it mostly works too! It is on 1997's 'Paint It, Blue: Songs of The Rolling Stones'.

[357] **(I CAN'T GET NO) SATISFACTION - Britney Spears** (2000)

(Jagger-Richards)

Rolling Stones original: Out Of Our Heads [US version] (1965) + UK/US A-side

Britney Jean Spears (b. 1981). Pop singer from McComb, Mississippi, USA.

Starting off very slowly with just vocals and acoustic guitar, Britney Spears' cover of '(I Can't Get No) Satisfaction' then develops into a very contemporary-sounding breathy Dance version. It was first released on the Japanese edition of her 2000 'Oops!... I Did It Again' CD.

[358] **(I CAN'T GET NO) SATISFACTION - The Heptones** (2001)

(Jagger-Richards)

Rolling Stones original: Out Of Our Heads [US version] (1965) + UK/US A-side

Leroy Sibbles (b. 1949), Earl Morgan and Barry Llewellyn (d. 2011). Rocksteady and Reggae trio from Kingston, Jamaica.

The Heptones' Reggae cover of '(I Can't Get No) Satisfaction' is far more modern (and far less impressive vocally) than Ken Boothe's version over 3 decades earlier. It was first issued on the 2001 various artists 'Reggae Rocks - The Tide Is High: A Tribute to Rock 'n' Roll' CD, also appearing on the following year's 'Paint It Black: A Reggae Tribute to The Rolling Stones' album.

[359] (I CAN'T GET NO) SATISFACTION - Jill Saward (2010)

(Jagger-Richards)

Rolling Stones original: Out Of Our Heads [US version] (1965) + UK/US A-side

(b. 1953). Jazz, Funk and Pop singer, flutist and percussionist from Tooting, London, UK. Best known for being the lead singer of Shakatak.

A light Jazz singer who has fronted one of the genres most successful bands for decades isn't going to cut a convincing cover of '(I Can't Get No) Satisfaction', right? Wrong! Backed by a band that closely follows the Stones' original template, Jill Saward's powerful, sassy vocals are a revelation. It's the highlight of 2010's various artists 'A Tribute To The Rolling Stones' album.

Whose idea was it to record this song?

"Our sound man Nick Smith was our engineer and producer on many Shakatak cuts. He loved the analogue way of recording and wanted to make some high quality tribute albums with full band and guest artists. He offered the cover to me and yes, 'Wow, love to do it' was the response. A large step away vocally for me but I enjoyed every minute of it."

Have you ever performed this or any other Stones song live?

"In my jazz rock days I was with a band called Fusion Orchestra who had something of a cult following 1970-75. We used to perform 'Honky Tonk Women' as an encore, it was always a showstopper!"

Were the Rolling Stones an influence on your own music, with or without Shakatak?

"The Stones are more of an influence to me these days in that their sheer resilience and longevity is inspiring. I watch their concerts and the energy they give, and try to bring some of that to our performances."

[360] **SHANG A DOO LANG - Adrienne Poster** (1964)

(Jagger-Richards)

Rolling Stones original: 1963 Demo: Bootleg only (excerpt)

Adrienne Luanne Poster (b. 1949). Pop singer and actress from Hampstead, London, UK.

A Spector-like Pop song that has more than a passing semblance to The Crystals 'He's Sure The Boy I Love', Adrienne Poster does a reasonable enough job on it. A flop single, she'd have far more success as an actress, appearing (under the name Adrienne *Posta*) in such cult '60s movies as 'To Sir With Love', 'Here We Go Round The Mulberry Bush' and 'Up The Junction'.

[361] SHATTERED - Rock City Morgue (2003)

(Jagger-Richards)

Rolling Stones original: Some Girls (1978) + US A-side (1978)

Rick Slave (vocals), Johnny Brashear (guitar), Sean Yseult (Shauna Reynolds, b. 1965 - bass and piano) and Keith Hajjar (drums). Rock band from New Orleans, Louisiana, USA.

The 'Some Girls' album was heavily influenced by the Punk, New Wave (and to a lesser extent Disco) of New York, with 'Shattered' being a prime example. Rock City Morgue's version ups the Punk quota with an increased tempo, attitude-filled vocals and noisier guitars, and is included on their 2003 album 'Some Ghouls'. [Interview is with Sean Yseult]

Whose idea was it to record this song?

"It was actually our singer's idea, Rik Slave. He's a punk from way back but loves The Rolling Stones."

Do/did you perform this or any other Stones songs live?

"Yes! We would play it live. Always a blast. I think that was the only Stones song we covered."

Were the Rolling Stones an influence on your own music?

"I'm sure I was influenced by the Stones, because I grew up hearing them for my entire childhood; my dad was a huge fan and would blast it, loud! The music that made me want to play in a band were The Cramps, The Ramones, and The Birthday Party. But I love the Rolling Stones, of course!"

[362] **SHE SMILED SWEETLY** - Love Affair (1967)

(Jagger-Richards)

Rolling Stones original: Between The Buttons (1967)

Steve Ellis (Stephen John Ellis, b. 1950 - vocals), Rex Brayley (Rex Charles Brayley, b. 1948 - guitar), Mick Jackson (Michael Jackson - bass), Maurice Bacon (b. 1952 - drums) and Lynton Guest (b. 1951 - keyboards). Pop and Soul band from London, UK.

A seldom-heard but excellent song from 'Between The Buttons', Love Affair's version of 'She Smiled Sweetly' has a slightly more adventurous organ (played by Keith on the Stones' original!), but is otherwise very similar in arrangement. It was released as the band's debut single in 1967, but failed to chart. [Interview is with Steve Ellis]

What made you choose this song in particular?

"We had three managers, two who worked at Decca, they brought it to rehearsals one night. We were 16 I did not have a clue about proper singing. We were a Soul band. We argued with them but as was the way then, we did not know any better. It was in the wrong key and it was dire. I am fairly confident we recorded it at Abbey Road so we were more interested to see if The Beatles or the like may turn up. We took it along to the BBC and Tony Blackburn was outside, we asked him to play it and he did. It made my ma very happy, but we all hated it, it was terrible."

Have members of the Stones ever commented on your version?

"Not to my knowledge."

Do you perform the song live?

"We did it a few times in 1967, but it stiffed, we hated it with a passion. Played with the Stones at Wembley a year later [NME Poll Winners Concert 1968], they were surprise guests and they were brilliant. When I went solo after Love Affair I covered 'Gimme Shelter'. People seem to like it, a great song."

[363] **SHE SMILED SWEETLY - Lindsey Buckingham** (2011)

(Jagger-Richards)

Rolling Stones original: Between The Buttons (1967)

Lindsey Adams Buckingham (b. 1949). Rock and Rock-Pop singer and guitarist from Palo Alto, California, USA. Best-known as a former member of Fleetwood Mac.

Similar to his cover of 'I Am Waiting' (included elsewhere in this book), Lindsey Buckingham's version of 'She Smiled Sweetly' is accompanied only by his impressive guitar playing. It is on his 2011 album 'Seeds We Sow'.

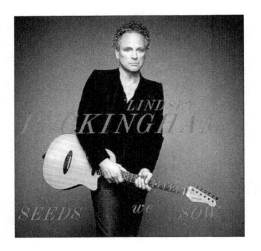

[364] **SHE WAS HOT - The Karl Hendricks Trio** (1992)

(Jagger-Richards)

Rolling Stones original: Undercover (1983) + UK/US A-side (1984)

Karl Hendricks (b. 1970 - d. 2017 - vocals and guitar), Tim Parker (bass) and Tom Hoffman (drums). Alternative Rock band from Pittsburgh, Pennsylvania, USA. Disbanded 2016.

One of the more straight-forward Rock songs on the 'Undercover' album, The Karl Hendricks Trio's frantic version is twice as fast and with none of the original's subtleties. It was included on their 1992 album 'Buick Electra'.

[365] SHE'S A RAINBOW - The Glass Menagerie (1968)
(Jagger-Richards)

Rolling Stones original: Their Satanic Majesties Request (1967) + US A-side (1967)

Lou Stonebridge (vocals and organ), Alan Kendall (b. 1944 - guitar), John Medley (bass) and Bill Atkinson (d. 1992 - drums). Psychedelic Rock band from Manchester, UK. Disbanded in 1970.

One of the less menacing and more commercial songs on 'Their Satanic Majesties Request', The Glass Menagerie's more straight-forward organ-dominated cover was released as a 1968 single.

[366] SHE'S A RAINBOW - Molly Tuttle (2020)
(Jagger-Richards)

Rolling Stones original: Their Satanic Majesties Request (1967) + US A-side (1967)

Molly Rose Tuttle (b. 1993). Bluegrass, Americana and Country singer, guitarist and banjoist from Santa Clara, California, USA.

A modern Folk-tinged Pop arrangement with impressive acoustic guitar picking, Molly Tuttle's cover of 'She's A Rainbow' is on her 2020 album '...But I'd Rather Be With You'.

[367] SHE'S SO COLD - Vitamin String Quartet (2003)

(Jagger-Richards)

Rolling Stones original: Emotional Rescue (1980) + US single (1980)

Modern Classical band from Los Angeles, California, USA.

A New Wave-inspired song from 1980's 'Emotional Rescue' album, it perhaps isn't the first Stones song that springs to mind as being suitable for a string quartet! Yet, amongst more obvious titles like 'Angie', 'As Tears Go By', 'Play With Fire' and 'Wild Horses', it is included on Vitamin String Quartet's 2003 album 'The String Quartet Tribute to The Rolling Stones'. [Interview is with VSQ creative director James Curtiss]

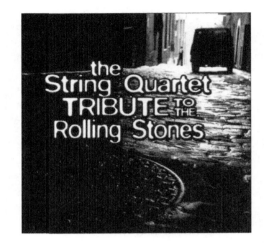

Whose idea was it to record this song?

"Vitamin String Quartet has been around for so long, with so many different people involved in creating what VSQ ultimately has become throughout the years, that the notion of whose idea it probably was in the first place has been lost to time. Sorry if that's not the most romantic answer, but it's true. Because VSQ is a collaborative effort between A&R creatives, producers, musicians, etc. it's also ultimately not the point - the point is for a string quartet to pay tribute to seminal rock, pop, and contemporary artists, and the Stones most definitely qualify for that distinction."

Do you perform this or any other Stones songs live?

"We've been known to break off a rendition of '(I Can't Get No) Satisfaction'. Honestly, we should add more Stones to our rep. There's just too much that is so essential, it's like, "where do you start?""

Were the Rolling Stones an influence on your own music?

"See the above answer on seminal artists. To elaborate, a lot of what we do stems from the work that artists create that transcends its original intention. The Stones influence VSQ as much as The Stones influenced every band that followed in their seismic wake. We wouldn't have so much of what VSQ is able to translate without the influence felt by The Rolling Stones. Like the family tree of artists who take from them is so massive it might as well be a forest. And at the top of the forest, surveying all, would be VSQ."

[368] **SHINE A LIGHT - Jennifer Warnes** (1976)
(Jagger-Richards)

Rolling Stones original: Exile On Main St. (1972)

Jennifer Jean Warnes (b. 1947), Country Rock and Pop singer from Seattle, Washington, USA.

A song initially written in 1968 by Mick Jagger as 'Get A Line On You' (allegedly about his concern over Brian Jones' worsening drug habit), it was later reworked for inclusion on 'Exile On Main St.'. Jennifer Warnes' polished orchestrated cover is on her 1976 'Jennifer Warnes' album.

[369] **SHINE A LIGHT - Allison Crowe** (2003)

(Jagger-Richards)

Rolling Stones original: Exile On Main St. (1972)

> Allison Louise Crowe (b. 1981). Rock, Pop, Folk, Jazz and Celtic singer, pianist and guitarist from Nanaimo, British Columbia, Canada.
>
> More intense and soulful than other covers, Allison Crowe's inspired rendition makes you believe every word of the song! It was initially released on Allison's 2003 EP 'Tidings', and then the following year on her album of the same name.

Whose idea was it to record this song?

"When coming up with ideas for songs for my Christmas album 'Tidings' all those years ago, my manager Adrian actually suggested it would be a good fit!"

Have you performed this (or any other Stones songs) live?

"I have performed 'Shine a Light' in concert, many times. It's more fun and full to play with a band in my opinion, just for that energy, but it's pretty fun to play solo too. Nice combination of rock and blues."

Were the Rolling Stones an influence on your own music?

"I'm not entirely certain, but I have always loved the Stones' sound. 'Sympathy For The Devil' has long been another favourite of mine, particularly when I heard it in 'Interview With The Vampire' in the '90s!"

[370] **SILVER TRAIN - Johnny Winter** (1973)

(Jagger-Richards)

Rolling Stones original: Goats Head Soup (1973) + UK/US B-side (1973)

John Dawson Winter III (b. 1944 - d. 2014). Blues-Rock singer and guitarist from Beaumont, Texas, USA.

An up-tempo song with slide guitar from 'Goats Head Soup' which was a bit *too* similar to the previous album's 'All Down The Line' to be an out-and-out classic, Johnny Winter heard an early demo, and issued his own single of the song several months prior to the Stones' release. Played a little slower, it features a good double-tracked vocal, as well as powerful twin slide guitars.

[371] **SILVER TRAIN - Carla Olson and Mick Taylor** (1990)

(Jagger-Richards)

Rolling Stones original: Goats Head Soup (1973) + UK/US B-side (1973)

(b. 1952). Rock singer and guitarist from Austin, Texas, USA.

Recorded with the man who played lead on the Stones' recording, Carla Olson and Mick Taylor's extended workout has basically the same arrangement. The guitar playing is impeccable of course.

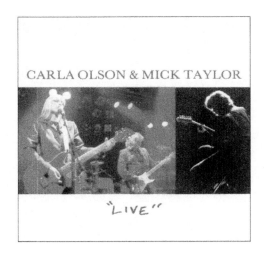

[372] SING THIS ALL TOGETHER - The Orange Bicycle (1968)

(Jagger-Richards)

Rolling Stones original: Their Satanic Majesties Request (1967)

Robb Storme (Robert Scales - vocals), Bernie Lee (guitar and vocals), John Bachini (bass, guitar and vocals), Wil Malones (Wilson Malone - keyboards, drums and vocals) and Kevin Currie (drums). Psychedelic Pop band from London. Disbanded in 1971.

Often compared unfavourably to The Beatles' 'Sgt. Pepper's Lonely Hearts Club Band', it is clear from the album's opening notes that 'Their Satanic Majesties Request' wasn't going to be cosy family-friendly entertainment. Lacking the darkness and faint menace of the Stones' original, The Orange Bicycle's cover of 'Sing This All Together' features stunning harmonies with simple but powerful guitar, bass, piano and drums backing. In fact, it sounds very much like The Tremeloes.

[373] THE SINGER NOT THE SONG - Pan's People (1974)

(Jagger-Richards)

Rolling Stones original: December's Children (and Everybody's) (1965) + UK B-side (1965)

Babs Lord (b. 1945), Dee Dee Wilde (b. 1946), Ruth Pearson (b. 1946 - d. 2017), Louise Clarke (b. 1949 - d. 2012) and Cherry Gillespie (b. 1955). Dance Troupe and occasional singing group from the UK.

As well as being the UK's most famous dance troupe, Pan's People recorded a few songs during the mid-'70s, including Jagger-Richards' 'The Singer Not The Song'. Throwing everything they could at it to make it a success (including strings, a saxophone solo and Peter Frampton-style 'Talk box' guitar), unfortunately nothing could disguise the fact that they couldn't really sing. It was released as the B-side of their 1974 single 'You Can Really Rock and Roll Me'.

[374] **THE SINGER NOT THE SONG - Alex Chilton** (1977)

(Jagger-Richards)

Rolling Stones original: December's Children (and Everybody's) (1965) + UK B-side (1965)

William Alexander Chilton (b. 1950 - d. 2010). Power Pop, Soul and Proto-Punk singer, guitarist and keyboardist from Memphis, Tennessee, USA. Best remembered as the leading member of The Box Tops and Big Star.

A little more aggressive yet also more polished than the Stones' slightly off-key original, Alex Chilton's excellent New Wave cover is on his 'Singer Not The Song' EP.

[375] **THE SINGER NOT THE SONG - Patti Palladin** (1994)

(Jagger-Richards)

Rolling Stones original: December's Children (and Everybody's) (1965) + UK B-side (1965)

Punk Rock and New Wave singer from New York, USA.

With an arrangement very similar to Alex Chilton's version, Patti Palladin's cover of 'The Singer Not The Song' first surfaced on 1994's 'Destination: Bomp! - The Best of Bomp Records' First 20 Years' various artists compilation, though it was probably recorded several years earlier.

[376] **SISTER MORPHINE - Marianne Faithfull** (1969)

(Jagger-Richards-Faithfull)

Rolling Stones original: Sticky Fingers (1971)

Marianne Evelyn Gabriel Faithfull (b. 1946). Pop, Rock, Folk and Jazz singer from London, UK.

Famously co-written by Marianne (something she wasn't initially credited with), her 1969 version features backing by Mick Jagger (acoustic guitar), Ry Cooder (slide guitar and bass), Jack Nitzsche (piano and organ) and Charlie Watts (drums). It is of course absolutely wonderful - not that many people in the UK heard it at the time: released as the B-side of 'Something Better', Decca quickly withdrew the single due to the drug references. In 1979 she re-cut the song, and if anything it was even better thanks to her more world-weary vocals.

[377] **SISTER MORPHINE - Ren Harvieu** (2011)

(Jagger-Richards-Faithfull)

Rolling Stones original: Sticky Fingers (1971)

Lauren Maria Harvieu (b. 1990). Pop, Rock and Soul singer from Broughton, Salford, UK.

Wisely keeping away from trying to copy Marianne Faithfull's version, Ren Harvieu's stunning cover of 'Sister Morphine' features her backed solely by piano. It is on 2011's various artists 'Sticky Soul Fingers: A Rolling Stones Tribute'.

[378] **SITTIN' ON A FENCE - Twice As Much** (1966)

(Jagger-Richards)

Rolling Stones original: Flowers (1967) (recorded in 1965)

Dave Skinner (David Ferguson Skinner, b. 1946) and Andrew Rose (Andrew Colin Campbell Rose, b. 1946). Pop duo from London.

As with the equally excellent 'Ride On Baby' (a minor hit for Chris Farlowe), The Rolling Stones' version of 'Sittin' On A Fence' was an 'Aftermath' outtake that wasn't released until the US 'Flowers' compilation in 1967. Twice As Much's harmonized version is in a higher key, with the duo sounding (and looking) like a more trendy Peter and Gordon. Released as a single, it peaked at No. 25 in the UK charts, and was their biggest hit. [Interview is with Dave Skinner]

How did you end up recording an exclusive Jagger-Richards song?

"In 1965, Andrew Rose and I were a duo playing in folk clubs like 'Bunjies' and 'Les Cousins' in London, private functions, restaurants and basically anywhere we could get a gig. We were playing at a private party at 'Ye Olde Cheshire Cheese' pub in Fleet St and there was a girl there called Linda Solomans whose family knew Andrew Oldham from the south of France days. She really liked what we were doing and said she would tell ALO about us. This led to a recording audition with him at IBC Studios in Portland Place with Glyn Johns engineering where we recorded 3 songs live - Just a 6-string acoustic and a 12 string acoustic and our voices - one of which we had written. This resulted in us signing a recording and publishing deal with Immediate records. ALO thought 'Sittin' On A Fence' suited us and that's how we came to record it for our first single."

Did you perform this or any other Stones songs live?

"We used to include the song in our set lists plus 'Play with Fire' and 'As Tears Go By'."

Were the Rolling Stones an influence on your own music?

"The Stones were an influence in so far as song structure and the art of 'crafting' a song were concerned. Also by opening us up to other artists and writers who we hadn't maybe listened to as much, like a lot more blues players both black and white, whereas ALO turned us on to more pop oriented writers and bands."

[379] **(WALKIN' THRU THE) SLEEPY CITY - The Mighty Avengers** (1965)
(Jagger-Richards)

Rolling Stones original: 1964 Demo: Metamorphosis (1975)

Tony Campbell (guitar and vocals), Kevin 'Bep' Mahon (guitar and harmonica), Mike Linnell (vocals and bass) and 'Biffo' Beech (drums and vocals). Beat group from Coventry, UK.

One of the better songs that Mick and Keith gave away, The Mighty Avengers' version is in a higher key than the Stones' demo (eventually released on 'Metamorphosis') but is otherwise similar. It was released as a non-charting single in 1965. *See [43] for interview!*

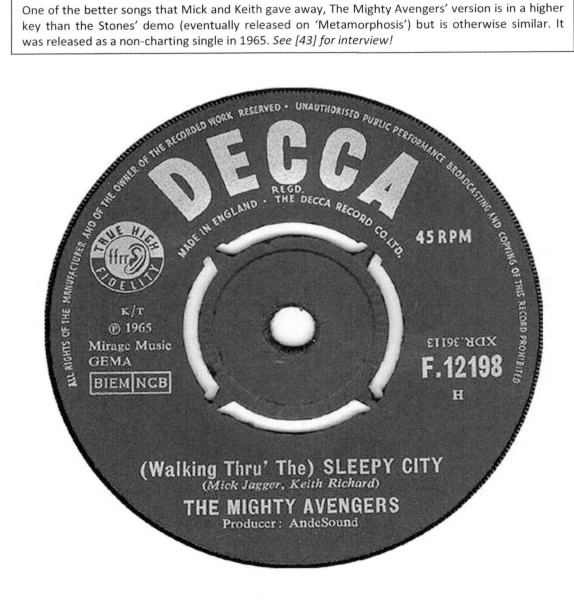

[380] **(WALKIN' THRU THE) SLEEPY CITY - Luna** (2017)
(Jagger-Richards)

Rolling Stones original: 1964 Demo: Metamorphosis (1975)

Dean Wareham (b. 1963 - vocals and guitar), Sean Eden (guitar), Britta Phillips (bass and keyboards) and Lee Wall (drums). Indie Pop and Indie Rock band from New York City, New York, USA.

Luna's interesting *extremely* slow ballad revival of '(Walkin' Thru The) Sleepy City' is on their 2017 album 'A Sentimental Education'. [Interview is with Dean Wareham]

Whose idea was it to record this song?

"It was my idea to record '(Walkin' Thru The) Sleepy City'. 'Metamorphosis' has long been one of my favourite Stones albums even if it's not 100% Rolling Stones."

Have you performed this (or any other Stones songs) live?

"We have not played this one live, but we have played 'Waiting On A Friend' (which we also recorded), and 'Just My Imagination (Running Away with Me)' which is the Smokey Robinson song but I discovered it via the Rolling Stones."

Were the Rolling Stones an influence on your own music?

"Yes. The Rolling Stones were most certainly a big influence on Luna, being a twin-guitar band. As Keith Richards likes to say, it's not about one guitarist, it's about how two guitars work together."

[381] **SO MUCH IN LOVE - The Mighty Avengers** (1964)

(Jagger-Richards)

Rolling Stones original: 1963 Demo: Bootleg only (excerpt)

Tony Campbell (guitar and vocals), Kevin 'Bep' Mahon (guitar and harmonica), Mike Linnell (vocals and bass) and 'Biffo' Beech (drums and vocals). Beat group from Coventry, UK.

One of Jagger-Richards' most convincing attempts at writing a Mersey-style Beat song, The Mighty Avengers' single was the band's sole UK hit at No. 46, though it did better in Australia at No. 22. *See [43] for interview!*

[382] SO MUCH IN LOVE - The Swinging Blue Jeans (1965) *(Not released until 2019)*

(Jagger-Richards)

Rolling Stones original: 1963 Demo: Bootleg only (excerpt)

Ray Ennis (Raymond Vincent Ennis, b. 1940 - vocals and guitar), Ralph Ellis (b. 1942 - vocals and guitar), Les Braid (b. 1937 - d. 2005 - bass) and Norman Kuhlke (b. 1942 - drums). Beat Group from Liverpool.

Along with The Searchers and Gerry and The Pacemakers, The Swinging Blue Jeans were one of *the* groups to come out of Liverpool in 1963. A few years back, an inspired BBC-recorded cover of 'So Much In Love' surfaced online - much to the surprise of former band members! It is on the digital-only 'On The Radio' collection. [Interview is with Ralph Ellis]

Where did you find the song? Was it something you performed on stage at the time and/or considered releasing on record?

"I don't remember anything about this song, where we got it from, or our involvement with it! It is definitely me singing the lead but other than that, I don't recall anything else about it. We did not include it in our stage performances and I don't remember making this recording."

Do you have any other memories of the Rolling Stones? I believe you toured with them?

"Although we toured a lot with the Stones, I do not have many tales to tell. This is because when we arrived at Venues, we had little time to meet due to sound checks, checking in hotels, clean up and a meal before performing. After the show, we were glad to get back to the hotel to rest or... on the road to the next venue!

One I remember, however, was when we were on the Chuck Berry tour in May 1964. I was standing backstage with Keith Richards (who was visiting), when Chuck came out of his dressing room on his way to the stage... he was sweating profusely. After him playing a couple of numbers, I said to Keith, 'Keith, his guitar is out of tune and he can't remember his words!' Keith said 'Yeah man, but that's Chuck Berry ain't it!!' It came as a shock to me, but to Keith, he couldn't do anything wrong."

[383] **SO MUCH IN LOVE - The Herd** (1966)

(Jagger-Richards)

Rolling Stones original: 1963 Demo: Bootleg only (excerpt)

Terry Clark (vocals and guitar), Gary Taylor (guitar and vocals), Louis Cennamo (Louis David Cennamo, b. 1946 - bass), Mick Underwood (Michael John Underwood, b. 1945) and Andy Bown (Andrew Steven Bown, b. 1946 - keyboards). Beat, Rhythm 'n' Blues and Psychedelic Pop band from London, UK.

A highly successful band when led by Peter Frampton in 1967-1968, an earlier line-up of The Herd released a nice organ-accompanied version of 'So Much In Love' as a 1966 single. [Interview is with Louis Cennamo]

Did you learn the song via The Mighty Avengers' version or a different source?

"I did play on the track but no recall of it. The Herd's hits came after I had moved on to my next project, the first James Taylor album on Apple Records."

Did you perform this or any other Stones songs live?

"In terms of their own songs, no. But my first band 'The Dimensions', a teenage band that included Rod Stewart, were influenced by the Stones before they had started doing their own material."

Were the Rolling Stones an influence on your own music?

"Rod and I went to Eel Pie Island a couple of times to watch them playing Chuck Berry, Bo Diddley and Jimmy Reed songs to a packed house, and we later used to support them at Eel Pie and Studio 51. Like many bands at the time, influenced by The Beatles and Stones, we became an R&B band, supporting the Stones at the above venues, and later with singer Jimmy Powell (and the Five Dimensions) at Alexandra Palace."

[384] **SO MUCH IN LOVE - The Inmates** (1980)

(Jagger-Richards)

Rolling Stones original: 1963 Demo: Bootleg only (excerpt)

Bill Hurley (vocals), Peter 'Gunn' Staines (Peter Ronald Staines, guitar and vocals), Tony Oliver (Anthony Oliver - guitar), Ben Donelly (bass) and Jim Russell (drums). Rhythm 'n' Blues band from North London, UK.

With just a hint of a modern guitar and drum sound without losing that 60s retro feel, The Inmates included a wonderful version of 'So Much In Love' on their 1980 'Shot In The Dark' album.

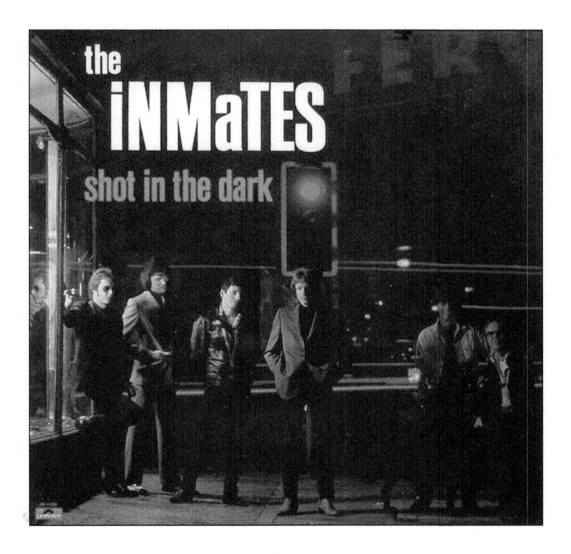

[385] **SO MUCH IN LOVE - Roxanne Fontana** (2018)

(Jagger-Richards)

Rolling Stones original: 1963 Demo: Bootleg only (excerpt)

Roseann Fontana (b. 1959). Blues-Rock, Rock 'n' Roll and Folk Rock singer and guitarist from Brooklyn, New York, USA.

A long-time Stones fanatic (she ran an officially-recognised Brian Jones fan club back in the '70s), Roxanne Fontana released a nice The Inmates-influenced version of 'So Much In Love' as a 2018 single.

Whose idea was it to record this song?

"It is my idea. I love the song, the version I heard by The Inmates, back in the late 1970s. I always wanted to record it, and loved their version so much, that when the time was right - meaning living in England with access to my friend Tony Oliver, rhythm guitarist of The Inmates - that I would ask him to produce it, play on it, etc. I am so happy he said yes because I love my version. Tony played guitars, bass... the video we done for it was some other musicians I have played with, so we could pull off the video as a band. I understand that at least Mick has heard it, and likes it."

Have you performed this (or any other Stones songs) live?

"I can't remember, if I did it would have been a New York City show I did right after it came out. I can't remember if it was on the set list or not. Yes, previously I have performed 'Till the Next Goodbye', at a show at Webster Hall, NYC, which I only remember because of how greatly it was received... but after all that is their ultimate NYC song. And I have performed '2000 Man' perhaps once or twice, or more. I'm actually planning another."

Were the Rolling Stones an influence on your own music?

"The Rolling Stones are an influence on more than my music, but yes they are. Growing up and reading all those books, the mythology... I am such a vagabond, I'm blaming them. Musically, as a performer, the diversity of their music: country, pop, psychedelia, rock... in the old era a lot of bands crossed genres, but it hasn't really been acceptable to do that since the 80s, or even late 70s. As an independent artist, I don't have to worry about anyone telling me that I can't do a French version, or a dance tune, etc... The first song I ever learned how to PLAY on acoustic guitar was 'Torn and Frayed', so no doubt that kind of chordal and melody structure (Keith) has influenced the songs I write myself."

[386] **SOME GIRLS - Kristi Argyle** (2019)
(Jagger-Richards)

Rolling Stones original: Some Girls (1978)

Artist and Rock singer from Orange County, California, USA.

Established painter and illustrator Kristi Argyle has covered a number of Rolling Stones and Mick Jagger songs for streaming sites. 'Some Girls' is suitably gender-reversed - the infamous line "Black girls just wanna get f*cked all night" becomes "Black *boys* just wanna get f*cked all night".

[387] SOME THINGS JUST STICK IN YOUR MIND - Vashti (1965)

(Jagger-Richards)

Rolling Stones original: 1964 Demo: Metamorphosis (1975)

Jennifer Vashti Bunyan (b. 1945). Folk and Pop singer from Newcastle-upon-Tyne, UK. Later known as Vashti Bunyan.

Along with 'As Tears Go By', probably the most accomplished song written by Jagger-Richards in the early (pre-1965) days was 'Some Things Just Stick In Your Mind'. It was first given to Vashti (Bunyan), a distinctive-voiced and attractive Folk-influenced singer, though it sadly failed to chart, despite some TV promotion.

How did you manage to get an exclusive Jagger-Richards song to record as your first single?

"I've just had a book published (called 'Wayward, Just Another Life to Live') which describes the way I came to record the Decca single in 1965, written by Jagger/Richards. It also shows how its failure and subsequent failures to get my own songs noticed sent me off out of London and away from the music industry for 30 years. My first album - 'Just Another Diamond Day', recorded in 1969 - was also ignored, but was re-released in 2000 to a much kinder generation and this time it worked. I made 2 more albums after that and have now written a memoir about it all. So, in answer to your question... it's a long story and is in the book."

Do you think this helped your career in the long run?

"No, not at all, but my more recent career (since 2000) has definitely benefitted from the story!"

For Andrew Oldham's 2013 album 'Play the Rolling Stones Songbook Vol. 2' you recorded 'Bittersweet Symphony' - an inspired choice! Whose idea was this?

"It was Andrew's idea. He sent me the backing track, and I recorded my vocals here. I loved being on an ALO track again... Just listening to it now for the first time for ages... Good isn't it?!"

Vashti performing 'Some Things Just Stick In Your Mind' on 'Shindig!', 1965 [US TV]

Vashti Bunyan's excellent 2022 memoir.

[388] **SOME THINGS JUST STICK IN YOUR MIND - Dick and Dee Dee** (1965)

(Jagger-Richards)

Rolling Stones original: 1964 Demo: Metamorphosis (1975)

Dick St. John (Richard St. John Gosting, b. 1940 - d. 2003) and Dee Dee Sperling (Mary Spelling). Pop duo from Santa Monica, California, USA.

Utilising The Rolling Stones' demo backing track, Dick and Dee Dee released their version of 'Some Things Just Stick In Your Mind' as the B-side of 'Blue Turns To Grey'... or was *this* the A-side? No-one seems too sure.

Dick and Dee Dee performing 'Some Things Just Stick In Your Mind' on 'Shindig!', 1965 [US TV]

[389] **SOMETHING HAPPENED TO ME YESTERDAY** - The Lairds (2004)

(Jagger-Richards)

Rolling Stones original: Between The Buttons (1967)

Russell Wilkins (guitar and vocals), John Gibbs (bass and vocals) and Lenny Helsing (drums and vocals). Garage Rock band from London, UK. The Wildebeests under a pseudonym.

One of The Rolling Stones' most untypical songs from arguably their most musically adventurous album, the Stones original of the Kinks-like Music Hall-inspired 'Something Happened To Me Yesterday' features Mick and Keith on duet vocals, prominent piano backing, and added brass instrumentation courtesy of Brian Jones . ~~The Wildebeests'~~ The Lairds' fun cover for Norton has simple guitar, bass and drums plus kazoo backing, but otherwise stays fairly faithful to the original - right down to recreating Mick Jagger's 'Dixon of Dock Green' impersonation. *See [311] for interview!*

[390] **THE SPIDER AND THE FLY** - James Cotton and Kenny Wayne Shepherd (1996)

(Jagger-Richards)

Rolling Stones original: Out Of Our Heads [US version] (1965) + UK B-side (1965)

James Henry Cotton (b. 1935 - d. 2017). Blues singer and harmonicist from Tunica, Mississippi, USA, and Kenny Wayne Brobst (b. 1977). Blues-Rock singer and guitarist from Shreveport, Louisiana, USA.

The UK B-side to '(I Can't Get No) Satisfaction', 'The Spider and The Fly' is an original Blues song with amusing lyrics. James Cotton and Kenny Wayne Shepherd's excellent authentic-sounding cover is on the 1996 various artists soundtrack album 'Michael - Music from the Motion Picture'.

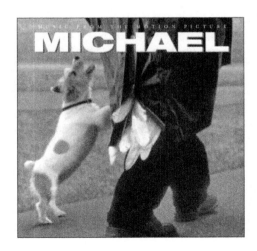

[391] **STAR, STAR - Joan Jett and The Blackhearts** (1983)

(Jagger-Richards)

Rolling Stones original: Goats Head Soup (1973)

Joan Jett (Joan Marie Larkin, b. 1958 - vocals and guitar), Ricky Byrd (Richard Scott Bird, b. 1956 - guitar and vocals), Gary Ryan (bass and vocals) and Lee Crystal (Lee Jamie Sackett, b. 1956 - d. 2013 - drums and vocals). Hard Rock band from USA.

Basically an X-rated update of Chuck Berry, the notorious 'Star, Star' (censored title!) was covered in fine style by Joan Jett and The Blackhearts. It first sneaked out on the cassette-only version of 1983's 'Album'.

[392] **STAR, STAR - Rikki Rockett** (2003)

(Jagger-Richards)

Rolling Stones original: Goats Head Soup (1973)

Richard Allan Ream (b. 1961). Glam Metal and Hard Rock drummer from Mechanicsburg, Pennsylvania, USA. Best known as the drummer for Poison.

Featuring Dick Swagger (b. 1963) from 'The Hollywood Stones' on vocals, Rikki Rockett's version of 'Star, Star' has a *very* stripped and minimal backing (often the only things heard are vocals and drums). It is on his 2003 album 'Glitter 4 Your Soul'.

[393] **START ME UP - Toots and The Maytels** (2001)
(Jagger-Richards)

Rolling Stones original: Tattoo You (1981) + UK/US A-side (1981)

Ska, Rocksteady and Reggae band from Jamaica, led by Frederick Nathaniel Hibbert (b. 1942 - d. 2020 - vocals and occasional guitar).

The Rolling Stones' final UK Top 10 hit, 'Start Me Up' began as a Reggae-styled 'Black and Blue' outtake. So who better to cover the song than Toots and The Maytels? Sounding more Ska than Reggae due to its lively tempo, their cover is on the 2001 various artists 'Reggae Rocks - The Tide Is High: A Tribute to Rock 'n' Roll' album, as well as the following year's 'Paint It Black: A Reggae Tribute to The Rolling Stones'.

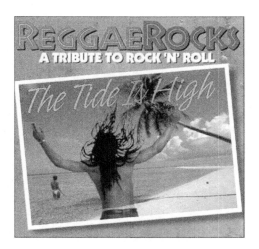

[394] **START ME UP - Beverley Skeete** (2011)
(Jagger-Richards)

Rolling Stones original: Tattoo You (1981) + UK/US A-side (1981)

Soul, Funk and Pop singer from the UK.

Surprisingly hard rockin', Beverley Skeete's Rock-Funk cover of 'Start Me Up' was first released on her 2011 'Personal' EP, and later on the album 'Good Times' in 2012. It's not the first time she's recorded a Stones song: Beverley was also a guest vocalist on Bill Wyman and The Rhythm Kings' 1997 cover of 'Melody'.

[395] **START ME UP - Manic Street Preachers** (2014)
(Jagger-Richards)

Rolling Stones original: Tattoo You (1981) + UK/US A-side (1981)

James Dean Bradfield (b. 1969 - vocals, guitar, piano and keyboards), Nicky Wire (Nicholas Allen Jones, b. 1969 - bass, piano and vocals) and Sean Moore (Sean Anthony Moore, b. 1968 - drums, percussion, trumpet and vocals). Alternative Rock band from Blackwood, Gwent, Wales.

Part Punk and part Glam, Manic Street Preachers' surprising cover is on the various artists 'Sounds of the 80s - Unique Covers of Classic Hits' album.

[396] **STONED - The Lyres** (1992)
(Nanker-Phelge)

Rolling Stones original: UK B-side (1963) + US B-side (1964)

Garage Rock band from Boston, Massachusetts, USA, led by Jeff Conolly (Jeffrey Lynn Conolly - vocals and organ).

A semi-instrumental that was released as the UK B-side to 'I Wanna Be Your Man', 'Stoned' was the Stones' first issued song that they wrote themselves, albeit it under the name 'Nanker-Phelge', used for all group compositions in the early days. The Lyres' cover has very little piano, and the occasional utterances ("Stoned", "Outta my mind") are more comical than Mick's, but otherwise it is similar. It was on their album 'Happy Now', as well as on a Norton single with 'Now I've Got A Witness' on the flip side.

[397] **STONED - Allah-Las** (2015)
(Nanker-Phelge)

Rolling Stones original: UK B-side (1963) + US B-side (1964)

Miles Michaud (vocals and guitar), Pedrum Siadatian (guitar and vocals), Spencer Dunham (bass and vocals) and Matthew Correia (drums and vocals). Psychedelic Rock, Garage Rock and Folk Rock band from Los Angeles, California, USA.

This time with no piano, and the whole group occasionally shouting "Stoned!", it is another strong version. It was very appropriately released on 'Stoned: A Psych Tribute to The Rolling Stones'.

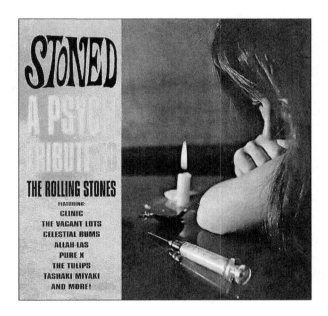

Whose idea was it to record this song?

"Our manager was joking that the only Rolling Stones song we were capable of covering was 'Stoned'."

Have you performed this (or any other Stones songs) live?

"We once covered 'Heaven' off of 'Tattoo You', and in high school Miles and Spencer both participated in a battle of the bands competition performing 'Jumping Jack Flash'."

Were the Rolling Stones an influence on your own music?

"Very much so. Ever since we saw 'Rock 'N' Roll Circus' as teenager's they've been one of our collective favourite bands of all time."

[398] **THE STORM - The Screws** (2001)

(Jagger-Richards)

Rolling Stones original: UK/US B-side (1994)

Mick Collins (b. 1965 - vocals and guitar), Terri Wahl (vocals and guitar), Jimmy Hole (bass) and Kerry Davis (drums). Garage Rock band from Detroit, Michigan, USA.

A stripped back Country Blues that was hidden away as the B-side to 'Love Is Strong' (which was also on 'Voodoo Lounge'), The Screws' remarkable cover sounds like a lost early Muddy Waters recording. It can be found on their 2001 album 'Shake Your Monkey'.

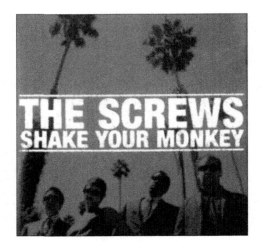

[399] **STRAY CAT BLUES - Johnny Winter** (1974)

(Jagger-Richards)

Rolling Stones original: Beggars Banquet (1968)

John Dawson Winter III (b. 1944 - d. 2014). Blues-Rock singer and guitarist from Beaumont, Texas, USA.

Those of a sensitive inclination (you know, the kind of people who are "offended" by 'Brown Sugar') shouldn't listen too closely to the tale of under-age groupies that is 'Stray Cat Blues'! Johnny Winter included a rather shouty Hard Rock version on his 1974 album 'Saints & Sinners'.

[400] **STRAY CAT BLUES - Soundgarden** (1991)
(Jagger-Richards)

Rolling Stones original: Beggars Banquet (1968)

Chris Cornell (b. 1964 - d. 2017 - vocals and guitar), Kim Thayil (Kim Anand Thayil, b. 1960 - guitar), Ben Shepherd (Hunter Benedict Shepherd, b. 1968 - bass) and Matt Cameron (Matthew David Cameron, b. 1962 - drums). Grunge and Heavy Metal band from Seattle, Washington, USA.

The whole thing is a lot noisier, but Soundgarden's cover basically sticks to the Stones' original arrangement. It was released as a bonus track on their 1991 'Jesus Christ Pose' single.

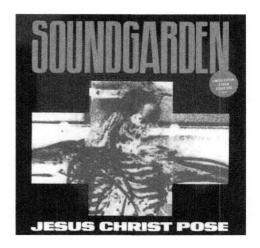

[401] **STRAY CAT BLUES - Chrissy Amphlett and Chris Cheney** (2006)
(Jagger-Richards)

Rolling Stones original: Beggars Banquet (1968)

Christine Joy Amphlett (b. 1959 - d. 2013). Rock and New Wave singer from Geelong, Victoria, Australia, and Christopher John Cheney (b. 1975). Rockabilly and Punk Rock singer and guitarist from Melbourne, Victoria, Australia.

Taken from an Australian TV show, this enjoyable duet is on the various artists 'RocKwiz Duets' album.

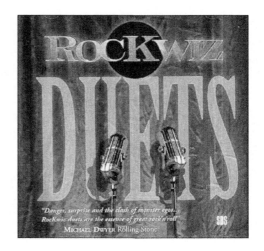

[402] **STREET FIGHTING MAN - Rod Stewart [with Ronnie Wood]** (1969)

(Jagger-Richards)

Rolling Stones original: Beggars Banquet (1968) + US A-side (1968)

Roderick David Stewart (b. 1945). Rock singer from Highgate, London, UK.

A song that was initially recorded as 'Did Everyone Pay Their Dues?', 'Street Fighting Man' is one of the Stones' relatively few forays into political comment. Rod Stewart's very different version - featuring future Stone Ronnie Wood on prominent slide guitar - was first released on 1969's US 'The Rod Stewart Album' (issued in the UK 3 months later as 'An Old Raincoat Won't Let You Down').

[403] **STREET FIGHTING MAN - The Ramones** (1985)

(Jagger-Richards)

Rolling Stones original: Beggars Banquet (1968) + US A-side (1968)

Joey Ramone (Jeffrey Ross Hyman, b. 1951 - d. 2001 - vocals), Johnny Ramone (John William Cummings, b. 1948 - d. 2004 - guitar), Dee Dee Ramone (Douglas Colvin, b. 1951 - d. 2002 - bass and vocals) and Richie Ramone (Richard Reinhardt, b. 1957 - drums and vocals). Punk Rock and Pop Punk band from Queens, New York, USA. Disbanded in 1996.

A fast and suitably Punked-up cover, this was on the 12" version of The Ramones' 1985 'Howling At The Moon' single.

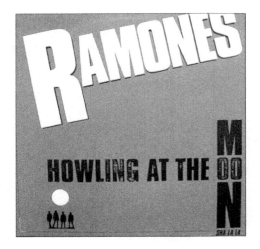

[404] **STREET FIGHTING MAN - The Chesterfield Kings** (1994)
(Jagger-Richards)

Rolling Stones original: Beggars Banquet (1968) + US A-side (1968)

Greg Prevost (b. 1959 - vocals, guitarist, harmonica, tabla, sitar, maracas, theremin and percussion), Andy Babiuk (Andrew Michael Babiuk, b. 1963 - bass, guitar, sitar, dulcimer, mellotron, recorder and percussion), Paul Rocco (b. 1962 - guitar, piano, zither and autoharp) and Brett Reynolds (drums, congas, bongos, tambourine, maracas and percussion). Garage Rock and Psychedelic Rock band from Rochester, New York, USA. Disbanded in 2009.

On other covers by The Chesterfield Kings (as well as Greg Prevost solo), they make the songs very much their own, but on 'Street Fighting Man' they go for pure imitation - albeit an extremely accurate one, right down to the sitar/piano fade. Sounding remarkably like the Stones' own backing track, if anything this has the edge thanks to the (arguably!) superior guitar solos. It is on their 1994 'Let's Go Get Stoned' album. *See [54] for interview!*

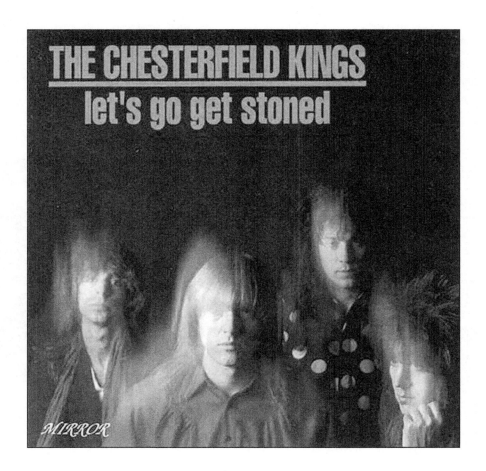

[405] **STREET FIGHTING MAN - Oasis** (1998)

(Jagger-Richards)

Rolling Stones original: Beggars Banquet (1968) + US A-side (1968)

Liam Gallagher (William John Paul Gallagher, b. 1972 - vocals and tambourine), Noel Gallagher (Noel Thomas David Gallagher, b. 1967 - guitar and vocals), Paul 'Bonehead' Arthurs (Paul Benjamin Arthurs, b. 1965 - guitar), Paul 'Guigsy' McGuigan (Paul Francis McGuigan, b. 1971 - bass) and Alan 'Whitey' White (Alan Victor White, b. 1972 - drums). Rock and Britpop band from Manchester, UK. Disbanded in 2009.

Oasis' cover is marred a little by the ridiculously over-driven guitars, but otherwise it's a nice enough version. It was included on their 1998 'All Around The World' single.

[406] **STREET FIGHTING MAN - Hayseed Dixie** (2013)

(Jagger-Richards)

Rolling Stones original: Beggars Banquet (1968) + US A-side (1968)

Rockgrass (Rock and Bluegrass) band from Nashville, Tennessee, USA, led by John Wheeler (John Christopher Wheeler, b. 1970 - vocals, guitar, piano and violin).

A fast 'Rockgrass' cover, Hayseed Dixie's version of 'Street Fighting Man' includes some fabulous fiddle and mandolin solos. It is on 2013's 'Grasswhooping Party Pack - Volume 1' album. *See [293] for interview!*

[407] **STREETS OF LOVE - Matthew Ryan** (2011)

(Jagger-Richards)

Rolling Stones original: A Bigger Bang (2005) + A-side (2005)

(b. 1971). Alternative Country singer and guitarist from Chester, Pennsylvania, USA.

A Rock-Ballad, 'Streets Of Love' was a highlight of 'A Bigger Bang', and was quite rightly released as a single. Unexpectedly, Matthew Ryan's version features Bono-esque vocals, along with synthesizer and drum machine backing. It has very little to do with Country music, but nevertheless, this refreshingly different cover can be found on 'Paint It Black: An Alt Country Tribute To The Rolling Stones'.

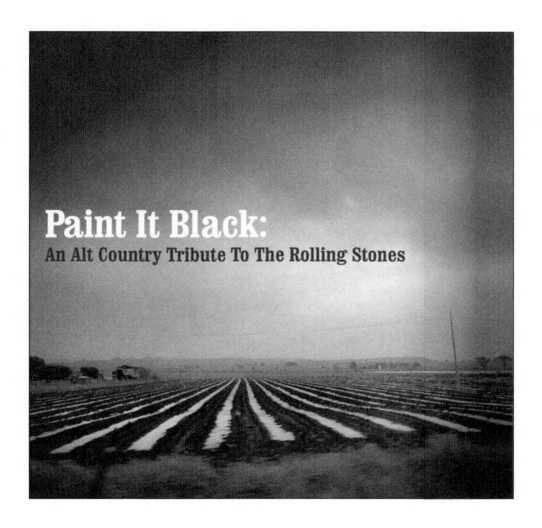

[408] **STUPID GIRL - Ellen Foley** (1979)
(Jagger-Richards)

Rolling Stones original: Aftermath (1966) + US B-side (1966)

(b. 1951). Rock singer and actress from St. Louis, Missouri, USA. Perhaps best known for her collaborations with Meat Loaf.

Curiously, some of Jagger-Richards' most sexist songs have inspired some highly memorable covers by women. 'Under My Thumb' is one such song, and 'Stupid Girl' is another. Ellen Foley's sassy New Wave cover was released on her 1979 'Night Out' album, as well as on the B-side of her 'Sad Song' single.

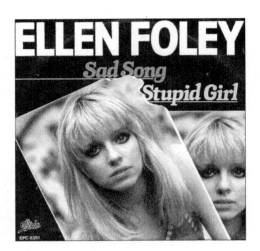

[409] **STUPID GIRL - Sue Foley** (2002)
(Jagger-Richards)

Rolling Stones original: Aftermath (1966) + US B-side (1966)

(b. 1968). Blues-Rock singer and guitarist from Ottawa, Ontario, Canada.

Not to be confused with Ellen Foley, Sue Foley's version of 'Stupid Girl' has the kind of mid-tempo Blues Boogie feel that the Stones might've used if the song was on 'Exile On Main St.' instead of 'Aftermath'. It is on her 2002 'Where the Action Is...' album.

[410] **STUPID GIRL - The Slow Slushy Boys** (1998)
(Jagger-Richards)

Rolling Stones original: Aftermath (1966) + US B-side (1966)

Benny Gordini (Denis Oliveres - vocals), Michel Breiller (guitar), Tello Maybe (bass), Lester Girard (Pascal Girard - drums) and Graham Mushnik (Axel Oliveres, b. 1985 - organ and vocals). Rhythm 'n' Blues and Soul band from Chambéry, France.

Although it probably wasn't their intention, The Slow Slushy Boys' organ-dominated stomping cover of 'Stupid Girl' sounds remarkably like Elvis Costello and The Attractions. It can be found on the various artists 'Standing in the Shadows - A Tribute to the Golden Days of The Rolling Stones 1963-1967' album. [Interview is with Benny Gordini]

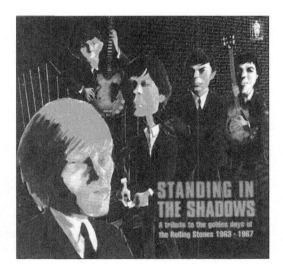

Whose idea was it to record this song?

"The great Australian label Corduroy asked us to record a Stones song for their tribute, and It was the right time to introduce in studio our 14 years new organist Teen' Axel, aka Graham Mushnik."

Do you perform this or any other Stones songs live?

"We never played this song on stage, only in the studio and recorded it as fast as possible, as we did in those times. If I do remember well, we only played 'The Last Time' in our early years."

Were the Rolling Stones an influence on your own music?

"They're surely one of the most important influences in my long musical story, as they were one of the first to introduce me to rhythm 'n' blues and soul."

[411] **SUMMER ROMANCE - The New Bomb Turks** (1993)
(Jagger-Richards)

Rolling Stones original: Emotional Rescue (1980)

Eric Davidson (vocals), Jim Weber (guitar), Matt Reber (bass) and Bill Randt (drums). Garage Rock and Punk Rock band from Columbus, Ohio, USA.

A punk-like song from 'Emotional Rescue' that would've sounded equally at home on 'Some Girls', The New Bomb Turks' cover is very fast and very Punk! It was the B-side of their 1993 single 'I'm Weak'. [Interview is with Eric Davidson]

Whose idea was it to record this song?

"We were asked to play a 'Stones-a-Thon' tribute event at a local club in our home base of Columbus, Ohio, and after knocking around some ideas, I think I suggested 'Summer Romance' just because we always find it more fun to find more seemingly obscure tunes from famous bands to cover; and we certainly figured no one else would ask to do that one. I think I had recently pulled out 'Emotional Rescue' and always liked that song. Seemed like something we could pare down to our standard 2 or 3 chords and play it fast."

Have you performed this (or any other Stones songs) live?

"Yes, so we played it at that 'Stones-a-Thon', circa late 1991. It was held at a sizable theatre club, and at that point we'd only played little dives. We'd only been a band for about a year or so. So here we were on this bill with a bunch of I guess you could say "popular" local bands, most (in our estimation) kind of cheesy cover bands or wannabe rock stars. And we went up and played our Stones cover about four times faster than any other that evening. Our friends piled in down front and cheered and laughed, but most people just stood there looking confused or pissed. So of course we jammed on it a bit longer than planned. I believe my quote at the end was, "Thank you all you classic rock motherfuckers!", middle fingers hoisted.

Considering we chose it on a lark for a one-time cover songs event, 'Summer Romance' became a pretty constant encore choice for us as the years went on (it was the B-side of one of our first 7" singles, and appeared on a singles comp we did too). We'd kind of jam on it and would sometimes bring in other tunes with similar-ish riffs before rocking out the end of it. I'm sure we drunkenly tried some other Stones covers over the years, but that was one we actually honed pretty well and did many times live."

Were the Rolling Stones an influence on your own music?

"TOTALLY, one of our absolute top main influences, along with the Ramones, Stooges, Saints, Devil Dogs, Geto Boys, and a few '80s Cleveland local bands, just to name a few. One of our very first songs we wrote, 'Out Of My Mind', I ripped some lyrics from 'Some Girls' for it. And later albums, we tried our half-baked attempt at aping the kind of roots genre twisting around the Stones did on 'Exile On Main St.', if not always consciously, just cuz it was in our DNA. We LOVE the Rolling Stones."

[412] **SURPRISE, SURPRISE - Lulu and The Luvvers** (1965)
(Jagger-Richards)

Rolling Stones original: The Rolling Stones, Now! (1965)

Marie McDonald McLaughlin Lawrie (b. 1948). Rhythm 'n' Blues and Pop singer (and band) from Glasgow, Scotland.

A song The Rolling Stones couldn't have thought much of (the first UK release of their demo-like original was on an obscure various artists collection), Lulu liked it enough to record and release it as a single. It failed to chart.

[413] **SURPRISE, SURPRISE - Rubber City Rebels** (1980)
(Jagger-Richards)

Rolling Stones original: The Rolling Stones, Now! (1965)

Rod Firestone (vocals and guitar), Buzz Clic (Elmer Charles Brandt - guitar), Johnny Bethesda (bass and vocals) and Brandon Matheson (drums). Punk Rock band from Akron, Ohio, USA.

Kicking off with a pounding drum intro and featuring a prominent guitar riff, Rubber City Rebels' almost unrecognizable mid-tempo cover is on their 2nd album, 1980's 'Rubber City Rebels'.

[414] **SWAY - Laurie Geltman** (1992)

(Jagger-Richards)

Rolling Stones original: Sticky Fingers (1971) + US B-side (1971)

(b. 1964). Pop, Rock and Country Rock singer and guitarist from Baltimore, Maryland, USA.

One of the less-celebrated songs from 'Sticky Fingers', 'Sway' was (allegedly) written by Mick Jagger and an uncredited Mick Taylor, with minimal contribution from Keith. Laurie Geltman's excellent Country Rock cover includes some prominent fiddle, and was included both on her 1992 debut album 'Departure' and the following year's 'Boston Gets Stoned' compilation.

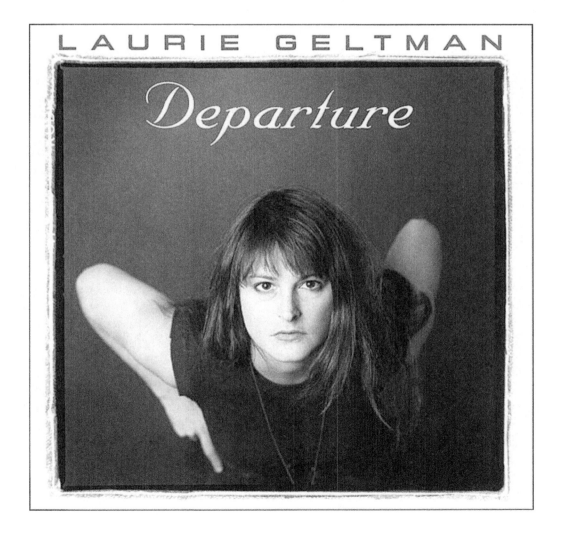

Whose idea was it to record this song?

"Sticky Fingers was one of my most played, influential and favourite albums as a kid. I would jump off my bed and writhe around on the floor with my stuffed animal as my mic (in elementary school) singing this song, so this choice to record it was always me. It was my mother's album, but I absconded with it as soon as she and my cousin ripped it open to see what was under the zipper. I consider that my first real rock and roll moment.

However, at the beginning of my career as a solo artist I was making my first album (Departure), while at the same time in Boston where I was living there was a compilation being put together by a couple local industry guys who had ties to Jimmy Miller (Stones producer). So he gets Producer credit cause he was supposedly part of the choosing of songs.

I called up one of the guys making 'Boston Gets Stoned' and said I'd like to record 'Sway.' He said, oh some other band is doing it. I said OK and did it anyway. I felt confidently that my love for the song would keep me from being dissuaded (hah Dis-SWAYED) and must've felt I was the rightful person to do it! They did pick mine obviously. I loved the rock churning electric version which later in the decade my mid to late 90s band did more like that, but due to circumstances and the band at the time it came out more rootsy and was noted by one rock critic as taking from the Gram Parsons' side of the Stones which is true, but that wasn't intentional. That was the organic result of what we had to work with in the studio and my band at the time. I played with an amazing violinist for many years (Daniel Kellar) and I was playing more acoustic then, but after the album I didn't even bring acoustic to gigs. Anyway, I did put it on my first album which came out right around the time of the Boston Gets Stoned Album, so I got a lot of cross over press locally because of it. It is to this day one of my most played songs."

Were the Rolling Stones an influence on your own music?

"The Stones were and are a huge influence. I don't play so much in Keith's open tunings, but the vibe and mix of soul, blues, rock is always in my rear view mirror."

Have you performed any other Stones songs live?

"I was mainly an original band because Boston was luckily not a cover band town, but on occasion we might've done 'No Expectations.' That was also earlier. 'Sway' was very much a part of my set and might be the only cover we'd do in most cases where cover songs might've been frowned upon. This song though represented, I felt, who I was as an artist, or at least a part of who I was. And we made it our own. When I did acoustic duo gigs with Daniel (violinist) he loved doing it."

[415] **SWAY - Alvin Youngblood Hart** (1997)
(Jagger-Richards)

Rolling Stones original: Sticky Fingers (1971) + US B-side (1971)

Gregory Edward Hart (b. 1963). Blues singer and guitarist from Oakland, California, USA.

Alvin Youngblood Hart's cover of 'Sway' sticks fairly close to the Stones' arrangement, though he does add his own distinctive guitar licks and solos. It is on the various artists 'Paint It, Blue: Songs of The Rolling Stones' album.

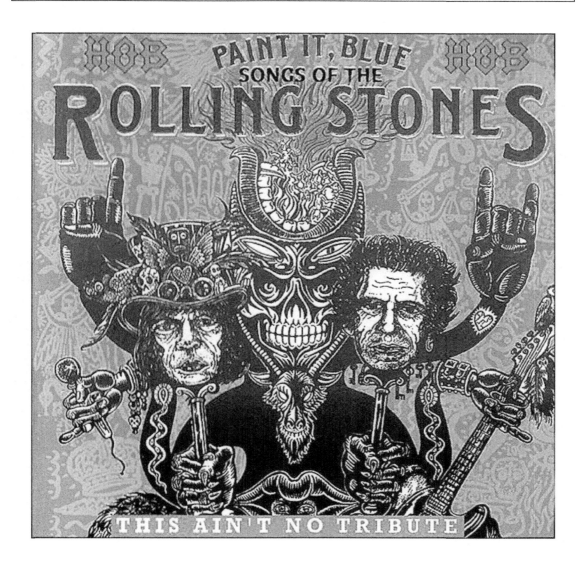

[416] **SWAY - Jesse Malin** (2008)

(Jagger-Richards)

Rolling Stones original: Sticky Fingers (1971) + US B-side (1971)

(b. 1967). Rock and Americana singer and guitarist from Queens, New York, USA.

Coming across like a grittier Pet Shop Boys, Jesse Malin's cover of 'Sway' is backed by 80s-style synthesizers and electronic drums. It is on his 2008 album 'On Your Sleeve'.

[417] **SWAY - Black Joe Lewis and The Honeybears** (2011)

(Jagger-Richards)

Rolling Stones original: Sticky Fingers (1971) + US B-side (1971)

Blues, Soul and Rock 'n' Roll singer and guitarist (and band) from Tucson, Arizona, USA.

Sounding like a Grunge-Soul hybrid, Black Joe Lewis' cover features his powerful voice backed by a loudly-mixed guitar and horns. It is on the 2011 compilation 'Sticky Soul Fingers: A Rolling Stones Tribute'.

[418] **SWEET BLACK ANGEL - The Wailing Souls** (1992)

(Jagger-Richards)

Rolling Stones original: Exile On Main St. (1972) + UK/US B-side (1972)

Rocksteady and Reggae band from Kingston, Jamaica, featuring vocalists Winston 'Pipe' Matthews and Lloyd 'Bread' McDonald.

A song written about black civil rights activist Angela Davis, the Stones' original has a distinct West Indian lilt to it. The Wailing Souls' relaxed and upbeat-sounding cover emphasise that West Indian Reggae-Calypso feel further, and it can be found on their 1992 album 'All Over The World'.

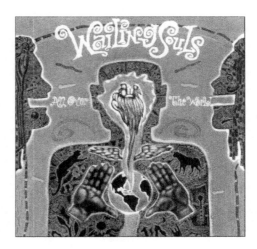

[419] **SWEET BLACK ANGEL - Otis Taylor** (2003)

(Jagger-Richards)

Rolling Stones original: Exile On Main St. (1972) + UK/US B-side (1972)

(b. 1948). Blues and Jazz singer, guitarist, banjoist, mandolinist and harmonicist from Chicago, Illinois, USA.

An electric Chicago Blues cover, Otis Taylor's version of 'Sweet Black Angel' can be found on 2003's 'Exile On Blues St.' various artists album.

[420] **SWEET VIRGINIA - Ronnie Lane and Slim Chance** (1974) *(Not released until 1997)*

(Jagger-Richards)

Rolling Stones original: Exile On Main St. (1972)

Ronnie Lane (Ronald Frederick Lane, b. 1946 - d. 1997 - vocals and guitar), Kevin Westlake (Kevin Patrick Westlake, b. 1947 - d. 2004 - guitar), Chrissy Stewart (Eric Christopher Stewart, b. 1946 - d. 2020 - bass), Billy Livsey (William Depew Livsey - keyboards) and Bruce Rowland (b. 1941 - drums). Folk Rock and Country Rock band from UK.

Along with 'Dead Flowers', 'Sweet Virginia' is the closest The Rolling Stones came to creating a Country music standard, and perhaps not coincidently, they both refer to illicit drug use. Ronnie Lane and Slim Chance performed a lovely version live in concert for BBC radio in 1974, and this can be heard on 1997's 'You Never Can Tell: The BBC Sessions' 2-CD set.

[421] **SWEET VIRGINIA - Jeff Lang** (2003)
(Jagger-Richards)

Rolling Stones original: Exile On Main St. (1972)

Jeffrey Lang (b. 1969). Folk, Blues and Rock 'n' Roll singer, guitarist, mandolinist and banjoist from Geelong, Victoria, Australia.

Jeff Lang's incredible solo version of 'Sweet Virginia' features just his vocals and open-tuned slide guitar. It's yet another highlight of 2003's various artists 'Exile On Blues St.' CD.

Whose idea was it to record this song?

"Someone got in touch through my website in 2002 or 2003, asking if I'd be interested in recording a song from 'Exile On Main St.'. It was for an album of cover versions of songs from that album they were putting together. My memory is that they asked specifically for that song, which was fine with me as I love the entire record. Initially I didn't think I was going to be able to do it as they needed it at fairly short notice and I was playing 5-6 shows a week touring across the States. But a few days after they asked I lucked out, playing a venue in Wisconsin which had a recording studio attached to the live room. It sounded great in the room I was performing in, so I played Sweet Virginia at the sound-check and they recorded it live to 2-track. The mix sounded good so I sent it off. It was only later that I realised I hadn't played the correct chords - a little embarrassing, seeing as there's only four in the whole song and I left one of them out! But I guess it counts as making it 'my own version', so I'll pretend I meant it. Nobody will ever know."

Have you performed this (or any other Stones songs) live?

"I might've played that song at the show straight after recording it, but I think that's the only time. As for others, I once played 'Just Wanna See His Face' in a band alongside a Malian kora player Mamadou Diabate, an Indian tabla player named Bobby Singh and a backing singer named Kellie Goldsmith. That was an interesting combination of instruments on a gospel style song like that one. 'Midnight Rambler' and 'Brown Sugar' have had a run in electric bands I've played in too from time to time."

Were the Rolling Stones an influence on your own music?

"Absolutely! The way the band has incorporated different genres - blues, rock and roll, country, folk - into their style, making those disparate influences blend together and sound like nobody but the Rolling Stones was definitely inspiring to me. Certain recordings of theirs sound absolutely perfect to me. 'Jumpin' Jack Flash' for instance, or 'Sympathy For The Devil', or 'Moonlight Mile' - I can't think of how they could be improved by changing a single thing, be it the way they played or the way the sounds were captured. Same with 'Gimme Shelter' or any number of their songs, I could go on for days. The quality of their songwriting has frequently been superb too, as much because of Jagger's lyrics as Keith's riffs. They've been an amazing songwriting team. And as a musician there are all manner of approaches which have been directly inspirational and influential on my guitar playing. Mick Taylor's beautiful touch with his slide playing and Keith Richards' raunchy rhythm guitar feel are two obvious ones, but the push and pull between the Wyman/Watts rhythm section and Keith's guitar has also been a touchstone for achieving that elusive 'loose-but-tight' band sound when playing with other musicians, and Sonny Rollin's soloing on 'Waiting On A Friend' contained many aspects which influenced my slide guitar playing, which I was only getting started with when that single was released."

[422] SWEET VIRGINIA - Jerry Lee Lewis [with Keith Richards] (2010)
(Jagger-Richards)

Rolling Stones original: Exile On Main St. (1972)

(b. 1935 - d. 2022). Rock 'n' Roll and Country singer and pianist from Ferriday, Louisiana, USA.

Jerry Lee Lewis and Keith Richards' enjoyably ragged duet is on The Killer's 2010 'Mean Old Man' CD, an album that also includes a duet with Mick Jagger on 'Dead Flowers' (featured elsewhere in this book).

[423] **SWEET VIRGINIA - The Cosmic Carnival** (2015)

(Jagger-Richards)

Rolling Stones original: Exile On Main St. (1972)

Rock, Pop, Folk, World and Country band from Rotterdam, The Netherlands. Members include Nicolas Schuit (vocals and guitar) and Indra Salima Kartodirdjo (violin, keyboards and vocals).

With Nicolas' husky voice nicely complimented by Indra's violin, 'Sweet Virginia' is a highlight of their 2015 double album 'The Cosmic Carnival Express - Live!'. [Interview is with Nicolas Schuit]

Whose idea was it to record this song?

"In 2014 we decided to record a live album in Country Rock/Americana style. The album was a tribute to our main influences and it was named The Cosmic Carnival Express, like 1970's Festival Express featuring The Grateful Dead and The Band. We had banjos on stage, pedal steel, fiddle, even a small flute, the whole thing sounded really great. With a 9 piece formation we performed songs like 'The Weight', 'Not Fade Away', 'Run Through The Jungle' and 'Outlaw Blues'. Because we had the fiddle and I loved it so much, I wanted to hear it on 'Sweet Virginia' and it worked really well! We received compliments from loads of Rolling Stones fans from all over the world, which was really great."

Do you perform any other Stones songs live?

"We used Steven Van Zandt's 'standing on the shoulders of giants' method, so yes, we played a lot of Rolling Stones songs early in our career. If you want to become a good artist, if you want to know how to play a song in a decent manner, you first need to experience it the way your heroes did. So we played every cool song we knew, we did The Band, Grateful Dead, Elvis Presley, Bob Dylan, CCR and of course The Rolling Stones. The songs we performed regularly as an encore were 'Miss You' and 'Happy'. And we learned more than a lot, it made us understand the music and we found out that we could play all these songs in our own, unique way. By changing harmonies, experimenting with tempo, playing the song in a different key and adding stuff. Profanity? Not at all, it's exactly the same The Rolling Stones did at the start of their career!"

Were the Rolling Stones an influence on your own music?

"The Rolling Stones played a big role in our own musical adventures from day one. We were really tired of popular music back in the days and we wanted to do it more like the sixties. Music shouldn't be polished and dull, it should be raw, groovy, colourful and full of emotion. So we tried to convince everyone that Creedence Clearwater Revival were way more badass than ALL music released since 2000, or maybe even since 1975. And that a pretty voice doesn't make you a good singer. And that sounds from a computer will never get any louder than a decent rhythm section. And that you can create music in your own special way, like... having a drummer like Charlie who always comes late with the snare, without slowing down, because he's right there on time with the next kick-drum. It's one of the magical ingredients of the Rolling Stones. So if anything, the Rolling Stones, along with a great bunch of artists from the sixties and seventies, taught us how to do it in our very own way, just like they did."

[424] **SYMPATHY FOR THE DEVIL - Sandie Shaw** (1969)

(Jagger-Richards)

Rolling Stones original: Beggars Banquet (1968)

Sandra Ann Goodrich (b. 1947). Pop singer from Dagenham, Essex, UK.

Almost from the beginning, thanks largely to Andrew Oldham's media manipulation, The Rolling Stones had a "bad boy" image. Eventually they started playing up to this, with 'Sympathy For The Devil' being the band at their most provocative and most brilliant. On Sandie Shaw's cover, she is backed only by drums, bass and a semi-audible piano apart from the occasional twin guitars, and sings with a wild abandon not heard on Sandie's hit singles. It is on her 1969 'Reviewing The Situation' album.

Whose idea was it to record 'Sympathy For The Devil'?

"Mine. The album 'Reviewing The Situation' was due for release in '69 and I wanted to do a kind of musical review of the Sixties' events, ideas, people that had resonated for me. I chose the song because I hoped it would shake people up a bit. It enabled me to be a bit of a devil myself! I chose songs because I felt that they and/or the artists who performed them would continue to have resonance over the next decades - I got some right!"

How did the collaboration with Cud for 'Gimme Shelter' come about?

"I was approached by the label and Cud's management. It was for a charity and I thought why not? It was a hoot recording it."

Did you ever perform any Stones songs live?

"Unfortunately no."

Did you get to know the band personally?

"Now that would be telling..."

[425] **SYMPATHY FOR THE DEVIL - Bryan Ferry** (1973)

(Jagger-Richards)

Rolling Stones original: Beggars Banquet (1968)

(b. 1945). Rock and Pop singer and pianist from Newcastle, UK. Best known as the front man of Roxy Music.

Semi-spoken, with girly singers, discordant keyboards and brass, Bryan Ferry's weird and wonderful cover is on his first solo album, 1973's 'These Foolish Things'.

[426] **SYMPATHY FOR THE DEVIL - Linda Kendrick** (1974)

(Jagger-Richards)

Rolling Stones original: Beggars Banquet (1968)

(b. 1951 - d. 2010). Rock and Pop singer from Dagenham, Essex, UK.

If you think Bryan Ferry's version is wacky, wait until you hear this. Starting off slowly with quasi-classical piano and church-like choir, Linda Kendrick is then joined by strings and brass whilst gradually reaching a vocal crescendo, until on the final verse she sounds like Suzi Quatro on helium! Released as a 1974 single, even in the Glam era it was just a little *too* weird to make an impact.

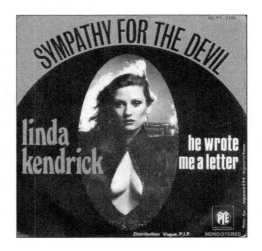

[427] **SYMPATHY FOR THE DEVIL - Guns N' Roses** (1994)
(Jagger-Richards)

Rolling Stones original: Beggars Banquet (1968)

Axl Rose (William Bruce Rose Jr., b. 1962 - vocals and occasional keyboards), Slash (Saul Hudson, b. 1965 - guitar and vocals), Gilby Clarke (Gilbert J. Clarke, b. 1962 - guitar and vocals), Duff McKagan (Michael Andrew McKagan, b. 1964 - bass and vocals), Matt Sorum (Matthew William Sorum, b. 1960 - drums and vocals) and Dizzy Reed (Darren Arthur Reed, b. 1963 - keyboards). Hard Rock band from Los Angeles, California, USA.

Guns 'n' Roses' version of 'Sympathy For The Devil' pretty much follows the Stones original template, except it is more hard-rocking and modern-sounding. It is on the 1994 'Interview with the Vampire' movie soundtrack album, and was also released as a single, peaking at No. 55 in the US and No. 9 in the UK.

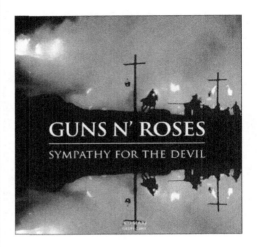

[428] **SYMPATHY FOR THE DEVIL - Ozzy Osbourne** (2005)
(Jagger-Richards)

Rolling Stones original: Beggars Banquet (1968)

John Michael Osbourne (b. 1948). Heavy Metal and Hard Rock singer from Marston Green, Warwickshire, UK.

Not the Heavy Metal scream-fest one would perhaps expect, Ozzy Osbourne's cover can best be described as 'Hard Funk' (think 80s group Cameo) though with an adventurous guitar solo (a bit like Brian May). It is on his 2005 album 'Under Cover' (great title!).

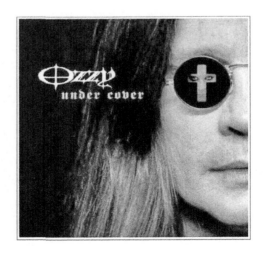

[429] **SYMPATHY FOR THE DEVIL - Motörhead** (2015)

(Jagger-Richards)

Rolling Stones original: Beggars Banquet (1968)

Lemmy Kilmister (Ian Fraser Kilmister, b. 1945 - d. 2015 - vocals and bass), Phil 'Wizzö' Campbell (Philip Anthony Campbell[1] (b. 1961 - guitar and vocals) and Mikkey Dee (Micael Kiriakos Delaoglou, b. 1963 - drums). Heavy Metal, Hard Rock and Speed Metal band from London, UK.

Sort of a Heavy Metal interpretation of the Stones' original arrangement, Motörhead's cover is pretty much as expected - right down to Lemmy's trade-mark gravelly vocals. It is on the band's final album, 2015's 'Bad Magic'.

[430] **SYMPATHY FOR THE DEVIL - Billy Branch** (2018)

(Jagger-Richards)

Rolling Stones original: Beggars Banquet (1968)

William Earl Branch (b. 1951). Blues singer and harmonist from Great Lakes, Illinois, USA.

Sounding like a restrained Billy Preston and with a steady (non-Samba) drum beat, Billy Branch's cover includes some superb slide guitar and harmonica. It is on the endlessly fascinating 'Chicago Plays The Stones'.

[431] **TAKE IT OR LEAVE IT - The Searchers** (1966)
(Jagger-Richards)

Rolling Stones original: Aftermath [UK version] (1966) + Flowers (1967)

Mike Pender (Michael John Prendergast, b. 1941 - guitar and vocals), John McNally (b. 1941 - guitar and vocals), Frank Allen (Francis Renaud McNeice, b. 1943 - bass and vocals) and John Blunt (born John David Blunt, b. 1947 - drums). Beat group from Liverpool.

One of the less Blues-orientated tracks on the UK edition of 'Aftermath' is 'Take It Or Leave It', a commercial Pop song that didn't really suit the band. So who better to give it to than Liverpool group The Searchers? Released a couple of days prior to the Stones' album, The Searchers' single, with its soaring harmonies, folky guitars and glossy production, quite frankly blew the original away. Sadly, it didn't do so well in the UK singles charts, though it did make No. 8 in Australia and No. 5 in The Netherlands. [Interview is with Frank Allen]

Two European picture sleeves for 'Take It Or Leave It'. Only the 2nd one features the correct line-up.

You released your single prior to the RS's own version (on 'Aftermath'), how did you get hold of the song?

"'Take It Or leave It' was acquired from The Stones during a tour of Australia and New Zealand in the Spring of 1966. They of course were headlining. Our status had dipped a bit by then and we closed the first half. Chris Curtis spent some time with Mick and Keith and they played him the demo of the new album. He liked 'Take It' very much and suggested we do it as our next single. Up to that point Chris Curtis was the main man for choosing our singles and had done a great job so we tended to accept whatever he thought was best.

At this time we were having quite a bit of trouble with Chris who was disenchanted at the way our career was going and had started to dabble in drugs although I believe it was not anything heavy, just some pills or cannabis. But he was certainly behaving very strangely throughout that tour. It was sad. Although we didn't know it till the latter part of the tour he had planned to leave and take on a role as an independent record producer. We tried to talk him out of this with no luck. It was a frightening time for us."

I believe it was your first recording with new drummer John Blunt, what was that like?

"Chris was pretty much the star of the show in our outfit. We even had a lunch in London on our return along with our manager Tito Burns to change his mind but he was adamant. He still however wanted to produce the song with us but we had decided that if there was to be a break then this was not an option. We went ahead and recorded the track with Tony Hatch as producer, as per all our other recordings up to that point.

Meanwhile Tito's assistant, Mike Rispoli, knew of a young drummer in his home town of Croydon and suggested we could give him a try out. John Blunt was taken on, essentially as a stop gap measure but in fact he stayed with us for three years. He was a nice guy although his actual persona was probably more suited to The Who than The Searchers. For a while we used to let him wear casual mod clothes on stage while we were the Searchers uniform of black suits, white shirts and black ties. He even kicked his kit around at the end of our show a la Keith Moon but we liked him and he settled in nicely, at least as a temporary measure.

John played well on the track and although it probably was not an ideal release for a single, it reached 17 I believe, it's still a very haunting sound and we have often received comments that it was better than The Stones' version. I've never heard what The Stones themselves thought of it. I'm still very fond of the song and our recording of it."

Do you still perform the song today?

"We revived it in our set list a few years ago but it didn't stay. We were oversubscribed with slower material from our recording catalogue and it had to make way for the more up tempo tracks like Have You Ever Loved Somebody which was a lesser hit but which livened up the show rather more."

[432] **TAKE IT OR LEAVE IT - Vinylbandet** (2013)
(Jagger-Richards)

Rolling Stones original: Aftermath [UK version] (1966) + Flowers (1967)

Danne Persson (guitar and vocals), Eddy Åbacka (guitar and vocals), Staffe Sundberg (guitar and vocals), Janne Widén (bass and vocals), Anders Jarkell (drums) and Peter Klaxman (Keyboards). Rock and Pop covers band from Stockholm, Sweden.

With its robust guitars and nice harmonies, Vinylbandet's cover sounds like a cross between the Stones' and the Searchers' versions. [Interview is with Anders Jarkell]

Was your version inspired by The Rolling Stones or The Searchers?

"We were inspired by the Rolling Stones when we included the song in our repertoire."

Do you perform this or any other Stones songs live?

"Besides 'Take It Or Leave It', we play live songs like 'Honky Tonk Women', 'Tell me', 'Satisfaction', 'Let's Spend The Night Together' and 'Out Of Time'. 'Take It Or Leave It' is the only song published."

Were the Rolling Stones an influence on your own music?

"The Rolling Stones are one of the bands from the 60s that have inspired us. We also play a lot of Beatles, Elvis and many more. We have around 150 songs in our repertoire."

[433] **TELL ME (YOU'RE COMING BACK)** - The Grass Roots (1966)

(Jagger-Richards)

Rolling Stones original: The Rolling Stones (1964) + England's Newest Hit Makers (1964) + US A-side (1964)

Willie Fulton (Willie James Fulton - guitar and vocals), Denny Ellis (guitar and vocals), David Stensen (bass and vocals) and Joel Larson (b. 1947 - drums). Folk Rock band from Los Angeles, California, USA.

'Tell Me (You're Coming Back)' always sounded a little out of place on The Rolling Stones' 1ˢᵗ UK album, being the only non-Rhythm 'n' Blues song, the only Jagger-Richards composition, and very likely the only track to feature Keith on harmony vocals. The Grass Roots' Folk-Rock version is on their 1966 album 'Where Were You When I Needed You'.

[434] **TELL ME (YOU'RE COMING BACK)** - Cassell Webb (1990)

(Jagger-Richards)

Rolling Stones original: The Rolling Stones (1964) + England's Newest Hit Makers (1964) + US A-side (1964)

(b. 1948). Psych, Folk and Pop singer and guitarist from Llano, Texas, USA.

With just keyboards and percussion backing, Cassell Webb's slow and beautifully sung Folk arrangement of 'Tell Me (You're Coming Back)' is on her 1990 album 'Conversations At Dawn'.

[435] **THAT GIRL BELONGS TO YESTERDAY - Gene Pitney** (1964)

(Jagger-Richards)

Rolling Stones original: 1963 Demo ('My Only Girl'): Bootleg only

Gene Francis Alan Pitney (b. 1940 - d. 2006). Pop singer and songwriter from Hartford, Connecticut, USA.

In late 1963, Mick and Keith wrote a song called 'My Only Girl'. No more than mediocre, it was intended for George Bean, who had previously recorded the equally mediocre 'It Should Be You' and 'Will You Be My Lover Tonight?' for a flop single. Andrew and the band then befriended successful US singer Gene Pitney, and when he heard 'My Only Girl' he knew it had further potential. Reworking the song as 'That Girl Belongs To Yesterday' (and very graciously refusing a co-writers credit), he recorded and released it himself as a single. Performed in his usual operatic Pop style, he took it to No. 7 in the UK charts, and in the process gave Jagger and Richards their first ever hit record as songwriters.

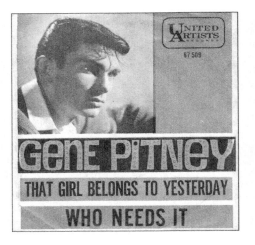

Gene Pitney performing 'That Girl Belongs To Yesterday' on 'Top Of The Pops', 1964 [UK TV]

[436] **THINK - Chris Farlowe** (1966)
(Jagger-Richards)

Rolling Stones original: Aftermath (1966)

Chris Farlowe (John Henry Dighton, b. 1940). Rhythm 'n' Blues, Soul and Pop singer from Islington, London.

A song released by the Stones on 'Aftermath', Chris Farlowe's version was issued on a single a full 3 months earlier, and instead of Keith's guitar fuzz features beefy saxes with a stomping Motown beat. His debut hit at No. 37, Chris Farlowe would issue four more Jagger-Richards songs as A-sides within the next couple of years, with variable degrees of success.

[437] **THIS PLACE IS EMPTY - Gilles Snowcat** (2020)

(Jagger-Richards)

Rolling Stones original: A Bigger Bang (2005)

Indie-Rock singer and keyboardist from Brussels, Belgium.

A gentle ballad from 'A Bigger Bang' that features vocals by Keith Richards on the original, Gilles Snowcat's version adds a nice percussive effect plus a gentle Reggae rhythm towards the end. Vocally though it is quite similar, with Gilles' gravelly voice sounding remarkably like Keef himself. It is available on his 2020 album 'You've Been Unboxing'.

Whose idea was it to record this song?

"It was me. 'This Place Is Empty' is one of those songs I wish I had written but someone did it before, Keef here, so my only choice was to record a cover of it. A few years ago, I was recording an album called 'Nama Time' and I asked the sound engineer to capture my voice the same way Don Was did for Keith's voice for 'This Place Is Empty' on 'A Bigger Bang'."

Do you perform this or any other Stones songs live?

"I did it live and funnily once I met a lady who was in the audience and she told me she discovered the Rolling Stones' version thanks to mine. As for other Stones songs, I recorded Keith's 'Crosseyed Heart' earlier this year, and played it live too. Besides, I did a demo for 'Oh No Not You Again' and 'Some Girls' but I never went further than that. I sometimes give a try to Ron Wood's 'I Got Lost When I Found You' and Mick Taylor's 'S.W.'", though I still haven't found a way to make them mine. Maybe they'll end up on an album sooner or later."

Were the Rolling Stones an influence on your own music?

"As a little kid, I was fascinated by the song 'Emotional Rescue' that was played quite often on the radio. I always felt a connection with the way the Stones have that 'loose' attitude while playing, that swinging groove, that 'dirty' way of playing, very natural. My music can sometimes be very different from the Stones', yet the way of playing owes a lot to them. I also feel a lot in common with how they included funk and reggae in their blues-infused rock."

[438] TILL THE NEXT GOODBYE - Human Drama (1993)

(Jagger-Richards)

Rolling Stones original: It's Only Rock 'N' Roll (1974)

Indie Rock and Gothic Rock band from Los Angeles, California, USA, led by singer and guitarist Johnny Indovina (b. 1957).

A really good but surprisingly overlooked ballad from the 'It's Only Rock 'n' Roll' album, Human Drama's version is mid-tempo and very Bowie-esque, with 'Heroes' styled guitar and a vocal that could almost pass for the great man himself. [Interview is with Johnny Indovina]

Whose idea was it to record this song?

"I personally compiled all the tracks on our 'Pinup's album. All of the tracks and artists included on the album were a part of the inspiration for my career. The Rolling Stones 'It's Only Rock and Roll' album would be my favourite of theirs. Also a big fan of the songs 'Wild Horses' and 'Ruby Tuesday', but I felt 'Till the Next Goodbye was the right one for us to cover for the album."

Have you performed this (or any other Stones songs) live?

"We have of course performed 'Till the Next Goodbye', most recently this year in Mexico City at the Human Drama anniversary concert. From time to time I would do 'Wild Horses' in my acoustic shows."

Were the Rolling Stones an influence on your own music?

"Absolutely. The way they evolved from a bluesy cover band, to an incredible pop band, and the growth and exploration over their career. It is what Human Drama wanted to do, and has done. Explore new areas of musical communication and feel, never allowing yourself to be limited to only one."

[439] **TOPS - Eight n' Up** (2017)

(Jagger-Richards)

Rolling Stones original: Tattoo You (1981)

Andrew O'Hazo (guitar and vocals), Michael O'Hazo (guitar), Paul Opalach (bass, keyboards and vocals), Bobby T Torello (drums and vocals), Teddy Yakush (saxophone and harp) and Jules (vocals). Rock and Alternative Country band from Washington Depot, Connecticut, USA.

'Tops' is a song that dates back to the 'Goats Head Soup' sessions and was then resurrected for 'Tattoo You' in 1981. A few years back, American band Eight n' Up did covers of every 'Tattoo You' song for their album 'Tattoo'. 'Tops' has been selected here and very good it is too, but really, the whole album is well worth checking out. [Interview is with Andrew O'Hazo]

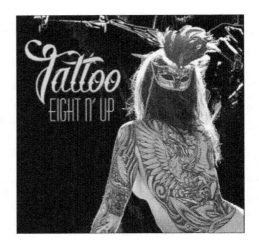

Why 'Tattoo You', rather than (say) 'Beggars Banquet' or 'Sticky Fingers'?

"I chose Tattoo You as it fit well with our rock band style. My band was anxious to record and I did not have any original material ready. I decided to do a cover album and The Stones were a foregone conclusion as they are my favourite band. I thought about all their albums and which songs may be harder or easier for us to record. 'Tattoo You' has great songs and it fit well with us. Some of the falsetto vocals were new for me, but came off well. I called our version 'Tattoo' because that is what Keith thought 'Tattoo You' was going to be called and he was angry when it was released and he saw the changed title."

What was the hardest song to reproduce?

"All of the tracks took a similar amount of work to reproduce, but in the process we realized how high the vocals were on 'Waiting On A Friend'. I had Jules, a skilled female vocalist record that part and she, myself and the engineer wondered how Mick did the original vocals."

Do you have any particular favourites from the album?

"My favourites off our version of the album are 'Worried About You', 'Slave', 'Neighbors' and 'Start Me Up'."

Do you perform any of these songs live?

"We have not played any of the songs live."

[440] **TORN AND FRAYED - The Black Crowes** (2009)

(Jagger-Richards)

Rolling Stones original: Exile On Main St. (1972)

Chris Robinson (Christopher Mark Robinson, b. 1966 - vocals, harmonica and guitar), Rich Robinson (Richard Spencer Robinson, b. 1969 - guitar and vocals), Luther Dickinson (Luther Andrews Dickinson, b. 1973 - guitar and harmonica), Sven Pipien (b. 1967 - bass and vocals), Steve Gorman (b. 1965 - drums and percussion and Adam MacDougall (b. 1974 - keyboards and vocals). Southern Rock, Blues Rock and Hard Rock band from Atlanta, Georgia, USA.

A song from the 2nd 'acoustic' side of 'Exile On Main St.', The Black Crowes' live cover is louder and heavier, but otherwise faithful to the original. It is on their 2009 album 'Warpaint Live'.

[441] TORN AND FRAYED - Blue Mountain (2011)

(Jagger-Richards)

Rolling Stones original: Exile On Main St. (1972)

Americana and Alternative Country band from Mississippi, USA, led by Cary Hudson (b. 1963 - guitar and vocals) and Laurie Stirratt (bass and harmony vocals). Disbanded in 2013.

Faster and more electric yet somehow a little more Country than the Stones' original, Blue Mountain's great cover is on 'Paint It Black: An Alt Country Tribute To The Rolling Stones'. [Interview is with Cary Hudson]

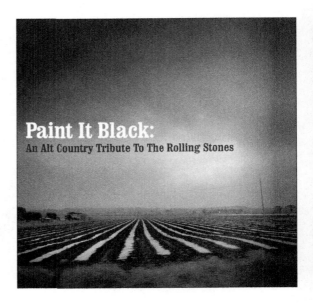

Whose idea was it to record this song?

"The idea to do the song was a joint decision with my partner Laurie from Blue Mountain... we smoked a joint and made the decision!"

Do/did you perform this or any other Stones songs live?

"I have played so many Stones songs in my years as a musician and they were and are an enormous influence on me. I was reading snippets of Keith's autobiography to my 20 year old daughter earlier this week."

Were the Rolling Stones an influence on your own music?

"I really owe it to the Stones for first turning me on to the blues. When I was a kid getting into their music and reading their interviews it slowly dawned on me that the music that had inspired so much of their sound and attitude was from my home state. This was life changing because it put me on the search to find the relics and hopefully some actual blues players, and I did find them, but that's another (very long) story."

[442] **TUMBLING DICE - Owen Gray** (1973)

(Jagger-Richards)

Rolling Stones original: Exile On Main St. (1972) + UK/US A-side

(b. 1939). Ska, Rocksteady and Reggae singer and keyboardist from Kingston, Jamaica.

One of the more commercial songs on 'Exile On Main St.', Owen Gray's cover of 'Tumbling Dice' is a good honest Reggae version, with none of the 'toasting' or 'dub' mixing that was starting to sneak into the genre by this time. It was released as a single in 1973, but it failed to sell.

[443] **TUMBLING DICE - Linda Ronstadt** (1977)

(Jagger-Richards)

Rolling Stones original: Exile On Main St. (1972) + UK/US A-side

Linda Maria Ronstadt (b. 1946). Rock, Pop, Folk and Country singer from Tucson, Arizona, USA.

An artist comfortable with a wide variety of genres, Linda Ronstadt's cover of 'Tumbling Dice' is a Country-Rock arrangement (perhaps more Rock than Country) that was released as a 1977 US single, when it peaked at No. 32 on the Billboard Pop charts.

[444] **TUMBLING DICE** - Diesel Park West (1992)

(Jagger-Richards)

Rolling Stones original: Exile On Main St. (1972) + UK/US A-side

---

John Butler (John Charles Butler, b. 1954 - vocals and guitar), Rick Willson (b. 1959 - guitar), Rich Barton (guitar and vocals), Geoff Beavan (bass) and Dave Anderson (drums). Alternative Rock band from Leicester, UK.

Diesel Park West's powerful cover stays fairly faithful to the original, though with the addition of some nice harmonies and an occasional jangling piano. It was released on their 1992 'God Only Knows' EP. [Interview is with John Butler]

Whose idea was it to record this song?

"Probably our lead guitarist Rick Willson."

Have you performed this (or any other Stones songs) live?

"Yeah we did 'Dandelion' and 'Salt Of The Earth'."

Were the Rolling Stones an influence on your own music?

"It's largely unavoidable to not be influenced in some way by them. Those early singles in the sixties with Brian Jones were pretty much transcendent recordings. Ok they were not as polished as the Beatles not even as creative and not as accomplished players in some areas but they were much closer to the real flame of rock 'n' roll and The Beatles knew it."

[445] **TUMBLING DICE - Johnny Copeland** (1997)

(Jagger-Richards)

Rolling Stones original: Exile On Main St. (1972) + UK/US A-side

John Clyde Copeland (b. 1937 - d. 1997). Blues singer and guitarist from Haynesville, Louisiana, USA.

Johnny Copeland's Blues-Rock cover features lots of (slightly over-the-top) lead guitar, and is on 1997's various artists 'Paint It, Blue: Songs of The Rolling Stones' album.

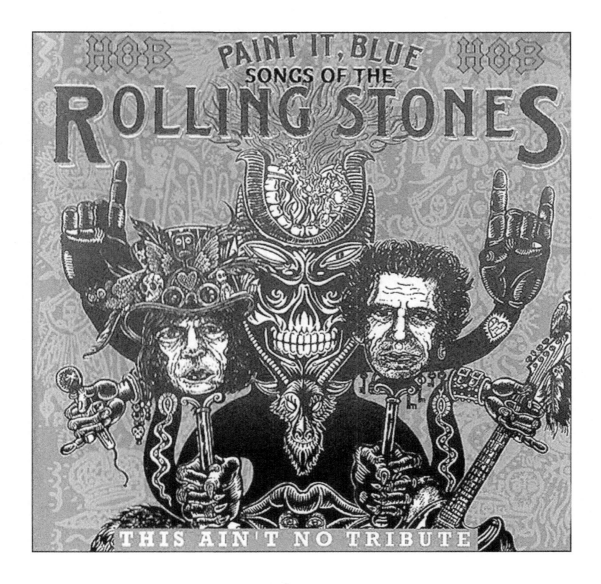

[446] **TUMBLING DICE - Julie Corbalis** (2013)

(Jagger-Richards)

Rolling Stones original: Exile On Main St. (1972) + UK/US A-side

Rock, Folk, Pop and Blues singer and guitarist from Port Chester, New York, USA.

In contrast to all the other covers featured here, Julie Corbalis' great version of 'Tumbling Dice' features just her alone with a guitar plus a washboard player. It is on Julie's 2013 album 'Songs In A Bottle'.

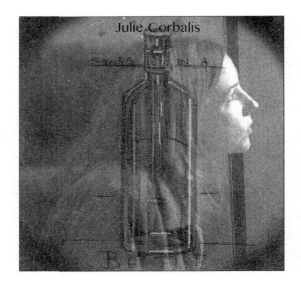

Whose idea was it to record this song?

"It was my idea to record a version of 'Tumbling Dice'. It's a fun groovin' song and I really wanted to stretch and grow my guitar playing skills for solo acoustic live performances. Part of this learning process was learning a couple of classic songs in open tunings. I first recorded an open tuned version of 'Tumbling Dice' just for fun and posted it on YouTube in 2011. Then after chatting with some guitar playing friends I revised my playing to open G and put it in on a covers record I released in 2013 called 'Songs In A Bottle'. Fred Gillen Jr. recorded it and played washboard on that version. I usually play it back-to-back with Joni Mitchell's 'Circle Game' because they are in the same tuning!"

Have you performed this (or any other Stones songs) live?

"I perform Rolling Stones songs all the time. 'Dead Flowers', 'Wild Horses', 'Sweet Virginia', 'Dear Doctor', just to name a few."

Were the Rolling Stones an influence on your own music?

"Yes, a big influence. My dad is a big Stones fan and we listened to them all the time growing up in the 80's-90's. 'Let's Spend the Night Together' and 'Ruby Tuesday' were on one of his mix tapes (I think they were originally on the same 45). I got to see them at Madison Square Garden about 20 years ago and they were so great."

[447] **2000 LIGHT YEARS FROM HOME - The Danse Society** (1983)

(Jagger-Richards)

Rolling Stones original: Their Satanic Majesties Request (1967) + US B-side (1967)

Steve Rawlings (Steven Victor Rawlings - vocals), Paul Nash (guitar), Tim Wright (bass), Paul Gilmartin (drums) and Lyndon Scarfe (keyboards). Gothic Rock and Post-Punk band from Barnsley, UK.

'2000 Light Years From Home' is The Rolling Stones (and anyone else's) finest ever slice of British Psychedelia, and one of the key tracks on 'Their Satanic Majesties Request'. Putting enough of their own stamp on the song to make it their own without moving too far away from the original, The Danse Society issued the song on a 1983 single, as well as on their album 'Heaven Is Waiting'. [Interview is with Paul Nash]

Whose idea was it to record this song?

"I believe the idea to cover '2000 Light Years' was mine (Paul Nash) and Lyndon Scarfes (keyboards), as 'Satanic Majesties' was one of our fave albums at the time. I not only loved the music but the cover (I had, still have, the lenticular one). After we signed our major label deal we got some pressure from the record company to be more commercial. We never wanted to be a singles band, and rarely did covers, but we decided to go with '2000 Light Year's as it was suitably obscure but fitted with the bands ethos, and we thought we had worked the Danse magic on it. It kept the label happy and they sprang for our first pro music video for it but sadly it didn't hit the top 40."

Have you performed this (or any other Stones songs) live?

"It has always been a song we play and still play live even now, it is always well received and a popular set choice."

Were the Rolling Stones an influence on your own music?

"Personally I love the stones my fave album is 'Let it Bleed', fave single (12") 'Sympathy For The Devil', and yes I am sure there have been influences seeping into our music over the years. Why not?"

[448] **2000 LIGHT YEARS FROM HOME - Robin Danar feat. Rachael Yamagata** (2008)

(Jagger-Richards)

Rolling Stones original: Their Satanic Majesties Request (1967) + US B-side (1967)

Producer, recording and mixing engineer and musician from New York City, USA, with Rachael Yamagata (b. 1977). Indie Pop singer and pianist from Arlington, Virginia, USA.

With haunting harmonies and a modern Dance beat, Robin Danar feat. Rachael Yamagata's cover of '2000 Years From Home' is on the 2008 album 'Altered States'.

[449] **2000 MAN - Kiss** (1979)

(Jagger-Richards)

Rolling Stones original: Their Satanic Majesties Request (1967)

Paul Stanley (Stanley Bert Eisen, b. 1952 - vocals and guitar), Gene Simmons (Chaim Witz, b. 1949 - vocals and bass), Ace Frehley (Paul Daniel Frehley, b. 1951 - guitar and vocals) and Peter Criss (George Peter John Criscuola, b. 1945- drums and vocals). Hard Rock and Glam Metal band from New York City, USA.

A wonderfully prophetic song from 'Their Satanic Majesties Request', Kiss lose the intricate acoustic guitar and syncopating drumming in favour of a straight-ahead Glam Rock stomper. This essential cover, sung by guitarist Ace Frehley, was first issued on Kiss' 1979 album 'Dynasty'.

[450] **2120 SOUTH MICHIGAN AVENUE - Joe Louis Walker** (2002)
(Nanker-Phelge)

Rolling Stones original: Five By Five [EP] (1964) + 12 X 5 (1964)

Louis Joseph Walker Jr. (b. 1949). Blues singer and guitarist from San Francisco, California, USA.

The Stones' instrumental tribute to Chess records (2120 South Michigan Avenue was the address of their Chicago studios and offices), Joe Louis Walker's cover is an excellent excuse for he and 2nd guitarist G.E. Smith to give their instruments a good work out. It is on Joe's 2002 album 'In The Morning'. *See [136] for interview!*

[451] **2120 SOUTH MICHIGAN AVENUE - George Thorogood and The Destroyers** (2011)
(Nanker-Phelge)

Rolling Stones original: Five By Five [EP] (1964) + 12 X 5 (1964)

George Lawrence Thorogood (b. 1950). Blues-Rock and Rock 'n' Roll singer, guitarist and harmonicist from Wilmington, Delaware, USA, with Jim Suhler (guitar), Billy Blough (bass), Jeff Simon (drums and percussion) and Buddy Leach (saxophone and piano).

Featuring guest musician Charles Musselwhite on harmonica, George Thorogood and The Destroyers faithful cover is on the 2011 album '2120 South Michigan Ave'.

[452] **THE UNDER ASSISTANT WEST COAST PROMOTION MAN - The Dream Syndicate** (1989)

(Jagger-Richards)

Rolling Stones original: US B-side (1965) + Out Of Our Heads [US + UK versions] (1965)

Steve Wynn (Steven Lawrence Wynn, b. 1960 - vocals and guitar), Paul B. Cutler (guitar), Mark Walton (bass) and Dennis Duck (drums). Alternative Rock band from Los Angeles, California, USA.

An amusing mid-tempo Rhythm 'n' Blues song that was the US B-side of '(I Can't Get No) Satisfaction', The Dream Syndicate's exciting live cover from 1988 was first issued on the 'It's Too Late To Stop Now' bootleg the following year - an album that got an official release in 2022.

[453] **UNDER MY THUMB - Wayne Gibson** (1966)

(Jagger-Richards)

Rolling Stones original: Aftermath (1966)

Edward William Allen (b. 1942 - d. 2004). Pop and Soul singer from London.

One of the better known tracks on 'Aftermath' is 'Under My Thumb', a song so well-loved that it was used to open every show on their US and European Tours in 1981/1982. Wayne Gibson's vaguely Tom Jones-styled single was all but ignored on release; however, it later gained popularity on the 'Northern Soul' circuit, and in 1974 got to No. 17 in the UK charts.

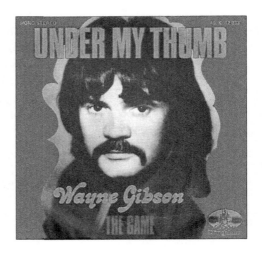

[454] **UNDER MY THUMB - Del Shannon** (1966)

(Jagger-Richards)

Rolling Stones original: Aftermath (1966)

Charles Weedon Westover (b. 1934 - d. 1990). Rock 'n' Roll and Pop singer and guitarist from Grand Rapids, Michigan, USA.

Del Shannon knew a good song when he heard one. The very first person to chart in the USA with a Lennon-McCartney song (a cover of 'From Me To You'), he went on to record *two* songs from 'Aftermath': 'Out Of Time' in 1981 (featured elsewhere in the book), and 'Under My Thumb'. Predictably excellent, it was released as a 1966 single (and was a minor Australian hit), as well as on his album 'Total Commitment'.

[455] **UNDER MY THUMB - The Who** (1967)

(Jagger-Richards)

Rolling Stones original: Aftermath (1966)

Roger Daltrey (Roger Harry Daltrey, b. 1944 - vocals and harmonica), Pete Townshend (Peter Dennis Blandford Townshend, b. 1945 - guitar and vocals), John Entwistle (John Alec Entwistle (b. 1944 - d. 2002 - bass and vocals) and Keith Moon (Keith John Moon, b. 1946 - d. 1978 - drums and vocals). Rhythm 'n' Blues and Rock band from London, UK.

The flip-side of their version of 'The Last Time' (also in this book), 'Under My Thumb' features a nice Pete Townshend high harmony part, as well as the usual no-holds-barred drumming from Keith Moon. The Who's greatest single!

[456] **UNDER MY THUMB - Tina Turner** (1975)

(Jagger-Richards)

Rolling Stones original: Aftermath (1966)

Anna Mae Bullock (b. 1939). Rhythm 'n' Blues, Soul and Rock singer from Brownsville, Tennessee, USA.

Tina Turner sings this wonderfully of course, but it is greatly marred by the horrible dated Rock-Disco backing. It is on her 1975 album 'Acid Queen'. Within a year she would leave husband Ike, and would no longer be under *anyone's* thumb.

[457] **UNDER MY THUMB - Terence Trent D'Arby** (1987)

(Jagger-Richards)

Rolling Stones original: Aftermath (1966)

Terence Trent Howard (b. 1962). Pop, Rock and Soul singer and multi-instrumentalist from Manhattan, New York, USA.

Sounding like he's been on a strict diet of Otis Redding records, Terence Trent D'Arby's fast live version of 'Under My Thumb' is on his 1987 'Sign Your Name' EP.

[458] **UNDER MY THUMB - Barrence Whitfield and The Savages** (1992)

(Jagger-Richards)

Rolling Stones original: Aftermath (1966)

Barry White (b. 1955). Rhythm 'n' Blues, Soul and Gospel singer (and band) from Jacksonville, Florida, USA.

Although a bit sluggish in tempo, Barrence Whitfield and The Savages' otherwise fine Soul version is on their 1992 album 'Savage Tracks'.

[459] **UNDER MY THUMB - Lucky Peterson** (1997)

(Jagger-Richards)

Rolling Stones original: Aftermath (1966)

Judge Kenneth Peterson (b. 1964 - d. 2020). Blues, Soul, Rhythm 'n' Blues and Gospel singer, guitarist and keyboardist from Buffalo, New York, USA.

A vocally-relaxed cover with wah-wah guitar and heavy-handed drumming, Lucky Peterson's Bluesy version is on 1997's 'Paint It, Blue: Songs of The Rolling Stones' various artists CD.

[460] **UNDER MY THUMB - Andrew Francis** (2002)

(Jagger-Richards)

Rolling Stones original: Aftermath (1966)

Reggae singer, probably using a pseudonym.

A pleasant Lover's Rock Pop-Reggae version, Andrew Francis' cover of 'Under My Thumb' is on 2002's 'Paint It Black: A Reggae Tribute To The Rolling Stones' various artists CD.

[461] **UNDER MY THUMB - Kim Carnes** (2015)

(Jagger-Richards)

Rolling Stones original: Aftermath (1966)

(b. 1945). Pop and Rock singer from Los Angeles, California, USA.

Amazingly, Kim Carnes' arrangement of 'Under My Thumb' is *very* similar to 'Bette Davis Eyes', her big hit from several decades earlier. It is on 2015's various artists '80's Re:Covered - Your Songs with the 80's Sound' album.

[462] **UNDERCOVER OF THE NIGHT - Cassandra Beck** (2018)
(Jagger-Richards)

Rolling Stones original: Undercover (1983) + UK/US A-side (1983)

Pop, Jazz, Dance and Bossa Nova singer from Boston, Massachusetts, USA.

One of the Stones' more memorable songs from the mid '80s and a rare latter-day foray into social commentary, Cassandra Beck transforms the Stones' song about political corruption into a gentle Bossa Nova. It was released as a 2018 single, as well as on the various artists 'Bossa n' Stones 3' album.

[463] **VENTILATOR BLUES - Clarence Gatemouth Brown** (1997)
(Jagger-Richards)

Rolling Stones original: Exile On Main St. (1972)

Clarence Brown Jr. (b. 1924 - d. 2005). Blues, Swing, Country, Cajun and Rhythm 'n' Blues singer and multi-instrumentalist from Vinton, Louisiana, USA.

A song inspired by the appalling hot and humid conditions in The Rolling Stones' temporary studio at Nellcôte, South of France, Clarence Gatemouth Brown's wonderful down-home Blues cover features his strong vocals backed by just acoustic slide guitar, bass and drums. It is on 1997's 'Paint It, Blue: Songs of The Rolling Stones'.

[464] VENTILATOR BLUES - Marie Martens and The Messarounds (2019)
(Jagger-Richards)

Rolling Stones original: Exile On Main St. (1972)

Marie Martens (vocals and guitar), Ronnie 'Two Times' Cacioppo (percussion and vocals), Jimmy B. Natural (bass) and Tom Selear (drums). Swedish-born and USA-based Rhythm 'n' Blues and Rock 'n' Roll singer and guitarist (and band).

With dirty, fuzzy, Z.Z. Top-styled guitar, Marie Martens and The Messarounds' powerful cover is on their 2019 album 'Travelled'. [Interview is with Marie Martens]

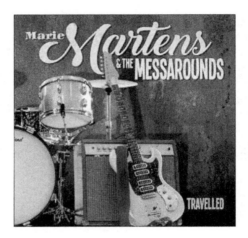

Whose idea was it to record this song?

"It was my idea, I had been toying around with this song for a while, loved the slide and the gritty-ness."

Have you performed this (or any other Stones songs) live?

"Yes, and yes. We play this song regularly on gigs when it fits the vibe! The Messarounds percussionist/ vocalist Ronnie 'Two Times' is a big Stones fan and he does a few Stones tunes. The Stones' version of Robert Johnson's 'Stop Breaking Down' is one of them."

Were the Rolling Stones an influence on your own music?

"Yes for sure. I grew up in Sweden and I listened a lot to blues and rock from England, like early Fleetwood Mac with Peter Green and Jeremy Spencer, Stones, John Mayall's Blues breakers, Cream and Jimi Hendrix and more. All those bands was for me the gateway to the original blues musicians and to this day I still listen to all of it. So yes the Stones has definitely had an impact on my music."

[465] **WAITING ON A FRIEND - Hu Jay** (2002)
(Jagger-Richards)

Rolling Stones original: Tattoo You (1981) + UK/US A-side (1981)

Reggae singer, probably using a pseudonym.

A song whose origins date back to the 'Goats Head Soup' sessions, with further work at the 'Black and Blue' sessions, 'Waiting On A Friend' was revamped and finally released on 'Tattoo You'. The mysterious Hu Jay (also known as Hugh J.) issued a nice relaxed Lover's Rock version on 'Paint It Black: A Reggae Tribute To The Rolling Stones'.

[466] **WAITING ON A FRIEND - Jeanne Newhall with Kazunori Koga** (2016)
(Jagger-Richards)

Rolling Stones original: Tattoo You (1981) + UK/US A-side (1981)

Jazz, Pop and Classical singer and pianist from Los Angeles, CA, USA, with Jazz and Pop guitarist from Osaka, Japan.

With Jeanne Newhall's Joni Mitchell-styled voice backed just by piano and acoustic guitar, this lovely cover of 'Waiting On A Friend' is on the 2016 album 'Still Loving You'.

[467] **WANDERING SPIRIT - Miranda Lambert** (2022)

(Jagger-Rip)

Rolling Stones original: Wandering Spirit [Mick Jagger solo album] (1993)

Miranda Leigh Lambert (b. 1983). Country and Country Rock singer and guitarist from Longview, Texas, USA.

A song that can only be described as modern Rockabilly, from Mick's excellent 1993 solo album of the same name, 'Wandering Spirit' was covered in very fine style indeed by Miranda Lambert for her 2022 'Palomino' album.

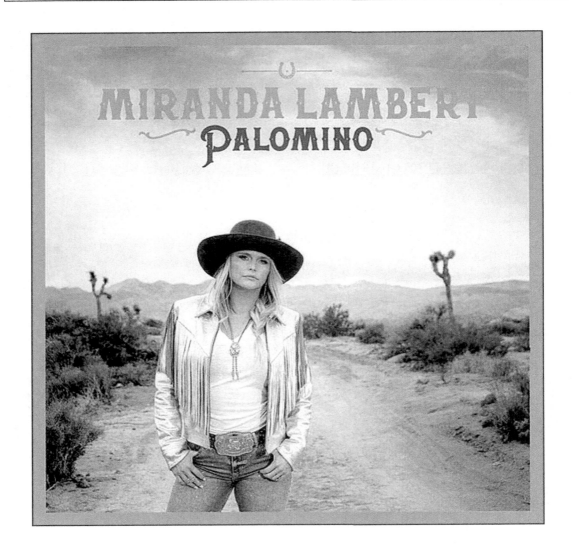

[468] **WE LOVE YOU - The Damned** (1984) *(Not released until 1993)*
(Jagger-Richards)

Rolling Stones original: UK A-side (1967) + US B-side (1967)

Dave Vanian (David Lett, b. 1956 - vocals), Captain Sensible (Raymond Ian Burns, b. 1954 - guitar, keyboards and vocals), Algy Ward (Alasdair Mackie Ward, b. 1959 - bass) and Rat Scabies (Christopher John Millar, b. 1955 - drums and vocals). Punk and Gothic Rock band from London.

Dismissed by many as a Beatles rip-off at the time, 'We Love You' was much more discordant, unsettling and dark than anything The Fabs were doing back in the Summer of Love. The Damned's revival kicks off with a piano intro, just like the Stones' original, before both the tempo and sarcasm is drastically increased for an incredibly powerful and tight cover. Recorded for the BBC in 1984, it was issued 9 years later on 'Sessions of The Damned'. *See [62] for interview!*

[469] **WE LOVE YOU - Nudity** (2016)
(Jagger-Richards)

Rolling Stones original: UK A-side (1967) + US B-side (1967)

Dave Harvey (vocals and guitar), Stephie Crist (guitar), Abigail Ingram (bass), Tanar Stalker (drums) and Rachel Carns (synthesizers). Psychedelic Rock band from Olympia, Washington, USA.

Mixing the modern with the retro, Nudity's cover has a trance-like repetitive riff and drum beat, combined with pleasant 60s-influenced female vocals. It is on 'Discover: Songs Of The Rolling Stones Vol. 1'.

[470] WE'RE WASTIN' TIME - Jimmy Tarbuck (1965)
(Jagger-Richards)

Rolling Stones original: 1964 Demo: Metamorphosis (1975)

James Joseph Tarbuck (b. 1940). Comedian, Presenter and occasional Pop singer from Wavertree, Liverpool, UK.

A song that can only be described as a fast waltz, 'We're Wastin' Time' was one of the stranger tracks when finally released on 'Metamorphosis'. Stranger still, the track was originally given to singing Scouse comedian Jimmy Tarbuck, as the B-side to his debut single 'Someday', and on the ultra-hip Immediate label no less. Although sung in a lower key than the Stones' demo, it isn't bad at all.

[471] WHAT A SHAME - Lorelle Meets The Obsolete (2015)
(Jagger-Richards)

Rolling Stones original: US B-side (1964) + The Rolling Stones No. 2 (1965) + The Rolling Stones, Now! (1965)

Lorelle aka Lorena Quintanilla (vocals, guitar and bass) and Alberto González (drums, guitar and bass). Garage and Psychedelic Rock duo from Guadalajara, México.

The Stones original of 'What A Shame' is a fine Rhythm 'n' Blues song with stinging Brian Jones slide guitar; Lorelle Meets The Obsolete's cover is an almost unrecognizable effects-laden drone work-out, and can be found on 'Stoned - A Psych Tribute to The Rolling Stones'.

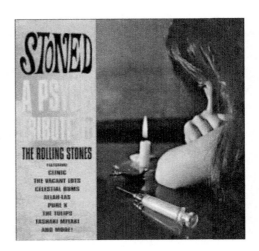

[472] **WHAT TO DO - Meat Puppets** (1984) *(Not released until 1999)*
(Jagger-Richards)

Rolling Stones original: Aftermath [UK version] (1966)

Curt Kirkwood (Curtis Matthew Kirkwood. b. 1959 - vocals and guitar), Cris Kirkwood (Christopher Kirkwood, b. 1960 - bass and vocals) and Derrick Bostrom (Derrick Edwin Bostrom (b. 1960 - drums). Alternative Rock, Psychedelic Rock and Cowpunk band Phoenix, Arizona, USA.

The UK edition of 'Aftermath' could've perhaps been improved further with a different running order, ending as it did with the restrained 'What To Do', a song not even released in the USA until the '70s. The Meat Puppets' cover is *very* laidback, sounding like stoned cowboys jamming. It stayed in the can for 15 years, surfacing as bonus track on a CD reissue of their 2nd album 'Meat Puppets II'. [Interview is with Derrick Bostrom]

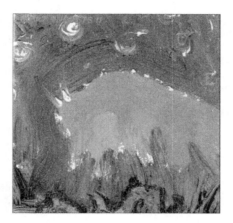

Whose idea was it to record this song?

"Our recording of 'What To Do' is an outtake from a session we did back in 1982. I (Bostrom) had always liked the song and it was probably me who introduced it to the band."

Have you performed this (or any other Stones songs) live?

"I don't believe we ever did this song live. We did a couple Stones songs just as one-off jams back in 1982, but we never added them to our set. I still have live recordings of 'Can You Hear Me Knocking', '2000 Light Years From Home' and 'I Can't Be Satisfied' from back then."

Were the Rolling Stones an influence on your own music?

"I never really took to the Stones until after I had already gotten into punk rock. I liked their earlier stuff, before Jagger/Richards crowded Brian Jones out of the leadership role. Around 1966, I lose interest. I can't say the Stones were much of an influence on the Meat Puppets, but anyone who listens to my drumming would have to assume I've spent time listening to Charlie."

[473] WHO'S BEEN SLEEPING HERE? - Hooyoosay (2011)

(Jagger-Richards)

Rolling Stones original: Between The Buttons (1967)

International music recording project, featuring a variety of loose and unnamed contributors.

One of many highlights on 'Between The Buttons' (heck, every song on 'Between The Buttons' is a highlight!), Hooyoosay's simple cover is nice enough. It can be heard via the usual streaming sites. *See [246] for interview!*

[474] WHO'S DRIVING YOUR PLANE? - Great White (1992)

(Jagger-Richards)

Rolling Stones original: UK/US B-side (1966)

Jack Russell (b. 1960 - vocals), Mark Kendall (b. 1957 - guitar and vocals), Michael Lardie (b. 1958 - guitar, keyboards and vocals), Dave Spitz (b. 1958 - bass) and Audie Desbrow (b. 1957 - drums). Hard Rock band from Los Angeles, California, USA.

Issued as the B-side to 'Have You Seen Your Mother, Baby, Standing In The Shadow?', 'Who's Driving Your Plane' is a heavy Blues song that probably owes more to Bob Dylan than it does Muddy Waters. Great White's unsubtle cover was issued on the B-side of their 1992 'Big Goodbye' single.

[475] **WILD HORSES - The Flying Burrito Brothers** (1970)
(Jagger-Richards)

Rolling Stones original: Sticky Fingers (1971) + US A-side (1971)

Gram Parsons (Ingram Cecil Connor III, b. 1946 - d. 1973 - vocals, guitar and keyboards), Bernie Leadon (b. 1947 - vocals, guitar and dobro), Chris Hillman (Christopher Hillman (b. 1944 - vocals, bass and mandolin), Sneaky Pete Kleinow (Peter E. Kleinow, b. 1934 - d. 2007 - pedal steel guitar) and Michael Clarke (Michael James Dick, b. 1946 - d. 1993 - drums). Country Rock band from Los Angeles, California, USA.

Despite their hard-riffing Blues-based Rock reputation, pretty much every Stones album features at least one slow ballad. 'Sticky Fingers' was no exception, though few songs are quite as memorable or eternally-popular as 'Wild Horses'. Thanks to Gram Parsons' friendship with Keith Richards, The Flying Burrito Brothers released their version of 'Wild Horses' almost a year before the Stones. A laid-back Country Rock arrangement, it is on their 1970 album 'Burrito Deluxe'.

[476] **WILD HORSES - LaBelle** (1971)

(Jagger-Richards)

Rolling Stones original: Sticky Fingers (1971) + US A-side (1971)

Patti LaBelle (Patricia Louise Holte, b. 1944), Nona Hendryx (b. 1944) and Sarah Dash (b. 1945 - d. 2021). Soul and Funk vocal trio from Philadelphia, Pennsylvania, USA.

Patti Labelle has a vocal style that makes Aretha Franklin sound shy and retiring, and this can be a bit unpalatable at times. That said, one can't help but also be impressed, especially when accompanied by Nona Hendryx and long-time Keith Richards collaborator the late Sarah Dash. Their cover of 'Wild Horses' is on the 1971 album 'LaBelle'.

[477] **WILD HORSES - Melanie** (1974)

(Jagger-Richards)

Rolling Stones original: Sticky Fingers (1971) + US A-side (1971)

Melanie Anne Safka (b. 1947). Folk and Pop singer and guitarist from Queens, New York, USA.

Very slow and with sweeping strings, Melanie makes the song very much her own as always. 'Wild Horses' is on 1974's 'Madrugada' album.

[478] **WILD HORSES - The Sundays** (1992)

(Jagger-Richards)

Rolling Stones original: Sticky Fingers (1971) + US A-side (1971)

Harriet Wheeler (Harriet Ella Wheeler, b. 1963 - vocals), David Gavurin (David Richard Gavurin, b. 1963 - guitar), Paul Brindley (Patrick Hannan - bass) and Patrick Hannan (drums). Alternative Rock and Indie Pop band from Bristol, UK. Disbanded in 1997.

A heartfelt and modern update, The Sundays' version of 'Wild Horses' was buried away on 1992's 'Goodbye' single. However, it was heard in the movie 'Fear' as well as in 'Buffy the Vampire Slayer', so it is quite well known despite having never been an A-side.

[479] **WILD HORSES - Blackhawk** (1997)

(Jagger-Richards)

Rolling Stones original: Sticky Fingers (1971) + US A-side (1971)

Henry Paul (b. 1949 - vocals, mandolin and guitar), Van Stephenson (Van Wesley Stephenson, b. 1953 - d. 2001 - guitar and vocals) and Dave Robbins (Charles David Robbins, b. 1959 - keyboards and vocals). Country band from Tampa, Florida, USA.

Blackhawk's up-tempo Bluegrass version (complete with a mandolin solo) is on 1997's various artists 'Stone Country' album.

[480] **WILD HORSES - Gregory Isaacs** (2002)

(Jagger-Richards)

Rolling Stones original: Sticky Fingers (1971) + US A-side (1971)

Gregory Anthony Isaacs (b. 1951 - d. 2010). Reggae and Lovers Rock singer from Kingston, Jamaica.

A mid-tempo Reggae cover that is very relaxed vocally, Gregory Isaacs' cover is on the 'Paint It Black: A Reggae Tribute To The Rolling Stones' various artists album.

[481] **WILD HORSES - Garbage** (2002)

(Jagger-Richards)

Rolling Stones original: Sticky Fingers (1971) + US A-side (1971)

Shirley Manson (Shirley Ann Manson, b. 1966 - vocals), Duke Erikson (Douglas Elwin Erickson, b. 1951 - guitar, bass and keyboards), Steve Marker b. 1959 - (guitar and keyboards) and Butch Vig (Bryan David Vig, b. 1955 - drums). Alternative Rock band from Madison, Wisconsin, USA.

A live, low key, version, Garbage's cover of 'Wild Horses' is on 2002's 'Shut Your Mouth' single.

[482] **WILD HORSES - Charlotte Martin** (2004)

(Jagger-Richards)

Rolling Stones original: Sticky Fingers (1971) + US A-side (1971)

Charlotte Ann Martin (b. 1976). Alternative Rock singer and pianist from Charleston, Illinois, USA.

Passionately sung, and backed just by her piano, Charlotte Martin's highly individual cover of 'Wild Horses' is on her 2004 'On Your Shore' album.

Whose idea was it to record this song?

"It was my idea to record Wild Horses. I was actually inspired by the Sunday's version of it from their sophomore album 'Blind'."

Do you perform this or any other Stones songs live?

"I have performed 'You Can't Always Get What You Want' and 'Gimme Shelter'!"

Were the Rolling Stones an influence on your own music?

"The Rolling Stones absolutely influenced me I grew up listening to them my entire childhood in life. I will always side them as an influence as I'm a huge fan."

[483] **WILD HORSES - Susan Boyle** (2009)
(Jagger-Richards)

Rolling Stones original: Sticky Fingers (1971) + US A-side (1971)

Susan Magdalane Boyle (b. 1961). Operatic Pop singer from Dechmont, West Lothian, Scotland.

Famously appearing on 'X-Factor' whilst looking very unlike a potential pop star - and then blowing everyone away with her beautiful voice, Susan Boyle's highly polished cover of 'Wild Horses' deservedly made it to No. 9 in the UK charts. But isn't the piano arrangement based on Charlotte Martin's version?

[484] **WILL YOU BE MY LOVER TONIGHT? - George Bean** (1964)

(Jagger-Richards)

Rolling Stones original: 1963 Demo: Bootleg only (excerpt)

(d. 1970). Folk and Pop singer from the UK.

As with the flip side 'It Should Be You', 'Will You Be My Lover Tonight?' was one of Jagger-Richards' earliest attempts at writing. It is no more than mediocre, and if anything it's the weaker of the two.

[485] **WINTER - Carla Olson (with Mick Taylor)** (2001)

(Jagger-Richards)

Rolling Stones original: Goats Head Soup (1973)

(b. 1952). Rock singer and guitarist from Austin, Texas, USA.

An epic ballad notable for some of Mick Taylor's finest guitar playing on a Stones record, he recreates that magic on Carla Olson's cover. 'Winter' is on 2001's 'The Ring Of Truth'.

[486] **WORRIED ABOUT YOU - Heikki** (2002)

(Jagger-Richards)

Rolling Stones original: Tattoo You (1981)

Maria Eriksson (vocals) and Jari Heikki Haapalainen (guitar). Indie Pop and Progressive Folk duo from Stockholm, Sweden.

A falsetto-sung ballad that dates back to the 'Black and Blue' sessions (and was even played live at a 1977 Toronto concert), it wasn't issued until 1981's 'Tattoo You'. Heikki's lovely cover features Maria Eriksson's clear Folk voice accompanied by just piano, acoustic bass and brushed drums. It is on the 2002 various artists 'We Love You - A Tribute To Rolling Stones' collection.

[487] **THE WORST - Sheryl Crow [with Keith Richards]** (2019)

(Jagger-Richards)

Rolling Stones original: Voodoo Lounge (1994)

Sheryl Suzanne Crow (b. 1962). Rock, Pop and Country singer and guitarist from Kennett, Missouri, USA.

Keith's latter-day crooned ballads tend to divide fans: some dismiss them as a bit of a snooze-fest, but Stones connoisseurs recognise these as the heart and soul of their later albums. Of these, 'The Worst' is one of the best, and if anything, Sheryl and Keith's beautiful duet has the edge over the 'Voodoo Lounge' original. It is on her 2019 'Threads' album.

[488] YESTERDAY'S PAPERS - Chris Farlowe (1967)
(Jagger-Richards)

Rolling Stones original: Between The Buttons (1967)

Chris Farlowe (John Henry Dighton, b. 1940). Rhythm 'n' Blues, Soul and Pop singer from Islington, London.

With fuller production than the Stones' original and sung in a higher key, Chris Farlowe's great cover was an undeserved flop single. Interestingly, when The Rolling Stones performed 'Yesterday's Papers' (as part of a medley with 'Get Off Of My Cloud') on their Spring '67 European Tour, Mick Jagger sang the song with the same phrasing and in the same key as Chris Farlowe's single.

Chris Farlowe performing 'Yesterday's Papers' on 'Beat Club', 1967 [German TV]

[489] YESTERDAY'S PAPERS - Wayne Gibson (1975)

(Jagger-Richards)

Rolling Stones original: Between The Buttons (1967)

Edward William Allen (b. 1942 - d. 2004). Pop and Soul singer from London.

Released a follow-up to his belated Northern Soul hit with 'Under My Thumb', Wayne Gibson's cover of 'Yesterday's Papers' lacked both the magic and popularity of its predecessor, and he quickly faded back into obscurity.

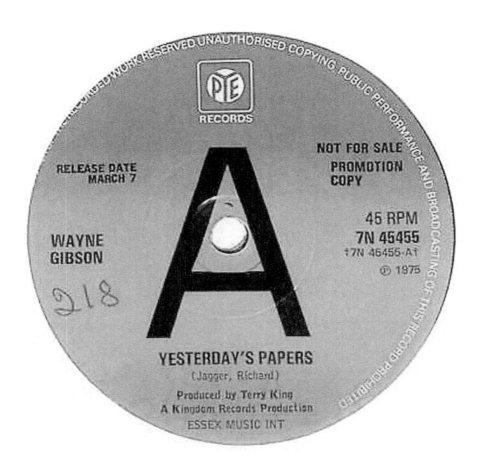

[490] **YOU CAN'T ALWAYS GET WHAT YOU WANT - P.P. Arnold** (1970) *(Not released until 2017)*

(Jagger-Richards)

Rolling Stones original: Let It Bleed (1969) + UK/US B-side (1969)

Patricia Ann Cole (b. 1946). Soul, Rock and Pop singer from Los Angeles, California, USA.

Supposed by some to be The Rolling Stones' answer to The Beatles' 'Hey Jude', 'You Can't Always Get What You Want' has remained a popular live number ever since. P.P. Arnold's sprightly cover with swirling organ fade-in is excellent, but sadly it remained in the can until 2017, when 'The Turning Tide' album from 1970 was finally released.

[491] **YOU CAN'T ALWAYS GET WHAT YOU WANT - Aretha Franklin** (1981)

(Jagger-Richards)

Rolling Stones original: Let It Bleed (1969) + UK/US B-side (1969)

Aretha Louise Franklin (b. 1942 - d. 2018). Soul, Gospel, Jazz and Pop singer and pianist from Memphis, Tennessee, USA.

Though there's nothing wrong with her singing, Aretha Franklin's cover of 'You Can't Always Get What You Want' is given a highly inappropriate and ill-fitting Disco treatment. It is on her 1981 album 'Love All The Hurt Away'.

[492] **YOU CAN'T ALWAYS GET WHAT YOU WANT - Luther Allison (1997)**

(Jagger-Richards)

Rolling Stones original: Let It Bleed (1969) + UK/US B-side (1969)

Luther Sylvester Allison (b. 1939 - d. 1997). Blues singer and guitarist from Widener, Arkansas, USA.

Luther Allison's gravel-voiced Blues-Funk cover of 'You Can't Always Get What You Want' is yet another worthwhile track on 1997's 'Paint It, Blue: Songs of The Rolling Stones' album.

[493] **YOU CAN'T ALWAYS GET WHAT YOU WANT - Steel Pulse (2002)**

(Jagger-Richards)

Rolling Stones original: Let It Bleed (1969) + UK/US B-side (1969)

David Hinds (b. 1956 - vocals and guitar), Clifford 'Moonie' Pusey (guitar), Alvin Ewan (bass), Selwyn Brown (keyboards and vocals), Sidney Mills (b. 1959 - keyboards and vocals), Conrad Kelly (drums and percussion). Reggae band from Birmingham, UK.

A fine Funk-tinged Reggae version, Steel Pulse's cover is on the 'Paint It Black: A Reggae Tribute to The Rolling Stones' CD.

[494] YOU CAN'T ALWAYS GET WHAT YOU WANT - Anastacia (2012)
(Jagger-Richards)

Rolling Stones original: Let It Bleed (1969) + UK/US B-side (1969)

Anastacia Lyn Newkirk (b. 1968). Rock, Pop and Soul singer from Chicago, Illinois, USA.

In an arrangement quite faithful to the Stones' version (albeit very different vocally), Anastacia's cover of 'You Can't Always Get What You Want' is on her 2012 album 'It's A Man's World'.

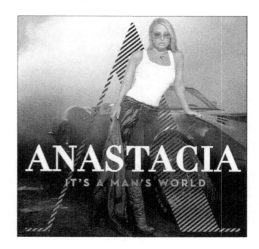

[495] YOU GOT ME ROCKING - Cassandra Beck (2018)
(Jagger-Richards)

Rolling Stones original: Voodoo Lounge (1994) + UK/US A-side (1994)

Pop, Jazz, Dance and Bossa Nova singer from Boston, Massachusetts, USA.

One of the lesser songs on 'Voodoo Lounge', Cassandra Beck transforms this typical rocker into a Blues-enthused mid-tempo dance song. It is on the various artists 'Bossa n' Stones 3' collection.

[496] **YOU GOT THE SILVER - Susan Tedeschi** (2005)

(Jagger-Richards)

Rolling Stones original: Let It Bleed (1969)

(b. 1970). Blues and Americana singer and guitarist from Boston, Massachusetts, USA.

Although Keith Richards had previously duetted with Mick (notably on 'Something Happened To Me Yesterday' and 'Salt Of The Earth'), it wasn't until 1969's Country Blues 'You Got The Silver' that he was featured on a song alone. Oddly, the song seems to mostly get covered by women (there's at least 8 different female-sung versions out there). Three of the best have been selected for this book. Susan Tedeschi's is probably the most Blues-orientated of them, and it is on her 2005 album 'Hope and Desire'.

[497] **YOU GOT THE SILVER - Anne Haigis** (2007)

(Jagger-Richards)

Rolling Stones original: Let It Bleed (1969)

(b. 1955). Rock, Blues and Jazz singer and guitarist from Rottweil, Germany.

Anne Haigis' version is mostly performed purely acoustically, though other instrumentation is heard occasionally. It is on her 2007 album 'Good Day for the Blues'.

[498] **YOU GOT THE SILVER - Barbara Kessler** (2011)

(Jagger-Richards)

Rolling Stones original: Let It Bleed (1969)

(b. 1962). Folk Rock singer and guitarist from Boston, Massachusetts, USA.

Barbara Kessler's clear, country-tinged voice is accompanied just by a couple of acoustic guitars (1 of them slide) for the first minute of the song; then electric slide (and what sounds like a distant fuzz), bass and drums kick in for much of the remainder. Her version is on the 'Paint It Black: An Alt Country Tribute to The Rolling Stones' various artists CD.

Whose idea was it to record this song?

"A Massachusetts-based producer named Jim Sampas who has a label called Reimagine Music which releases tribute/cover compilations told me he was creating this collection of alt-country Stones covers. Jim and I knew each other from the Boston scene, and I knew that he was known for keeping the literary estate of his uncle, Jack Kerouac, alive. As a folkie singer-songwriter type myself, I thought "which tune could I believably 're-imagine'" and I was just drawn to the dreamy, sort of loose guitar layers and song-form of 'You Got The Silver'. It has a kind of sweetness in the lyric, where a lot of the well-known Rolling Stones songs I grew up with have a more brash, swaggering quality. And of course, most of them are sung by Mick Jagger! But I loved discovering Keith Richards' voice on this cut and thought I'd take a shot covering it. Both the bass [Rick O'Neal] and slide guitar player [Charlie O'Neal] are friends from another Boston-based band, The Delta Generators. And my husband [Phil Antoniades] plays drums on the track. Jim and I produced. Super fun session."

Have you performed this (or any other Stones songs) live?

"Not really; I remember doing 'Wild Horses' a few times with bands in the past (and as a guitar/voice teacher now, I can tell you students still want to learn this song!). And 'As Tears Go By' was a song I learned at a guitar lesson back when I was a kid."

Were the Rolling Stones an influence on your own music?

"I would say originally my own music was more directly influenced by the singer-songwriter types I grew up listening to. I played guitar from a very young age, but was quite a late bloomer (especially by today's standards!) in terms of performing and creating music - I didn't start writing original tunes until my late 20's. I remember when I was little, one of my older cousins was really into the Stones and told me "I'm into hard rock, you like soft rock better..." Over the course of my song-writing career I've delved more deeply into my more "rockin'" side, and the better I get as a player (and the more I work with guitar students figuring out the riffs and the open tunings etc) the more I appreciate the Stones' music for its originality and attitude and absolute hook-hammering longevity."

[499] YOU MUST BE THE ONE - The Greenbeats (1964)

(Jagger-Richards)

Rolling Stones original: 1963 Demo: Bootleg only (excerpt)

John Keogh (vocals and piano), Paul Williams (d. 1967 - guitar), Brian Lynch (bass) and Maurice Mog Ahearne (drums). Showband and Rhythm 'n' Blues band from Dublin, Republic of Ireland.

Fronted by a Jerry Lee Lewis-influenced piano pounding vocalist, The Greenbeats were one of Ireland's biggest and best beat groups. They were gifted with one of Jagger-Richards' better earlier songs, though unfortunately they hid it away on the B-side of the far inferior 'If This World Were Mine'.

[500] YOU MUST BE THE ONE - Tommy Vance (1966)

(Jagger-Richards)

Rolling Stones original: 1963 Demo: Bootleg only (excerpt)

Richard Anthony Crispian Francis Prew Hope-Weston (b. 1940 - d. 2005). DJ and Pop and Rhythm 'n' Blues singer from Eynsham, Oxfordshire, UK.

Eschewing the group sound of The Greenbeats' version, Tommy Vance's version features a full brassy orchestra, similar to some of Tom Jones' early hits. The highlight is a guitar solo that may or may not be Jimmy Page.

UNDERCOVER

INDEX

The following websites have been invaluable to the research of this book:

www.45cat.com

www.discogs.com

www.iorr.org

www.nzentgraf.de

www.secondhandsongs.com

(Not forgetting YouTube, Bandcamp, Amazon, Spotify and Wikipedia!)